MOURNING IN AMERICA

MOURNING IN AMERICA

Race and the Politics of Loss

David W. McIvor

CORNELL UNIVERSITY PRESS   ITHACA AND LONDON

Cornell University Press gratefully acknowledges receipt of a subvention from Colorado State University which aided in the publication of this book.

First published 2016 by Cornell University Press

Printed in the United States of America

Library of Congress Cataloging-in-Publication Data

Names: McIvor, David Wallace, author.
Title: Mourning in America : race and the politics of loss / David McIvor.
Description: Ithaca, New York : Cornell University Press, 2016. | Includes bibliographical references and index.
Identifiers: LCCN 2016021191 | ISBN 9781501704956 (cloth : alk. paper)
Subjects: LCSH: African Americans—Violence against—History—20th century. | African Americans—Violence against—History—21st century. | Bereavement—Political aspects—United States. | Grief—Political aspects—United States. | Collective memory—Political aspects—United States. | United States—Race relations—Political aspects.
Classification: LCC E185.615 .M3537 2016 | DDC 305.800973—dc23 LC record available at https://lccn.loc.gov/2016021191

Cornell University Press strives to use environmentally responsible suppliers and materials to the fullest extent possible in the publishing of its books. Such materials include vegetable-based, low-VOC inks and acid-free papers that are recycled, totally chlorine-free, or partly composed of nonwood fibers. For further information, visit our website at www.cornellpress.cornell.edu.

Contents

Acknowledgments

This book has been in development for a number of years, so the list of people to thank is long. I have to start with my family: my mother, Merrie McIvor; my father, D. William McIvor; and my sister, Kristen McIvor. Their encouragement and support have been unswerving. Even as I pursued an uncertain career, they never evinced a moment of doubt. If they were delusional, it was a loving (and necessary) form of delusion.

My passion for the study of politics was kindled while I was an undergraduate student at Western Washington University. I owe a special gratitude to Gerard Rutan, with whom I spent countless office hours arguing and puzzling over the state of the world. Ken Hoover provided a less combative yet just as essential form of support. Vernon Damani Johnson, Butch Kamena, and Sara Weir each provided inspiration and mentorship. Outside the political science department, I owe special thanks to Brenda Miller and Gary Geddes. Gary in particular had a foundational impact, not least because his seminars cultivated a camaraderie and bonhomie that is all too rare in academic spaces. Finally, I need to thank the friends and intellectual companions I met during this time, including Lee Gulyas, Jeremy Pataky, Carter Hasegawa, Janel Davis, Ian Buchan, Trevor Sargent, and Brian Mapes Skywalker.

At Duke University, I was fortunate to fall into an intellectual community that provided the right mixture of rigor, humor, passion, and commitment. The beating heart of this community was Peter Euben. Peter is everything a mentor should be: generous, supportive, attentive, and lovingly critical. None of this would have been possible without him. I also owe an incalculable debt to Rom Coles, Ruth Grant, and George Shulman. Each of them provided guidance, support, and critique in their own unique way, and I am deeply appreciative of their individual and collective efforts. In addition to stellar faculty members, I was part of a cohort at Duke that pushed, prodded, and supported one another. Special thanks are due to Laura Grattan, Stefan Dolgert, Alisa Kessel, P. J. Brendese, Ali Aslam, James Bourke, and Joel Schlosser.

I would also like to show my appreciation to the staff at the Kettering Foundation, where I spent a wonderful stretch of time as a postdoctoral research associate. Derek Barker made my time at Kettering possible, and for this and many other reasons, I am deeply indebted to him. I also thank David Mathews, John Dedrick, Randy Nielsen, Sara Mehltretter-Drury, Noëlle McAfee, Jack Becker,

Connie Crockett, David Holwerk, Paloma Dallas, and Alice Diebel for making my time at Kettering so fruitful and intellectually stimulating. While at Kettering I also had the great fortune to meet Michael Neblo, who has become a wonderful mentor and friend.

This project was completed at Colorado State University, where I have been extremely lucky to find yet another group of supportive colleagues. I owe special thanks to Brad Macdonald, who has done so much to make political theory a vibrant presence at CSU and whose passion for the vocation of political theory is infectious and inspiring. Thanks also to Michele Betsill and Bob Duffy, who, as chairs, have guided me through the early years of an academic career. In addition I am grateful to Steve Mumme, Gamze Cavdar, Marcela Velasco, and the other members of the CSU political science department for creating such a collegial and exciting place to work.

A small part of chapter 2 was originally published as "Bringing Ourselves to Grief: Judith Butler and the Politics of Mourning" in *Political Theory* (August 2012), and is reprinted here with permission. In addition, this project was developed through various conference presentations, and I owe a debt of gratitude to a string of discussants and copanelists who pushed me to sharpen or deepen my arguments. In particular, I must single out the Association for Political Theory working group convened by Jill Frank in 2012, which helped me to develop the arguments made in chapter 4. Special thanks also to the other members of that group: Steven Salkever, Arlene Saxonhouse, Thornton Lockwood, Jeff Miller, and Joel Schlosser. I was also very fortunate to be selected for the APT first book manuscript workshop in 2013. Deep and abiding thanks to the organizers of and participants in that workshop: Mark Rigstad, Andrew Murphy, Melissa Schwartzberg, Simon Stow, Christina Tarnopolsky, W. James Booth, Libby Anker, Michaele Ferguson, and Joel Schlosser. Bonnie Honig has read pieces of the manuscript and has been very generous with suggestions and support. I also thank the anonymous reviewers and my editor at Cornell, Roger Haydon, for seeing the potential in the manuscript and helping to bring it to the finish line.

A connective thread runs between all of these spaces. My wife and companion, Hollie Johnson, is a remarkable person with whom I am blessed to share a life. Hollie has been there for me since before this project began, and her love and support have been steady sources throughout the course of its completion.

And finally, this is a book about the pain of loss and the potential for repair, and as it happens its genesis is rooted in a personal calamity. In December 2006, I was hit and then run over by a dump truck while on my bike commute to the campus of Duke University. In an irony that I only later appreciated, the vehicle struck me while I was on my way to deliver the final exam for a class I was teaching entitled Politics and Tragedy. I avoided permanent disability or death by a matter of inches.

It is a cliché that near-death experiences fundamentally alter one's perspective, and it is a cliché because we can never fully live (or live fully) in awareness of life's fragility. Yet this experience remains a presence in my life, and it serves as a potent reminder of vulnerability and interdependency. To be tossed by a vehicle like a cheap toy is to realize the contingency and chanciness of life. But beyond this I learned that recovery only happens with and through others. After the crash I was instantly surrounded and supported by a community of friends, mentors, family members, health professionals, and even strangers who had witnessed the accident. One should not romanticize communities too much, of course, but one also should not underestimate their importance. This book is dedicated to all those who brought me back to life.

MOURNING IN AMERICA

> **Not everything that is faced can be changed, but nothing can be changed until it is faced.**
>
> —James Baldwin

On December 3, 2014, the mayor of New York City, Bill de Blasio, held a press conference to discuss the decision by a Staten Island grand jury not to indict the police officer Daniel Pantaleo in the death of Eric Garner. Garner had died the previous July while being arrested for selling untaxed cigarettes, his death caused by asphyxiation as the result of a chokehold applied by Pantaleo, despite Garner's repeated exhortation to the arresting officer—captured by amateur video—"I can't breathe!" De Blasio began by remarking how the decision of the grand jury had served to refresh the loss occasioned by Garner's death. As he put it, "We are grieving, again, over the loss of Eric Garner." The Garner incident, de Blasio continued, touched on painful and pressing issues such as police-community relations and civil rights, and he claimed that American citizens now faced "a national moment of grief."[1]

As if in verification of this national moment of mourning, in the days and weeks following Garner's death, multiple "die-in" protests were held locally in Staten Island, Manhattan, and Brooklyn, and as far afield as Boston; Washington, D.C.; and London. At many of these events protesters chanted "I can't breathe" in unison before silently prostrating themselves on the ground in a kind of mournful sit-in. Several of the protests were organized under the slogan and nascent social movement of "Black Lives Matter," which began as a social media hashtag coined by three young African American women in response to the 2013 acquittal of George Zimmerman in the Trayvon Martin case—another incident in which an unarmed African American had been killed without the killer having to face legal repercussions.[2] Black Lives Matter quickly became a rallying cry for national protests, not only over the deaths of Trayvon Martin and Eric Garner but also over the deaths of Michael Brown in Ferguson, Missouri; Tamir Rice in Cleveland; Walter Scott in North Charleston, South Carolina; Jamar Clark in Minneapolis, Minnesota; and Freddie Gray in Baltimore.

The Black Lives Matter protests and the repeated instances of death and disregard that have continued to motivate them imply that we face less a "moment" of grief than an enduring situation of loss, pain, and vulnerability—a situation that has not been adequately faced by public institutions or ordinary citizens. For Claudia Rankine, the Jamaican-born poet and the author of *Citizen: An American Lyric*—an award-winning reflection on everyday experiences of racial disrespect—the Black Lives Matter protests represent nothing less than an "attempt to keep mourning an open dynamic in our culture."[3] Only a "sustained state of national mourning," Rankine argues, can provide witness to the ongoing "devaluation . . . [of] black lives."[4] In making these arguments, Rankine cited the example of Mamie Till Mobley, whose refusal to "keep private grief private" when her son Emmitt was murdered in 1955 reflected a desire to "make mourning enter our day-to-day world . . . as a method of acknowledgment" in the struggle for equality—a desire that needs to be rekindled in the post–civil rights context of mass incarceration, enduring poverty, social neglect, and deep interracial mistrust.[5]

A chorus, then, of public officials, concerned citizens, and social critics is converging at the time of this writing on the themes of loss, grief, and mourning, and the fraught connection between painful social realities and avowed democratic ideals. Yet some important questions remain unanswered. What precisely would it look like for citizens to keep mourning as an "open dynamic" in American politics and culture? What would it mean if mourning were envisioned as a kind of civic or democratic obligation? What might that say about mourning, and what might it mean for democracy? Mourning is typically envisioned as a finite course to be run, a temporary retreat from the outside world, and a staggered process by which one returns.[6] And democracy implies coexistence amid plurality, occasional cooperation between strangers, and tolerance for differences—not the kind of intimacy or empathy that inspires feelings of deep grief. So what, then, would it mean for citizens to practice a *politics* of mourning?

The chapters that follow directly address these difficult and urgent questions. They offer a way of thinking about public mourning as less a means of getting past or moving on from traumatic experiences than as an ongoing democratic labor of recognition and repair. This labor is what I refer to as the *democratic work of mourning*, which is both a theory and a set of practices that, together, can form the basis for an open and ongoing response to experiences of social disrespect and marginalization. The democratic work of mourning takes seriously the idea of a civic obligation of mourning, yet it also offers a properly *political* understanding of mourning itself. Democratic mourning is not reducible to rituals of grief in response to experiences of public loss or trauma, such as the flowers or flags (soon to fade) left at the scene of a calamity. It is not reducible to the speeches and eulogies given for the fallen. Instead, democratic mourning is an ongoing labor of recognition and repair—of recognizing experiences of social trauma and cultivating civic repertoires of response. This labor is ongoing because it is an accompaniment to the (endless) work of building democratic commonwealth. Democratic citizens and communities need spaces and practices through which the damages of disrespect and the complexities attendant to public history and identity can be confronted and to some extent worked through. The democratic work of mourning responds to these urgent needs by identifying the meaning and means of—along with the obstacles to—these political and social labors.

The Black Lives Matter movement is perhaps the most recent reminder of the connection between loss and social grievance, or between mourning and politics, but this is a timeless topic for political communities and therefore a frequent concern for political theorists. In exploring these themes, we are drawn back to the experience of Attic tragedy and Greek democracy of the fifth century BCE. Within the tragic festival and performances, the ancient Athenians displayed a keen sensitivity to issues of trauma, loss, and suffering that continues to illuminate and inspire our own political dramas. For such reasons, the names of Antigone, Orestes, and Electra still populate contemporary reflections on the politics of loss and mourning. Rankine herself, visiting Ferguson during the protests for Michael Brown, explicitly drew a connection between the pathologies of American democracy and the stories of Greek tragedy:

> It almost felt Greek. Predetermined, and hopeless. And then you had all these police cars with white policemen and policewomen, just sitting inside the cars, looking out at you. It was like you were in a theater, and they were this encased audience. It made me think of *Antigone*. And so that's what I'm working on—a rewriting of *Antigone*, as a way of discussing what it means to decide to engage. The dead body's in the street. What do you do now?[7]

If the politics of loss and grief is at least as old as *Antigone*, however, these questions have also taken on new poignancy and urgency in the context of what many scholars refer to as the "age of apology," which has been heralded by the appearance of a variety of formal and informal mechanisms of acknowledgment for historical traumas and injustices.[8] Foremost among these mechanisms are the rapidly proliferating truth and reconciliation commissions (TRCs) that have been initiated in a variety of national and local contexts, ranging from the famous South African Truth and Reconciliation Commission to the Truth and Reconciliation Commission of Canada (completed in 2015) to lower profile processes such as the Maine-Wabanaki State Child Welfare TRC.[9] Truth and reconciliation processes seem to embody the idea that acknowledging or "facing up" to historical traumas is the only way to advance efforts toward social repair. Perhaps, to paraphrase James Baldwin, not everything that is faced can be changed, but to disavow the work of confrontation is to radically preclude the possibility of change.[10]

In this book, I bring conversations within and beyond political theory about the connection between mourning and politics together with the literature on truth and reconciliation processes in order to explore and theorize the democratic promise of the latter. Ranging from the time of *Antigone* to our own, this book explores the democratic politics of mourning. At the heart of this project is the example of the Greensboro Truth and Reconciliation Commission (GTRC), a grassroots-organized TRC that operated in Greensboro, North Carolina, from 2004 to 2006. The GTRC, like other TRCs, was not a magical device of social repair. Yet it did mark the creation of public space for dialogue and deliberation about a painful event in the city's history—the so-called Greensboro Massacre of November 1979—and the complicated pathways between that event and the present life of the community. I argue that the GTRC, when contextualized within a democratic theory of mourning, can provide a model for similar means and mechanisms of responding to the frustrations, blockages, and confusions within our contemporary politics of grief.

Mourning or Morning in America?

It should be acknowledged at the outset, however, that the idea that mourning might be a kind of civic obligation or an open democratic dynamic cuts against a powerful current in American political and cultural life. American political identity, in fact, has in some ways been predicated on the ability to *overcome* the past, to start anew or begin again. Alexis de Tocqueville, for instance, argued that America's culture of democratic inventiveness owed a great deal to the fact that it was unburdened by an aristocratic past. The absence of a burdening tradition allowed for outsized expectations of upward mobility and ever-expanding well-being.[11] Nearly two hundred years after Tocqueville's visit, the idea that Americans are not beholden to the past remains a potent political trope. This trope was perhaps wielded most effectively in the reelection campaign of Ronald Reagan in 1984, which featured the famous political advertisement, "Morning in America." The ad implied that the strength, confidence, and indefatigable optimism of American citizens are reflected in the collective unwillingness to dwell on the past and to eagerly greet each day as a new opportunity to be seized and exploited—"It's morning, again, in America."

It is easy to dismiss this optimism as delusional or naïve, yet such ideas have political utility because they have deep cultural resonance. In a different form from the Reagan advertisement, they are reflected in the classic Bob Dylan song, "It's All Over Now, Baby Blue," in which the listener is implored to "forget the dead you've left, they will not follow you," and to "strike another match, go start anew."[12] The myth of self-invention and perpetual innovation paints the country as a collective of ingenious individuals full of audacious hopes, capable at any moment of a sudden break into unanticipated territory. Dwelling on the past is not only a waste of precious energy; it is practically un-American.

If the power of this myth is understandable, it is nonetheless powerfully misleading and profoundly problematic in a country marked by historical brutalities and by ongoing realities of disrespect and despair. This myth reflects a political and psychological investment in innocence, a belief that each new dawn is a potential rupture from the past. It is Baldwin, again, who testified to the problematic nature of American innocence, when he wrote that Americans "have destroyed and are destroying hundreds of thousands of lives and do not know it and do not want to know it."[13] The historical crimes are one matter, but Baldwin faults his fellow citizens more for the attitude of blithe disregard *about* those crimes. As Baldwin put it in 1962, the "problem of American identity has everything to do with all the things that happened in this country but never have been admitted or dealt with."[14] The collective inability or unwillingness to mourn the past—and the presence of the past—poisons American politics and identity.

Mourning, however, should not be viewed in terms of an endless dwelling on the past. As I see it, democratic work of mourning is also inherently future oriented, because it is animated by an aspirational politics of recognition that compels us not only to face down the complexities that brutality has produced and continues to produce for American identity, but also to think about and locate practices of respect and recognition that might establish this identity on surer footing. To provide witness to the compromised state of democratic ideals is not to practice a cynical or sharp-eyed realism about the hollowness of those ideals— it is an *exercise* of those ideals. The nonmanic hope for a more democratic future in a country marked by both a brutal past and a troubled present is connected, I argue, with the collective ability to craft spaces and norms of mourning that in turn provide occasions for democratic efforts of recognition and repair.

The connection between politics and mourning is old, but the meaning of this connection remains contested and complex. The following chapters work through these complexities and offer a way of thinking about and practicing social mourning in ways that might honor democratic ideals while acknowledging the complex history, uneven enactment, and uncertain future of those ideals. To keep mourning an open dynamic in a democratic society is a difficult charge, made even more difficult by powerful myths of innocence and perpetual renewal. It requires a psychological and practical reorientation toward democratic identity and civic responsibility. Yet as the Black Lives Matter protests demonstrate, this reorientation is both urgently needed and long overdue. It's mourning, then, in America.

This is the faith from which we start:
men shall know the commonwealth again
from bitter searching of the heart.

—Leonard Cohen, *Villanelle for Our Time*

THE POLITICS OF MOURNING IN AMERICA

From the Greensboro Massacre to the Greensboro Truth and Reconciliation Commission

It is across great scars of wrong / I reach toward the song of kindred men.

—Robert Duncan

In the late morning on Saturday, November 3, 1979, a caravan of Ku Klux Klansmen steered its way through the streets of Greensboro, North Carolina. The thirty-five individuals packed into nine automobiles were on their way to disrupt a scheduled rally in a black public-housing neighborhood that had been planned by the Communist Workers Party (CWP), which had been organizing mill and cafeteria workers along with the Greensboro Association for Poor People (GAPP). Ostensibly, this disruption was to be limited to throwing eggs and making speeches, but the pistols and shotguns packed into the Klansmen's vehicles bespoke other possibilities. As the first car—with its Confederate flag license plate—pushed its way amid the protesters, a shouting match broke out. The verbal confrontation between the demonstrators and the white supremacists quickly escalated to violence, and five CWP members and activists were shot dead. Ten others were wounded. The event came to be known as the "Greensboro Massacre."

The deadly confrontation on November 3 quickly set off a period not only of grief but also of conflict within Greensboro and beyond over the meaning and larger significance of the event. For instance, in the immediate aftermath of the shooting, the CWP issued a pamphlet entitled "Turn Grief into Strength! Avenge the CWP Five!"[1] The pamphlet described the formation of the Committee to Avenge the Communist Workers Party Five, whose first order of business would be to plan a funeral and protest march to take place the following Sunday. A flyer for the proposed march depicted an idealized CWP member smashing the butt of a shotgun into the chin of a figure marked "capitalism" (who was surrounded on either side with figures depicting the FBI and the KKK). During the funeral procession, nearly eight hundred activists marched in support of the CWP (several activists brandished shotguns in a show of defiance),[2] shadowed by as many as one thousand law enforcement officials.[3]

The Communist Workers Party implored local citizens to mourn and "remember the CWP 5," and to see the events of early November as "the turning point of class struggle in the U.S." This latter statement was engraved onto a large granite monument in the Maplewood Cemetery in Greensboro, where four of the five deceased members of the CWP were buried. The monument declared that the CWP Five had been murdered by "the criminal monopoly capitalist class," and that their deaths—while a "tremendous loss to the CWP and to their families," amounted to a "clarion call to the U.S. people to fight for workers' rule." The revolutionary rhetoric of the CWP continued throughout the subsequent trials against members of the KKK—activists interrupted the first trial with a stink bomb and refused to participate in what they described as a "sham"—and in both the following state court and federal criminal trials, the Klansmen were acquitted on all charges, each time by an all-white jury.[4]

The Communist Workers Party was not the only active participant in the struggle to comprehend or publicly narrate the meaning of the Greensboro Massacre. Immediately, the CWP's struggle to memorialize their dead encountered heavy resistance from city officials and local business and civic leaders in Greensboro. In the eyes of these officials, the Greensboro Massacre was little more than an ugly incident between two extremist groups. Framed by city officials not as a "massacre" of vulnerable citizens but as a "shootout" between out-of-town radicals, the massacre was seen to have little if anything to do with Greensboro itself. The city, on this account, was an "innocent victim" caught between the equally unsavory radicalism of the CWP and the KKK.[5]

The struggle to mobilize public action and to shape public discourse on the basis of the Greensboro Massacre took place against the backdrop of Greensboro's official civic narrative as a vanguard city for civil rights progress. Greensboro officials had worked assiduously in previous decades to cultivate a progressive image of the city with regard to race relations. For instance, Greensboro was one of the first cities in the South to announce that it would comply with the 1954 Supreme Court ruling in *Brown v. Board of Education*. Greensboro was also the site of the famous Woolworth's sit-in in February 1960, in which the so-called Greensboro Four occupied spots at the segregated downtown lunch counter and refused to leave. The nonviolent, direct action of the Greensboro Four was widely credited as the spark for the broader sit-in movement across the South.[6] Their actions contributed to a sense of Greensboro exceptionalism in the area of civil rights and helped facilitate what historian William Chafe called Greensboro's "progressive mystique."[7] At the core of this mystique was the notion of "civility," which encapsulated the belief that racial disparities and conflicts were best addressed through indirect means—sublimated into a gradual process of eroding inequalities and achieving mutual respect.[8]

The Greensboro Massacre and its aftermath clearly did not fit into this larger civic narrative about racial moderation and gradual progress, nor did the image of a Death to the Klan rally organized by self-avowed communists being shot up by white supremacists reflect the supposedly consensual norm of civility. Many prominent citizens—both black and white—could not reconcile their image of civil rights progress with the revolutionary rhetoric of the CWP or with the ugly violence of the Greensboro Massacre. The massacre and its aftermath, then, seemingly had to be split off from the official narrative of race relations and civil rights in Greensboro.

Efforts to split off the trauma were largely successful. In downtown Greensboro, for instance, the narrative of the 1960 sit-in is memorialized in the International Civil Rights Center and Museum, which opened on the site of the former Woolworth's building in 2010.[9] The museum, funded in part by the state of North Carolina, the U.S. Department of the Interior, and the City of Greensboro, dramatizes the experience of the Greensboro Four before and during their courageous challenge of segregation. It also contextualizes the sit-ins within the broader struggle for civil and human rights, including in its exhibition space not only artifacts from the period of slavery and Jim Crow but also tokens from U.N. peacekeeping missions. Missing from the museum, however, is any mention of the Greensboro Massacre of 1979, or the subsequent protests or trials. In this respect, the museum seems to embody the official civic narrative that emerged in the aftermath of the Massacre—namely, that it had "nothing to do" with Greensboro or, by implication, the struggle for civil rights and racial equality. Although the Greensboro Four of the Woolworth's sit-in are justly lauded for their bravery, the CWP Five are simply not part of the picture.

These omissions within the civil rights museum are all the more striking when we consider what happened twenty-five years after the massacre. In 2004, after extensive grassroots organizing, seven individuals were sworn in during a public ceremony to create the Greensboro Truth and Reconciliation Commission (GTRC). The GTRC, in striking contrast to both the strident politics of the CWP and the amnesic community cover story, was designed as a public process by which citizens in Greensboro could deliberatively engage the events of 1979 and their aftermath. Charged with investigating the causes and consequences of the Greensboro Massacre, the commission heard public testimony over the following fifteen months from surviving members of the CWP, the KKK, and others associated with the events of 1979. On completion of a final report, the organizing forces behind the commission sponsored a series of public dialogues to discuss the process and its results. The memory of the GTRC continues to have a presence in Greensboro (although, as previously noted, not in the international civil rights museum) and has inspired similar grassroots, unofficial reconciliation efforts in other places.

Greensboro, since the events of 1979, dramatizes the full range of what could be described as the *politics of mourning*. To speak about the politics of *mourning* is to acknowledge the fact that many salient political issues are strongly linked with experiences of pain and loss.[10] If mourning is the process by which individuals and collectivities respond to loss, then to speak of the *politics* of mourning is to acknowledge the ways that these responses often feed into and are fed by broader social struggles for redress, recognition, or reparation. From AIDS activist and Black Lives Matter "die-ins" to the transnational "women-in-black" protest movement, countless political struggles in a variety of cultural contexts have been waged through the rhetoric and the iconography of mourning.[11]

Yet the idea of a politics of mourning also reflects a deeper problematic—namely, that what counts as socially legible pain and loss is *itself* a political question. *Which* and *whose* losses will be commemorated or honored are questions that touch on the struggle within all societies over collective values. Jeffrey Stout, for instance, has argued that the question of what is to be publicly mourned is answered by the values that are held by citizens to be socially nonnegotiable or "sacred."[12] The struggle over the sacred requires public memorialization of triumphs and losses according to shared norms, which—in a democracy—are ideally those of nondomination, accountability, and shared agency.[13] Mourning is inescapably a part of politics because politically, just as much individually, we are what (or who) we mourn. It matters a great deal, to name just one example, whether banks close in honor of Martin Luther King Jr. or Jefferson Davis. Who sacrifices what for whom, whose pain is publicly registered and honored, and how those losses are commemorated—these are unavoidable and imperative political questions.

The need for rituals and processes of public mourning reflects the fact it is impossible to conceptualize collective life without corresponding practices that identify certain losses as significant and worthy of remembrance. However, as many observers have pointed out, public acts of remembrance often conceal a simultaneous request for forgetting. Mourning the losses of some often involves an explicit or implicit silencing of those who fall outside the circle of socially legible loss. For instance, Judith Butler has shown how some deaths appear to be more readily "grievable" than others, depending on dominant social frameworks.[14] In-group biases, prejudices, and power relations often circumscribe who or what can be mourned. On Butler's reading, it was this form of mourning that typified American public life in the months following the terrorist attacks of September 11, 2001. For Butler, the mediated public spectacle of the attacks shaped citizens of the United States into the image of a nation unified in grief, but at the cost of idealizing the attacked homeland and demonizing the perpetrators as freedom-hating "evil-doers."[15] Pressures of idealization, moreover, intensified feelings of distrust and unease with perceived outsiders—Muslims, Arab Americans, or anyone who looked vaguely "foreign." This in turn fed what Libby Anker has described as "melodramatic" political discourse, which interpreted the losses of 9/11 in terms of sullied innocence and injured sovereignty that could only be redeemed through a heroic, violent response.[16] For Anker, such responses are ultimately self-defeating because the "lost" objects of sovereignty and innocence are themselves the product of an idealizing fantasy or collective illusion. What appears to be a response to felt loss or trauma, then, seems closer to a form of social melancholia or blocked grief. Yet what is undeniable is that grief over the trauma of 9/11 has ramified through a variety of political issues and contests, ranging from the controversy over the so-called Ground Zero mosque in 2010 to the presidential primaries of 2016.[17]

Whether polities can avoid what Butler calls the "dry grief of endless political rage" or what Anker sees as a self-defeating melodrama of impossible sovereignty depends on how the politics of mourning is taken up and practiced.[18] Critics of regnant forms of public mourning and memorialization therefore carry a responsibility to articulate not just what is problematic with how we mourn but how we might mourn better—more inclusively, more democratically. The alternative is not to pretend that we can do otherwise than mourn, because what these events and their contested aftermaths reveal most clearly are the bedrock assumptions of this book, namely, that *politics is intertwined with mourning and mourning has a politics.*

Greensboro proves to be a fruitful site for the investigation of mourning's politics because the recent history of the city reflects the broad range of ways in which mourning can manifest itself within public life. In the reactions of the CWP to the shooting deaths of their members, we can see the intimate connection between mourning and an activist politics of resistance directed against the state or other agents of social oppression. In this respect, the CWP's efforts fit into a long tradition. Funerals have repeatedly served as occasions for popular mobilization against injustice, from the context of the civil rights struggle in Mississippi to antiapartheid activism in Johannesburg, South Africa, to Northern Ireland's most intense period of sectarian strife, to the "dirty war" period of Argentina and to pre- (and post-) revolutionary Iran.[19] Political demands have often flowed directly from funerary practice, and public mourning has, again and again, served as a site for political mobilization and as a mode of political resistance aimed at challenging or toppling the reigning order of things.[20] In 2015, for instance, protests erupted in Baltimore after the funeral for Freddie Gray, a local man who died as a result of a "rough ride" administered by the Baltimore Police Department following Gray's arrest. In these instances of protest or direct action, social divisions are reinforced or named—such as the CWP's uncompromising rhetoric of the "capitalist monopoly class"—providing an affectively charged, agonistic frame for politics.

Alongside this form of activist and often militant resistance, however, are the civic rites, rituals, and narratives of memorialization that attempt to provide an authoritative interpretation for social traumas. Through eulogies or commemorative events, public officials and other prominent voices shape the discourse surrounding social trauma.[21] Such rituals offer a collective means of mourning by incorporating traumatic events into narratives of civic life. As was the case in Greensboro, civic norms (such as "civility") provide a mechanism of selection by which certain events can be actively remembered or mourned while others are to be split off or left behind. Moreover, these norms often set the terms of political membership, such that belonging to a community (or to the "real" community) can be seen in light of whose losses we take seriously or honor.

With the Greensboro Truth and Reconciliation Commission, however, a relatively novel process of public mourning presents itself. The GTRC was a grassroots-organized, unofficial truth commission designed to facilitate public dialogue on a traumatic event, its historical context, and its long reach into the present. Reducible to neither an agonistic process of articulating social divisions nor to a consensualist ritual of amnesic commemoration, the GTRC staged a public process of identifying and clarifying the conflicts and differences within the community, including testimony from unrepentant Klan members alongside social justice advocates. The process included the voices not only of victims and perpetrators but also of witnesses and bystanders, along with citizens who only had an indirect connection to the event but who could testify to its lingering aftereffects. The commission clarified the differences between black and white citizens' perceptions of the massacre, revealing both the plurality and complexity within the city and the fact that social norms such as civility had acquired very different meanings depending on one's social position.[22]

In this respect, the GTRC did not simply name social divisions, nor did it paper over them. Instead, it provided an inclusive public space within which those divisions could be articulated and acknowledged, with the result that citizens of Greensboro were presented with an opportunity to face up to and deliberate about the massacre and its afterlife. The opportunity to engage in public dialogue is by itself, of course, a form of social action, but the GTRC also provided space and occasion for citizens to take concrete steps to address social issues revealed by the GTRC—

such as inequality, violence, and community distrust. I refer to these concrete actions as the GTRC's democratic "ripple effects." The aftereffects of the GTRC include new and strengthened associational networks and civic capacity in Greensboro, which—while not heralding an imminent end to racial discrimination or disrespect—sow the seeds of a more robust and resilient form of democracy in Greensboro and in those communities that might learn from its example.

In this book, I use the recent experiences of Greensboro as a means of thinking through the paradoxes, pathologies, and possibilities surrounding the politics of mourning. This is a particularly urgent task at this moment. It is urgent in part because the discourse of grief and mourning remains generative for activist politics—as demonstrated by the "die-ins" following the 2014 grand jury decisions in the cases of Michael Brown and Eric Garner in Ferguson and Staten Island, respectively, and by the way in which the funeral for Freddie Gray in Baltimore became a flashpoint not only for localized direct actions but for broader protests against police brutality, the war on drugs, concentrated poverty and racial mistrust. Yet a conceptualization of the politics of mourning is also timely insofar as countries and communities are increasingly attuned to the politics of memory and memorialization. We are living in what some scholars are calling the "age of apology," in which national and local communities are showing a greater willingness to revisit dark and violent episodes in their recent and not-so-recent history.[23] The GTRC, for instance, built on previous models of truth and reconciliation processes in South Africa and elsewhere, and the GTRC has in turn become a model for how communities can self-organize processes of examining violent episodes in their histories and the living legacies of those events. Over the past three decades, local and global pressures have conspired to make "dealing with the past" an essential component of national and international politics.[24] The politics of mourning, then, is intensifying and proliferating, which invites reflection as to its limitations and potential.

Some might argue, however, that an analysis of the situation of Greensboro in terms of mourning is misguided. These voices might claim that what Greensboro reveals is a clear-cut case of miscarried justice, in which long-standing racial prejudices perverted the judicial process and led to the Klansmen's acquittal, which in turn entrenched social divisions and intensified racial mistrust in Greensboro. By approaching the case of Greensboro from the perspective of a theory of justice, our attention would be directed toward the maldistribution of basic goods such as police protection, adequate housing, living wages, or to the presence of racial stereotypes and discrimination, all of which contributed to the tragic conflict in Greensboro and the inadequate response by public officials. The rhetoric of mourning, on the other hand, might seem to confuse a responsibility of the individual or the group (for a therapeutic or healing response to loss) with the responsibilities of the state or of its citizens (for the administration of fair procedures and the fair provision of basic goods).[25]

The value of the language of mourning, however, is precisely that it draws our eye toward a messier, multilayered struggle for recognition that exceeds—although it is not fully separate from—the struggle for justice, and it shows that the state is not the only important figure in this struggle. Fair, formal juridical procedures and the provision of basic goods are essential to supporting a democratic culture of equal respect. However, the emphasis on neutral principles of justice and the pursuit of liberal rights are, by themselves, insufficiently strong foundation stones for democratic society. As Axel Honneth has argued, the "load-bearing structures" for democratic culture consist less in juridical or legal relations than in "practices, customs, and social roles" within the everyday lifeworld.[26] Legally guaranteed rights and the institutions that support them are essential mechanisms by which democratic citizens can experience feelings of social respect. Yet, if we see democratic society in broader terms as a layered arrangement of recognition relationships, then we can appreciate these mechanisms as merely one of the many sets of institutions and practices through which the struggle for just recognition is waged.[27] Along these lines, Danielle Allen argues that a community's "civic etiquette"—which includes an understanding (often implicit) about whose losses are to be honored—has a significant effect on social trust and political engagement.[28] Civic etiquette is shaped but not determined or exhausted by positive laws or by the actions of the state. Hence for Allen as for Honneth, the process by which citizens acknowledge both seismic social traumas and mundane experiences of disrespect is a significant aspect of the broader work of cultivating democratic *Sittlichkeit*, a responsibility that is social or collective by its nature.[29]

Let us imagine a historical counterfactual as a way of bringing out these issues. Imagine that the members of the KKK had been found guilty during the initial trial in Greensboro. Imagine shackled Klansmen being led off to serve prison sentences of various lengths, as a chorus of concerned citizens cheers the verdict on the courthouse steps. One can then imagine some of those affected by the massacre—though not the members of the CWP themselves—speaking outside the courtroom about "justice being done." The local and national media would have amplified this message of resolution, before turning off the cameras and focusing their attention elsewhere. But with justice having been executed, the perpetrators having been convicted and sentenced, would the multilayered trauma of the Greensboro Massacre and the still simmering conflicts surrounding race and class in the city have been resolved? Would the need to narrate and interpret the events of 1979 have somehow evaporated? Would the "progressive mystique" surrounding congratulatory public narratives have been challenged or disrupted? More importantly, would the civic etiquette of a city like Greensboro—stratified by race and class, and replete with misrecognitions, mistrust, and deadly hostilities—have dramatically shifted? Rather, it is likely that such an outcome would have desocialized the events of November 1979 by focusing on the particular perpetrators and victims. The trial would have isolated these individuals from the broader social context that made the event possible in the first place and that had been reshaped by the event in ways that the trial could not fully unpack or undo. The larger, messy and internally contested story of the massacre would have faded away untold. From the angle of a theory of justice, this scenario might be seen as unproblematic or unavoidable. Yet as Iris Marion Young has argued, a narrow liability framework of justice—while appropriate in many instances—unduly limits the reach of social responsibility in situations of complex or structural injustice.[30] More importantly, from the perspective of a struggle for recognition, the failure to take into account the larger story of the event marks a continuation of social injury. Official or social silence surrounding historical traumas is a *heavy* silence; it is a wounding silence.[31]

The dominant discourses and practices of justice, then, while necessary to a democratic society committed to norms of equal respect, are an insufficient means of responding to traumatic events like the Greensboro Massacre, in part because traumatic events are never discrete phenomena isolated in time and place.[32] Instead, these events often reflect enduring patterns of misrecognition within social and political life. As such, the challenge of recognition will necessarily exceed the challenge of justice. Justice, in the words of Luc Boltanski, is that which "brings disputes to an end"; it is aimed at the authoritative resolution or settling of conflicts.[33] Yet what is important in situations of chronic social misrecognition is less an authoritative closing of accounts than the cultivation of democratic capacities for recognition and respect.[34] Struggles for coexistence in contemporary American life are intensified by lingering resentments born of legacies of misrecognition. For instance, in Greensboro, the massacre and its aftermath further entrenched social disparities and mistrust, making positive and mutualistic social relations more difficult.[35] For these reasons, democratic citizens need to be oriented less toward the resolution of conflict and more toward the *ongoing* struggle for recognition in the face of deep differences and amid the living legacies of social traumas.[36]

In this book, I show how the vocabulary of mourning can usefully draw our attention toward these multilayered struggles for recognition and the practices and spaces in which they take place. In so doing, I am stepping into and contributing to a lively conversation within political theory, among other disciplines, about the meaning and mechanisms of social mourning. Within contemporary political theory (perhaps ironically), the politics of mourning have been persistently filtered through two classical figures: Antigone and Pericles. Antigone, the ill-fated daughter of Oedipus, has come to embody the penchant for mourning to crystallize into direct actions or protests that challenge the dominant social-political order. Antigone's burial of her fallen brother Polyneices and her defiance of Creon serves as a model for how marginalized citizens can mobilize counter-publics of resistance, and in recent years political theorists such as Judith Butler and Bonnie Honig have repeatedly turned to Antigone in order to theorize a radical or agonistic account of politics.[37]

On the other hand the figure of Pericles—the Greek statesman and general dur-ing the so-called golden age of classical Athens—has come to stand in for the work of shaping public discourse surrounding social traumas by filtering such traumas through consensual civic norms and narratives. Pericles provides the ideal type for this activity, which is concerned with incorporating public traumas into the living traditions and shared values of the polity (or, by contrast, splitting off traumas because they *cannot* fit into the dominant narratives of these traditions or values). In his oration as represented in Thucydides's account of the Pelopon-nesian War, Pericles justifies the sacrifice of the Athenian soldiers by magnifying the glory and greatness of the polis. The surviving community subsumes or in-corporates its dead, who in turn become representatives of supposedly consen-sual norms. Although the Periclean funeral oration has been criticized practically from its point of origin, its basic tropes persist.[38] Contemporary funeral orations, as Simon Stow has argued, often "demand little" of their audience beyond an un-critical patriotism that reaffirms the social-political status quo.[39] Stow has charted the appearance of this "romantic" style of public grief in the wake of pub-lic traumas such as September 11 and Hurricane Katrina, while showing how the Periclean politics of mourning reappear within the ongoing struggle over the pub-lic meaning of the civil rights movement.[40] Public commemorations of civil rights icons often subsume these figures within a national narrative of inevitable progress. Commemorative events and discourses incorporate the story of civil rights into a story about the unique greatness of the American polis, yet only by excising the contentiousness, contingency, and (often) the unfinished nature of the struggle.[41] In this way, civic rituals of memorialization carry forward the tropes of the ancient funeral oration, which, as Nicole Loraux has argued, was an at-tempt to discursively transform Athenian democracy "into a beautiful, harmo-nious whole."[42] Funeral orations therefore depict the city not as it is and was, but as it "wishes [itself] to be."[43]

Antigone and Pericles, then, serve as figures for dominant modes of public mourning. Each of these modes, however, is shadowed by pathologies or internal excesses that make them problematic for democratic societies. Antigone has be-come exemplary in part because she stands for an insistent remembrance of in-justices in opposition to hasty foreclosures and a shrinking of the public space for contestation over the meaning of past traumas.[44] Strong-necked insistence on

justice aims to disrupt both practices of oppression and discourses of false reconciliation.[45] Antigone is inspiring in part because she does not capitulate, despite
the difficult circumstances of and steep penalty for her resistance. As a result,
Sophocles's heroine has enjoyed a very busy afterlife, as the performance of *Antigone* has galvanized resistance to state silence surrounding social traumas in a
dizzying variety of locations.[46]

The Antigonean insistence on justice over and against social forgetting, however, seemingly requires both the drawing of clear lines of division and an absolute commitment to the struggle. Yet the all-or-nothing fanaticism of memory
justice quickly encounters a paradox, expressed sharply by Robert Meister: "In
revolutionary justice the victim is to become victor; the problem with this concept
is that nothing counts as winning except continuing the fight. But the problem
with abandoning it is that nothing counts as justice if it is not worth the struggle."[47]
The absolute commitment to memory justice can cultivate a rigid moral-political
identity that cannot imagine "ways of winning" and therefore insists above all
else on the continued necessity of the fight, regardless of how the other "combat-
ant" may respond or how the terrain of struggle may shift.[48] The paradox resides
in the fact that memory justice both makes a claim for recognition and develops
a moral-psychological subject position that makes the settlement of recognition
claims difficult if not impossible: if the commitment to the struggle is given up,
then the internalized object has been compromised. Yet because this object has
served as the fixed source of identity, its compromise represents a mortal threat
to the self. The moral-psychological position of memory justice, then, requires
fresh reasons to carry on the (endless) fight, lest it forsake the (wounded) superego.[49] Every resistant Antigone requires an inflexible Creon, and if the latter
changes his ways, then a substitute Creon must quickly be found.

These difficulties have not gone unnoticed. Victims of social trauma can suffer from what Wendy Brown has described as "wounded attachment," a form of
political subjectivity that remains perversely tethered not only to its social injuries but also to the social order that produced those injuries.[50] For Brown, this
form of subjectivity settles for a "cathartic reaffirmation of victimhood" and aban-
dons riskier positions and mobilizations that might challenge oppressive forms
of political life.[51] An inordinate focus on past injuries, as Frantz Fanon put it,
threatens to turn the victim into a "prisoner of history" locked in the "Tower of
the Past."[52] Antigonean, agonistic resistance can coalesce into a rigid, heroic political posture that obscures the slower, patient work of democratic resistance.[53]
Like Antigone, wounded activists can spurn potential allies along with the difficult work of persuasion, given that they might feel charged with the moral righteousness activated by experiences of victimhood.[54] For instance, witness the CWP
activists in the wake of Greensboro Massacre, whose refusal to participate in the

subsequent trial helped facilitate the Klan members' acquittal. If an Antigonean style of mourning is an essential means of retaining the memory of misrecognition within public narratives, it is not without its potential pathologies.

The Periclean mode of public mourning, however, can also generate political pathologies. Commemorative discourses apply subtle moral pressure that can stigmatize political contestation. When "the community" is unified in grief, those who challenge the social actions undertaken on the basis of this consensus can be split off as dangerous outsiders, opposed to the "real" members of the group. Moreover, consensualist practices of memorialization can depoliticize the past by seeing contingent victories through fantasies of inevitable progress. Doing so promotes a false picture of social cohesion and closure, which in turn disciplines a society's civic etiquette.[55] Commemorative rituals can cultivate a benumbing amnesia over the past and a befogging romanticism about the present. For instance, insofar as the International Civil Rights Center and Museum in Greensboro passes over the Greensboro Massacre and the radical distrust and disparities that preceded and were intensified by that event, it contributes to the construction of a narrow narrative of civil rights struggle and progress that excludes the messier, more conflicted aspects of race and class relations in the South and the broader American polity—both past and present.

The kernel of moral and political truth within Periclean practices, however, is that processes of meaning making over the past and of articulating continuity between the past and present are unavoidable features of collective life and essential components of political identity. Communities do not exist without rituals and narratives of commemoration or remembrance—in fact, communities can be loosely defined by what they ask their members to remember or to forget.[56] The democratic challenge is to engage in this labor in ways that mitigate temptations toward idealization, splitting, or denial, which inspire pathologies of democratic life. Namely, these defenses can exaggerate social differences, reify identities, and make collaborative action unlikely or impossible. The dual-sided struggle is to resist hasty foreclosures on traumas of social misrecognition while remembering that insistent memory justice can preclude an awareness of possibilities for civic agency and social transformation.

Pericles and Antigone, then, stand in for ambiguous tendencies within political communities. Both the counsel of selective forgetting in the name of social cohesion and the insistence on remembrance in the name of social contestation can lead to pathological social formations, feeding either pernicious practices of denial or manic cycles of inflexible resistance. Yet both are also *unavoidable* sociopolitical orientations (practically and normatively). A society without insistent voices of memory justice risks a slide into barbarism; yet a society without norms of commemoration that provide a sense of (relative) cohesion is simply unimaginable. In the chapters that follow, once again, I attempt to navigate the paradoxes, pathologies, and possibilities that surround consensualist and agonistic practices of public mourning. In the process I articulate a theory and practice of a *democratic work of mourning* that attempts to theorize a tricky middle space that joins agonism and consensualism. I argue that this articulation is essential for seeing the promise and understanding the limitations of the Greensboro Truth and Reconciliation Commission as a democratic practice and space of mourning, by which citizens in Greensboro engaged in a public examination of a traumatic event—an examination that was significant in and of itself but also because of its democratic aftereffects. The GTRC—when situated in a theory of democratic mourning—testifies to and gives us hope for the ongoing labor of social recognition.

To understand the full meaning of the politics of mourning, we have to utilize resources both within and beyond political theory. The reason for this is that the struggle for recognition of which public mourning is an indispensable part is neither *strictly* a political nor a psychological phenomenon, but both at the same time. As Pamela Conover argues, recognition demands are "ultimately psychological in nature," because they reach out for patterns of reliable attention in which individual identities can develop and flourish.[57] However, with this formulation Conover elides the fact that the psychological demands of recognition are articulated and achieved within political contexts marked by inequalities of power, differential experiences of justice, and varying levels of mistrust, which inherently complicates both the articulation and the satisfaction of these claims. Recognition is therefore a complexly social, political, and psychological phenomenon. Along these lines, the drive for legal recognition embodied in the expansion and protection of human rights should be seen as a necessary part of a larger struggle for an intact identity, a struggle that assumes agents to have determinate needs and desires following from unavoidable experiences of interdependency. The legal or political subject is also a needy subject, and legal subjectification must therefore be understood in the context not only of political but psychological needs.

The work of Axel Honneth reflects eloquently on this interconnection between the psychological and the social. In fact, it is because of this interconnection that Honneth roots his theory of recognition in object relations psychoanalysis, which illuminates the interpersonal developmental trajectories by which various needs for recognition are fulfilled or denied.[58] According to Honneth, the satisfaction of interpersonal needs for recognition results in the acceptance of a difficult balancing act between independence and merger. For example, following the work of D. W. Winnicott, Honneth argues that the "capacity to be alone"—to have confidence in oneself as an agent—is inseparable from the internalization of relationships of care reflecting our undeniable dependency on others.[59] Navigating this terrain successfully leads to the development of basic self-confidence, a prerequisite for experiencing oneself as an object of legal respect or social regard.

While Honneth limits his use of psychoanalysis to his conceptualization of the interpersonal sphere of recognition, he argues that this sphere has significant implications for social and political life. Although the recognition accorded to legal and social subjects does not resemble the affection and intimacy through which interpersonal recognition is communicated, the need for the former is ultimately inseparable from the interdependencies and desires revealed by the latter. Once again, the legal or civic subject cannot be cleanly separated from the needy subject. Moreover, the interpersonal sphere is where the abilities to tolerate anxiety and ambiguity, to live constructively and respectfully with others, to handle differences and conflicts, are first tested and developed.[60] The interpersonal sphere can therefore be seen as protopolitical, insofar as it can be seen as a preparatory space for political engagement. The interpersonal sphere, however, is also properly political because the question of who can legitimately occupy the interpersonal sphere reflects a struggle over the kinds of intimacy that are socially legitimate and legible.

The interconnection between the psychological and the social within recognition struggles, once again, requires that we reach beyond disciplinary boundaries in an effort to understand the politics of mourning.[61] Psychoanalytic frameworks, I argue, are especially well suited to address this intermediate space at the intersection of personal and collective practices. Nancy Luxon, for instance, has argued that the "combative collaborative" within psychoanalytic practice contains a form of civic education that makes individuals more mindful of cultural and social codes and can "introject these individuals into the authorial practice of originating and revising" these codes.[62] Psychoanalytic settings exist "to the side" of normal social interactions, but they help cultivate relationships through which individuals can exercise their interpretive skills and develop a greater capacity for participation in public life. Going even further than Luxon, Honneth argues that psychoanalytic frameworks draw our attention to "emancipatory moments in our normal human life"—moments in which we clarify our internal and external conflicts and deepen capacities for mutual respect, tolerance, and trust.[63] In other words, the qualities of democratic citizenship that might enable a politics of just recognition are inextricably linked with intersubjective developmental trajectories (and misdevelopments) that psychoanalytic approaches can help to illuminate. The work of mourning, in this light, can be seen as a psychopolitical process. How communities and citizens process or memorialize loss, and how they act together in the wake of social traumas, will depend on both psychological and social capacities. This does not reduce the polis to the psyche, but shows their intertwinement.

Psychoanalytic approaches are of course already active within theoretical conversations about the politics of mourning. For instance, Sigmund Freud's seminal 1917 essay, "Mourning and Melancholia," has become a significant touchstone for social theorists who deploy (or challenge) Freud's famous distinction between pathological melancholia and healthy attempts at "working through" or mourning a lost object.[64] In his essay Freud recognized the potential political nature of mourning, noting that we mourn not only significant others but lost or compromised ideals and other collectively shared objects. Yet Freud's approach is problematic for conceptualizing a democratic politics of mourning and the larger struggle for recognition, in part because it depicts mourning as the process by which a socially withdrawn ego relinquishes and replaces what it lost through a process of detachment from failing investments and a reattachment to more responsive objects. As compelling as this narrative might seem, it creates false expectations about the politics of mourning, which is never characterized by a unified (or isolated) subject who can sovereignly survey the ramifications of its loss. Social mourning is a relational and public process, not an isolated or private task. Moreover, the traumas connected to an ongoing struggle for recognition are often not so much lost objects as they are enduring patterns or habits of disregard. To say that these damages must (or even that they can) be relinquished without taking into consideration asymmetries of power and representation is to risk continuing, rather than disrupting, these habits. The emphasis on "getting over" or relinquishing the lost object beckons a wounding silence. Finally, social mourning is not, contrary to Freud's narrative, primarily about *overcoming* loss; it is about finding ways of *living with* social traumas, their ongoing legacies, and the disagreements and conflicts within every political space that are often revealed by these traumas and by everyday experiences of loss, suffering, and grief.

If a Freudian approach is insufficient, then, this does not imply that we have to leave the psychoanalytic terrain in an effort to conceptualize the politics of mourning. Object relations psychoanalysis, in distinction to an orthodox Freudian account, provides a framework that takes into account both the relational nature of the politics of recognition and the latter's intertwinement with mourning. In particular, the work of Melanie Klein and D. W. Winnicott can be used to theorize both the obstacles and the preconditions for what I am calling the democratic work of mourning. Object relations approaches offer political theorists a conceptual vocabulary that sensitizes us to the ways in which social practices of mourning can feed vicious cycles of persecution, stereotyping, and misperception. Informed by this perspective, I show how instances of public mourning can activate certain cognitive-affective schemas characterized by mundane yet socially problematic defenses against anxiety, uncertainty, and frustration. The turn toward Klein and Winnicott, then, provides a diagnostic vocabulary that illuminates the pathologies attendant to both agonism and consensualism, including the common tropes of idealization and demonization and associated practices of splitting and denial. A psychoanalytically informed approach to the politics of mourning can reveal how agonism and consensualism each trade on and activate these defenses, which inspires a frozen politics of either endless struggle or fantastical harmony.

Yet the turn to object relations psychoanalysis is inspired by more than critique. Object relations approaches can also move us beyond a diagnosis of public mourning's pathologies and indicate alternative practices and spaces that might allow citizens to unwind these pathologies. Klein's concepts of the "depressive position" and the "good object" and Winnicott's understanding of "potential space" (discussed later in this chapter) form the conceptual kernel of an aspirational politics of mourning in which social conflicts are identified, clarified, and more openly engaged. This aspirational politics of mourning does not transcend agonistic or consensualist practices, but it contextualizes and, ideally, filters the struggle for memory justice and the search for civic narrative through a broader politics of recognition, based on the facilitation of intergroup contact and collaborative civic action. *Working through*, as it were, requires *public work*—democratic labors of recognition and repair.[65]

To encapsulate this aspirational democratic work, I put forward a third classical figure for the politics of mourning—that of Orestes. In Aeschylus's tragic trilogy, *The Oresteia*, Orestes both undergoes an experience of trauma (the murder of his father) and enacts one himself (the murder of his mother). Based in part on Klein's interpretation of Aeschylus, I argue that an Oresteian politics of mourning embodies a tragic awareness of a traumatic past alongside an optimism about democratic agency and the possibilities of social recognition. The image of Orestes, then, can inspire a democratic work of mourning that is irreducible to either agonism or consensualism, but that operates instead in the difficult space between them.[66] The Greensboro Truth and Reconciliation Commission can be usefully situated within this image, which magnifies its potential—and the potential for similar practices—as a space of democratic mourning.

In this chapter, I outline the steps of this argument in more detail, including the reason why the turn toward Klein and object relations psychoanalysis is crucial for the formation of an adequate account of the politics of mourning. Subsequent chapters develop critiques of agonism (chapter 2) and consensualism (chapter 3), before turning to the development of the theory of the democratic work of mourning and its accompanying objects and spaces (chapters 4 and 5). Each of the three middle chapters also unpacks concepts drawn from the object relations tradition: the depressive position (chapter 2), the good object (chapter 3), and potential space (chapter 4). Therefore, the value of this approach will be elaborated as the book unfolds. In the final chapter, I return to Greensboro in order to contextualize the GTRC within the broader politics of truth and reconciliation. In the afterword, I turn this conversation back to the recent deaths of unarmed black citizens such as Eric Garner, Michael Brown, and Freddie Gray and to the Black Lives Matter protest movement that has mobilized in response to these deaths and to enduring patterns of misrecognition.

Antigone and the Agonistic Politics of Mourning

The image and story of Antigone have been remarkably resilient within the western political tradition and beyond.[67] Antigone's exemplarity derives from the way that her narrative of resistance legitimates struggles by marginalized individuals and groups to achieve social redress. Antigone is a model activist mourner. She steadfastly insists that her losses should be honored, she refuses to cede on her claims, and she does not shy away from the struggle for hegemony that this commitment inspires. In this respect, Antigone has become a fitting representative for agonist political theory, which insists that antagonism and a struggle for hegemony reside at the very root of political life.[68] As Bonnie Honig puts it, the struggle between Antigone and Creon "is probably for most political theorists the template for what is meant by agonism."[69] From the work of Judith Butler—who turns to Antigone to theorize a performative politics of repudiation that can challenge dominant norms and discourses—to Honig's own appropriation of Antigone as a lively, demanding agonistic figure, Antigone and the politics of her mourning have been essential components of contemporary agonist approaches.

But what are agonists taking on board when they identify with Antigone and her particular politics of grief? What are the potential pathologies attendant to a view of mourning as agonistic mobilization, with its friend/enemy distinction and the associated tropes of idealization and demonization? For Gail Holst-Warhaft, grief offers a "unique opportunity for social mobilization and political action" because "grief is probably the most powerful emotion we ever feel."[70] Grief's passion, according to Holst-Warhaft, is excessive and ecstatic; it carries us "to the edge of madness."[71] At this edge, grief and anger collapse together in ways that can spark powerful political resistance. The power of Antigonean mourning, then, rests on the energy created by what Holst-Warhaft calls the "unity of shared rage."[72] The unity of shared rage fashions solidarity out of sorrow and channels grief into public grievance.[73]

Shared rage is then an essential aspect of an agonistic politics of grief. Political psychologists describe this in terms of the "psychology of outrage," which enables individuals and groups to overcome obstacles to collective action by inciting resistance against an oppressive social order.[74] As we have seen, the ability of groups such as the CWP to mobilize supporters in the wake of November 3 traded on the connections between grief, outrage, and vengeance. Yet this also indicates clearly the potential drawbacks of agonistic rage. The psychology of outrage can feed a process of abjection and debasement, which might be necessary in order to shore up a political identity of resistance, but which does so often at the cost demonizing the other toward whom the resistance is directed.[75] Social traumas filtered through an agonistic, friend/enemy distinction thereby support the formation of rigid and moralistic political identities, and the troubling or contesting of these identities is then *itself* a potential trauma that must be warded off. Becoming sensitive to the depth or complexity of the other would threaten the integrity of a self that is formed through outraged differentiation, and hence the other *must* stay debased or cruel if the self is to sustain its identity.[76] Yet rigid, polarized identities supported by a psychology of outrage and abjection can all too easily slide toward fantasies of the violent elimination of the other, an outcome that is psychologically less threatening than the acceptance of the other because fantasies of annihilation reinforce feelings of omnipotence and ward off anxieties of vulnerability.[77] As Julia Kristeva argues, the idea of the enemy is immediately and viscerally reassuring, and the hated object (unlike the loved object) "never disappoints."[78]

We can witness a politics and a psychology of outrage, and the associated tropes of abjection, idealization, and omnipotence, within the CWP's organizing efforts both before and after the Greensboro Massacre. The CWP's efforts to organize members of the working class in the Piedmont and Triangle regions of North Carolina were typified by polarizing rhetoric, and a cornerstone of their strategy were their repeated provocations of the KKK. Months before the events of November 3, the CWP had broken up a Klan rally in China Grove, North Carolina, burning a confederate flag in the process. The march on November 3 was itself advertised as a "Death to the Klan" rally, and it was publicized in an open letter to the KKK in which Klansmen were referred to as "scum" and a "temporary pest." All of these actions were part of the CWP's attempt to associate the Klan with the more immediate targets of labor organization, namely (in their words), the "monopoly capitalist class." The CWP's polarizing rhetorical strategy created an image of the abject enemy that collapsed the differences between owners of local textile mills and the KKK. Within the CWP's rhetoric, there was no effective difference between the KKK and local business leaders; the latter's "three piece suits," in their eyes, might as well have been "hooded sheets."[79] Identifying other social institutions and actors with the white terrorist violence of the Klan reveals the CWP's strategy of cultivating a large-scale working-class movement through the definition of an abject other to be resisted. After the massacre in November 1979, the CWP's rigid, polarized distinctions between the abject capitalist/Klan enemy and the idealized fallen members (who represented the "invincible Communist spirit") supported their refusal to cooperate with the state criminal trial, which, once again, helped to facilitate the KKK members' acquittal. Psychologically, of course, the acquittal could be seen as a more satisfactory outcome because it allowed the CWP and its allies to maintain the purity of their distinctions between the inherently corrupt system and the pure spirit of Communist opposition.[80]

The pathologies attendant to an agonistic politics of grief may seem obvious, but the difficulty is that the drawing of lines between friend and enemy *can* be democratically generative.[81] Just as abolitionists sought to sharpen the contradiction between a country (ostensibly) committed to equality and the practice of chattel slavery and legal discrimination, so too can the agonistic work of differentiation help to identify sources of social misrecognition and trauma. Yet insofar as the practice of differentiation reinforces social-psychological tendencies toward abjection and idealization, the politics of Antigonean mourning are precariously perched between democratic performance and pathology. Once again, political subjects that have internalized at their core a righteous struggle for justice can find it difficult to cede this internal object regardless of external circumstances. To quote Meister again, without an envisioned "way of winning," the only alternative is to ceaselessly continue the fight, which reifies both the opposition and the (heroic) self.[82] As the former CWP member Signe Waller later reflected, the organization's "stiff-necked polemical stance made united fronts difficult and isolated us from potential allies in the mainstream." What appeared in the moment as a principled stand against injustice based on the group's "moral authority" was later identified by Waller as a "smug sectarianism" that "had isolated us from much of the community." According to Waller, the CWP's moral authority itself relied on defenses of denial and splitting, only later recognized: "We were not as good or as dedicated or as right as we sometimes claimed to be, and the others were often not as bad or as wrong." As Waller concludes, in a line impossible for Antigone, "If you survive, you learn circumspection."[83]

Pericles and the Politics of Memorialization

If Antigone has come to stand in for a resistant, agonistic politics of grief, then the figure of Pericles can stand in for a concurrent mode of mourning in which civic rituals and discourses attempt to place public traumas within (or to displace them from) the polity's dominant narratives and norms. Periclean mourning rituals provide a context of public meaning making that sublimates felt grief and the disruptions of trauma into forms of civic identification and social coherence. As Nicole Loraux has argued, classical funeral oratory aimed to transform the democratic polity from a fractious mixture into "a beautiful, harmonious whole."[84] The idealization of the polis aims to dissolve the anxieties provoked by social trauma or loss, and the enduring values of the community provide a means of situating and comprehending the dislocating effects of painful events. In this light, rituals of commemoration must also be seen as civic rites of *forgetting*.[85] As Simon Stow has pointed out, this style of public mourning demands little from its audience beyond an uncritical attachment to the polity. By demanding little more than a recommitment to consensual civic norms, however, these rituals and discourses can conceal the contested nature of public traumas and the larger struggle for social recognition.

For instance, consider the Periclean politics of mourning surrounding the memorialization of African American enslavement, de jure discrimination under Jim Crow, and the struggle for legal recognition and social standing represented by the civil rights movement. The civil rights movement has moved into a central place within American public memorialization during the latter half of the twentieth century, yet this has seemingly come at the cost of a simultaneous sacralization and temporal restriction of the movement. Civil rights icons such as Martin Luther King Jr. and Rosa Parks are idealized and increasingly placed alongside other consensualist objects of admiration within American history such as Abraham Lincoln.[86] Yet the lionization of King and the Southern Christian Leadership Conference (SCLC) means that other relevant figures and movements (The Student Nonviolent Coordinating Committee [SNCC], for instance) are relegated to the position of bit players within the cosmic-political drama through which what King called the moral arc of the universe was bent toward justice.[87] Even that lionization is often highly amnesic. For instance Rosa Parks is repeatedly memorialized as someone whose "tired feet" inspired her resistance, which neglects the years of focused activism and training that preceded her direct action.[88] The focus on SCLC leadership, moreover, displaces traditions of grassroots organizing and democratic capacity building in the Deep South that were essential factors in the struggle toward racial equality.[89]

Public acts of memorialization are always selective, and they are additionally political insofar as they shape civic etiquette—the range of expected behaviors, norms and possibilities of democratic life. Consensualizing practices of civic memorialization, then, can dehumanize history's protagonists (seeing them as superhuman rather than all too human) and depoliticize the past. Retrospective claims about consensual norms displace the contentious struggles and contingent victories of civil rights, as the politics of civil rights become absorbed by a liberal story of pressure groups and steady legislative advance. Consensual practices of civic memorialization also restrict the broader agenda of civil rights, which involved not only the fight against legal discrimination but also against poverty and low wages, along with a developing critique of imperialism and colonialism.[90] This broader and more contentious agenda is displaced, if not defeated, by an ongoing politics of memory that endlessly replays "I Have a Dream," but skips over "I've Been to the Mountaintop," in which King conjoined the struggle for civil rights in the United States to the struggle against economic injustice and a transnational movement for human rights. Dominant modes of remembering civil rights reveal an impoverished understanding of the full range of the struggle, its contingent successes, and its unfinished business.[91]

Memorialization is a high-stakes game. A public space such as the International Civil Rights Center and Museum in Greensboro memorializes the struggle for civil rights in a particular way and through a particular lens. Through its selection of various objects and the presentation of particular narratives, it charts the pain, strife, and sacrifice by which social gains have been made. Yet as with all such efforts, the memorialization of civil rights in Greensboro is just as noteworthy for what it leaves out of the story. In this instance, the Greensboro Massacre of 1979 and the disparities and distrust within and between different communities in Greensboro that the events both reflected and served to entrench have been studiously avoided.[92] The result is a less contentious, less difficult, and less complex political history, etiquette, and identity.

If the agonistic politics of mourning imply a lively, activist rage, then the consensualist politics of mourning recommend civic passivity. Museum visitors are asked to be witnesses to history and to accept or absorb the lessons of the historical struggle for civil rights. Just as with Pericles's funeral oration, such practices shape their audience into carriers of a corrected, consensual version of social progress and civic identity. Civil rights actors are turned into superhuman figures, and the daily, lived struggle of organizing behind civil rights successes—the slow, patient building of capacity and courage that made democratic change possible—is made fugitive.[93] Moreover, events that do not fit the script are split off and left unacknowledged. As a result, communities are politically impoverished by these narratives and their associated rituals.

Nevertheless, the contested meaning of social traumas and the contours of consensus with respect to civil rights are not struggles from which we can easily retreat. The stories that are told about the dead—the meaning that is ascribed to social traumas and struggles, and the practices that are commonly associated with those struggles—inevitably shape political identities, imagination, and outcomes in the present.[94] In fact, the very question of which lives are "grievable" is a political question of the highest importance.[95] Cognizant of these facts, some political theorists have attempted to draw distinctions between rituals of commemoration that uncritically reinforce dominant social norms and reinforce patterns of social stratification, versus critical or politicizing forms of memorialization that can serve as the basis for sustained challenges to an amnesic consensualism.[96] Stow, for instance, has drawn a distinction between Periclean, "romantic" forms of public mourning and a "tragic" style of memorialization that emphasizes social contestation and contingency over consensual norms and narratives of progress.[97] For Stow, the exemplars in this latter tradition—ranging from Frederick Douglass to Joseph Lowery—provide a necessary "agonistic antidote" to consensualist practices of public mourning.[98] Yet, as I will argue in more detail in chapter 3, Stow's tragic exemplars are not so much playing a different, nonconsensualist game as they are attempting to play the game of democratic memorialization better—more inclusively, more honestly, and with a sharper sense of the contingency of progress and the inevitability of contestation. Figures such as Douglass excoriated dominant practices of memorialization, but their critique was aimed at displacing these narratives, not at displacing the process of collective narrativization itself.

As Paul Ricoeur has argued, "consensus is a dangerous game," but it is also one in which we are unavoidably engaged.[99] To argue otherwise involves more than the useful application of an agonistic antidote to manic consensualism; it risks a counterpathology that idealizes disruption as such.[100] Again, to criticize the dominant rituals of civic memorialization in Greensboro for their exclusion of the Greensboro Massacre and its aftermath is not to play a different, agonistic game; it is an attempt to play the game of consensus in ways that include difficult, traumatic events alongside those that are "easier" to remember, in the interests of cultivating a more honest and capacious public memory. An enriched public memory can help citizens to acknowledge conflicts in the past and democratically address problems in the present. This is the promise of the Greensboro Truth and Reconciliation Commission as a democratic practice of mourning. The GTRC cannot be adequately approached under either the agonistic or consensualist figures of mourning just drawn. Hence the need for a new interpretive lens, which I sketch out in the following section.

Object Relations Psychoanalysis and the Democratic Work of Mourning

It may be argued that the turn to psychoanalysis risks the reduction of political struggles for recognition to the internal dramas of the psyche. Yet in actuality, the turn toward Melanie Klein and object relations enriches social theory, by showing the interconnection between political objects, psychological defense mechanisms, and deep-seated cognitive-affective schemas (or what Klein calls "positions"). This does not reduce the political to the psychological, but it shows the depth of the political and the inevitable intertwinement between the dramas of social and psychic life.[101] As Fred Alford has argued, psychoanalytic accounts of social interaction are not so much in competition with institutionally or materially oriented approaches; instead these approaches can complement one another by examining relevant phenomena through different, or multiple, lines of sight.[102] Psychoanalysis can never completely explain political events, but political life cannot be adequately interpreted without an understanding of psychological defenses and dramas.[103] As Joel Kovel puts it, psychoanalysis "widens the semantic range" and sensitizes political and social theory to the interactions between the psyche and the political.[104] Object relations psychoanalysis is a particularly powerful investigative tool for political theory, because it dislodges Freudian assumptions about asocial drives and focuses attention on the ways that external and internal dynamics reciprocally shape each other. Because it challenges the orthodox Freudian picture of an asocial psyche, the concepts and categories of object relations psychoanalysis are inherently social concepts.[105] For instance, as Meister argues, Klein's work both "sociologizes the individual" and "psychologizes the group."[106] And while many social theorists—Meister included—argue that Klein's focus on the subject's internal world disqualifies her as a theorist of the political, for Klein this inner world is always in dialogue and tension with the external world of objects and experiences. This makes the work of Klein and of those she influenced, such as D. W. Winnicott, especially valuable for theorizing the interactions between psychological defenses and social phenomena.[107]

In this work, I use Kleinian concepts to articulate a social-psychological theory concerned with how communities and citizens can democratically work through and address the legacies of social traumas of misrecognition. I argue that, with respect to both the typical and possible politics of mourning, Klein can give us a vantage point onto social experiences of trauma, loss, and grief. Kleinian concepts, while originating in the seemingly cloistered world of analyst and analysand, can be used to illuminate broader political processes in ways that other, less psychologically attuned theories cannot do.

Klein's contribution to our understanding of the politics of mourning will be developed through each of the following chapters, but it is worth lingering on some of her concepts at this point, beginning with her understanding of mourning. For Klein, mourning is a repeated developmental challenge or "crossroads" that we encounter "again and again" throughout our lives.[108] Mourning is not primarily or merely the terminable process of accepting the loss of our attachments. Rather, it is the interminable process of mitigating a form of affective-cognitive dogmatism, which perverts our relationships to others and to ourselves. For Klein, the uncertainty and dislocation that accompany loss and pain trigger powerful psychological defenses including splitting, idealization, demonization, and omnipotence. These defenses mitigate anxieties by denying the loss in the first place or by exaggerating the power of the self to master its dependency on others. Through a labor of mourning, however, the ego is (ideally) able to work through these defenses by acknowledging the complexity and ambivalence of both its internal and external worlds. For Klein, then, mourning is less a finite process of putting to rest our lost objects than a broader, ongoing challenge of facing down the complexities and ambivalence of self, other, and world.

Klein's concept of mourning grows out of her idea of the "positions." For Klein, individuals experience reality from different cognitive-affective schemas, which she labels the "paranoid-schizoid" and the "depressive" positions. Unlike Freud's notion of hard developmental stages, Klein's positions are neither (strictly) chronological nor progressive; instead they refer to the ego's oscillation between different forms of perceiving internal and external realities depending on environmental stresses and internal capacities. For Klein, the positions are an unavoidable inheritance of the earliest months of life, and they coalesce into different cognitive-affective modes of perception, with associated defenses, that recur periodically throughout life. The positions, in short, are ways of organizing the self, its internal anxieties and fantasies, and its experiences in the world.[109]

The paranoid-schizoid position originates at birth, when the ego is relatively unintegrated and incapable of distinguishing sharply between inner and external worlds.[110] During the earliest weeks of life, under normal conditions, the unintegrated ego experiences recurrent episodes of both nurturance and deprivation, and these experiences interact with rudimentary cognitive capacities to create powerful fantasies that infuse perceptions and emotions. Within the infant's psyche a complex inner world is gradually built up through the interactions of fantasy and experience. Initially, the inner world is characterized by a bifurcation between "all-good" and "all-bad" figures reflecting the oscillatory experience between experiences of comfort and extreme stress. The frustration of bodily needs leads to fantasies of an "uncontrollable, overpowering object,"— and these anxious experiences establish "unavoidable grievances" at the heart of relationality.[111] In Klein's terms, the early ego splits the world between the all-giving "good breast" and the persecutory "bad breast," which serves as a receptacle for the negative affects associated with stress and deprivation. The early ego deploys this splitting defense—along with corollary defenses of idealization and demonization—as a hedge against an intolerable reality. Lacking object permanency, the paranoid-schizoid ego splits apart the reassuring and terrifying parts of its environment. Discomfort is projected out onto the fantastical "bad" objects, which are then reinternalized to form the kernel of the first superego, which rages against the subject with all the frustration and anxiety that the ego itself could not contain.[112] For Klein, then, early and unavoidable experiences of deprivation and impotency condemn the individual to a (temporary) pathological state of mind whereby their objects of perception are infused with the polarized passions of love and hate. Within the paranoid-schizoid position, the good and bad parts of both self and other are hermetically sealed from each other through fantastical constructs and psychological defense mechanisms. From within this space, the other either merges with and protects the fragile ego (in its role as the "good breast"), or it threatens the self with disintegration or annihilation (i.e., the "bad breast"). This latter figure must be purged out of the system, only to return in the form of the punishing, cruel superego around which persecutory anxieties constellate.

The paranoid-schizoid position is characterized by feelings of persecutory anxiety and by manic defenses that distort the perception of self and other in order to protect the fragile ego. Within the depressive position, on the other hand, the ego overcomes these defenses and develops a capacity to integrate the heretofore-polarized aspects of its internal and external worlds. The depressive position is first heralded by the development of object permanency, which marks a cognitive and affective watershed insofar as it permits the discovery that the heretofore-separated good and bad objects are merely parts of the same object—the caregiver. The depressive position, therefore, marks the first appearance of loss—namely, the loss of the protective good breast, which up to this point had been invested with all the feelings of warmth, care, and goodness within the child's early life. The good breast was a fantasized object that is in reality part of a larger whole. Recognizing the whole other, then, inspires a "psychical weaning" from the compromises and defenses of the paranoid-schizoid position and the bifurcated world of good and evil.[113]

The first loss is not the death of the loved object, then, but the death of the early "part objects" as pure sources of love or hatred. As Klein puts it, "With the introduction of the complete object . . . the loved and hated aspects of the mother are no longer felt to be so widely separated and the result is an increased fear of loss, states akin to mourning, and a strong feeling of guilt."[114] Mourning is the means by which the child can "work over in his mind [the] sense of loss entailed in the mother's actual imperfections."[115] By this labor, the ambivalence of self and other is first experienced, which liberates feelings of guilt and allows for efforts to repair the damages done through persecutory attacks (in fantasy and otherwise) against the other. The liberation of guilt forms the basis for acts of "reparation": "When the infant feels that his destructive impulses and phantasies are directed against the complete person of his loved object, guilt arises in full strength and together with that, the overriding urge to repair, preserve or revive the loved injured object."[116]

Reparation is the gift of mourning. For Klein, reparation is born within the depressive position by the recognition of the "wholeness" and ambivalence of self and other, and the corollary recognition of the harm done by the persecutory splitting of experience into all good and all bad parts. Nurtured by the labor of mourning, reparation is not a simple empathy for others so much as the recognition that we have damaged the other (and ourselves) by maintaining a fantastical construct that cast them as objects of pure loathing or perfect love. The reparative impulse is essential for building relationships outside paranoid-schizoid fantasies of blissful merger or sheer antagonism. Within the depressive position, the individual has to let go of the image of an ideal or pure object. As a result, conflicts with one's objects and within one's self can be made conscious for the first time. As the ego increases its ability to live with the competing and conflicted demands of its objects and its passions, the individual cultivates a deeper capacity for tolerance and generosity. The depressive position in this respect marks a mitigation of cognitive and affective dogmatism, and the overcoming of the compromises and defenses by which the ego keeps the complexity and ambivalence of self and other out of its conscious awareness. As Klein puts it, steps in ego integration result "in a greater capacity . . . to acknowledge the increasingly poignant psychic reality."[117]

Mourning opens up a space of mediation between self and other outside the paranoid-schizoid terms of merger or antagonism. In the paranoid-schizoid position, by contrast, there is no gap between the ego and its relational objects. The compromised ego creates "larger than life" people and emotions, "unmodified by their opposites."[118] Splitting the objects in this way is the infant's first means of defense against the bewildering array of internal and external stimulations, and the feelings of disintegration that these stimulations provoke. The sanctity of both enemies and friends is protected as a defense against the more complex, ambivalent reality; the loved and hated aspects of experience are isolated from each other through a willful act of negation.[119] Within the paranoid-schizoid position, the pain of persecution is preferable to the perplexity of lived experience.[120]

Paranoid-schizoid defenses are an unavoidable side effect of human development, and the paranoid-schizoid position is a continual temptation throughout the course of life. For Klein, experiences of loss—in fact, *any* painful experience such as uncertainty, frustration, or anxiety—invoke the original instability and chaos of the paranoid-schizoid position. The defenses of this position enable the splitting of internal and external worlds into flat part objects that can be manipulated into a consolatory narrative of demons and angels. Insofar as loss and trauma provoke paranoid-schizoid defenses, they lead to an anxious search for receptacles of focused aggression or outsized love.

However, the internalization of part objects beneath the intense pressures of idealization and demonization comes at high cost: the disavowal of both the in-

ternalized objects' and the self's ambivalence, and the collapse of a space of mediation between self and other. The work of mourning interrupts the baleful circuit
of the paranoid-schizoid position, with its outsized affects of persecutory guilt,
resentment, and disintegrative anxiety. In mourning—again, responding not merely
to the loss of an object but to the loss of an object as a one-sided persecutory or
angelic object—the capacity for reflecting on loss and damage improves and the
defenses of idealization, splitting, or denial are mitigated. The alternative pathway
of the depressive position allows for the ego's identification with whole, ambivalent others. These objects then repopulate the individual's inner world—
threatened or destabilized by experiences of loss—which in turn becomes an "assembly" of different voices.[121]

But Klein's story is more complicated than this. Some measure of idealization,
Klein implies, is unavoidable as a defense against anxiety. The so-called "good
object," first integrated under paranoid-schizoid pressures, later becomes the center or "focal point" of the integrated ego.[122] The good object is not the good breast
because the good object is a "whole" object. Still, the good object is not entirely
distinct from the all-giving, reassuring good breast. Klein implies that the idealization defense that brought into being the latter is in part transformed and in
part transferred to the whole, "good" object. It is due to the good object that the
ego can become integrated, which implies a "measure of synthesis between love
and hatred" in self, other, and the surrounding world.[123]

The integrated ego, according to Klein, is better able to understand and navigate the conflicts that exist within the self and between self and other. The good
object licenses this work of mediation because it reflects a deep-seated experience
of "being understood."[124] Without this internalized (and partly idealized) object,
the ego is more liable to become unintegrated when faced with internal and external pressures. Experiences of being understood, by contrast, can strengthen the
ego and increase its ability to bear the conflicts and misunderstandings between
and within selves.[125] Somewhat paradoxically, then, the internalized ideal other
(established under paranoid-schizoid pressures) is what permits the process of
deidealization—the diminishment of an anxious need for inherently ideal part
objects. Something in the self has to be beyond reproach in order for us to reproach ourselves, and if this object were to disappear so too would the work of
self-understanding and the capacity for recognition. The establishment of the good
object facilitates a work of mourning through which that object's wholeness and
ambivalence are acknowledged and the consolations of perfection and purity are
overturned. Instead of an exaggeration of the goodness of the other (or the self)
under the pressures of persecutory anxiety, the integrated ego has insight into its
own shortcomings or imperfections.[126] On this basis, the integrated ego is increasingly tolerant of the complexities and ambivalence of its internal and external

objects and experiences.[127] As Klein puts it, the insight gained from integration means that "potentially dangerous parts [of ourselves and others] . . . become bearable and diminish."[128] By contrast, a failure of integration occurs when we project the discomforting parts of the self out into a persecutory other.

Klein's language and categories seem primarily focused on the intimate world of early life, leading some to assume that her concepts have little, if any, direct political relevance. I argue, however, that this view is a misunderstanding of her work. Klein does locate the first source of intersubjective conflict in life's earliest moments, and she spends a great deal of time depicting the inner world of the psyche. Yet the inner world of fantasy (conscious and unconscious) is in constant interaction with the external world.[129] Moreover, the early conflicts of the protoself continue to manifest themselves throughout life. According to Klein, we are split at the core by competing passions of love and hate, which are directed toward and reflected in the world around us, yet which also shape our experience of this world and inflect the array of defenses at our disposal for navigating relations with others. On this reading, Klein's depiction of the struggle by which we come to terms with the fractious nature of the self and the ambivalence of our inner and external worlds is protopolitical in the way that interpersonal experiences of recognition are for Honneth or combative collaboration is for Luxon because it represents a developmental possibility with implications for political life. At the root of this developmental possibility is our capacity to mourn. Mourning in the depressive position allows suffering to "become productive," and it stimulates an "enrichment" of a self that is "more capable of appreciating people and things, [and] more tolerant in their relation to others."[130] We are not just what or whom we mourn; we are also, in a significant and powerful way, *how* we mourn.

As with Honneth's theory of the interpersonal sphere of recognition, however, Klein's understanding of mourning as a lifelong praxis is both protopolitical and properly political. Social misrecognition, as much as interpersonal misrecognition, can cause a regression to paranoid-schizoid defenses.[131] The challenge of integration therefore expands outward from the early moments of interpersonal life into political discourses and civic relationships. In the words of Gal Gerson, the world of attachments is "concentric, extending from the infant's first cry to the broadest achievements and failures of civilization."[132] In this light, Klein's theory of the positions also captures key differences between how the space between subjects—between legal and political subjects as much as intimate subjects—is understood and negotiated. According to Eve Sedgwick, for instance, Klein's positions offer distinct pictures of political agency. Within the paranoid-schizoid position, agency is "all or nothing" because it is colored by fantasies and anxieties of omnipotence and splitting.[133] Agency is all or nothing because the self and its others "can only be experienced as powerless or omnipotent."[134] By contrast, the depressive position is constructed on an appreciation for ambivalence, or for the awareness of multiple powers, presences, and possibilities.[135] We might call this a mournful vision of agency, which accepts the difficult copresence of ambivalence and complexity within self and other. For Sedgwick, then, the depressive position gives off an image of power as "a form of relationality that deals in, for example, negotiations (including win-win negotiations), the exchange of affect, and other small differentials, the middle ranges of agency—the notion that you can be relatively empowered or disempowered without annihilating someone else or being annihilated."[136]

The agency of the depressive position is "a fragile achievement that requires discovering over and over."[137] Klein's positional account of life makes integration a precarious achievement more than a stable outcome. Integration and depressive agency are always susceptible to rupture or failure based on the interactions between external circumstances and internal capacities. The paranoid-schizoid position is a cognitive-affective state to which we habitually return throughout life, as strains and stresses provoke its characteristic defenses and collapse the space of mediation within the self and between self and other. Because any painful experience can set off this process, mourning is an activity that can never be fully finished. Mourning, then, is less a momentary response to loss than it is a way of living in the world with a greater and more tragic sense of appreciation, understanding, and generosity.

The work of Klein's student and successor D. W. Winnicott helps to further develop these ideas in the direction of a social theory of mourning. Winnicott referred to the integrated ego in the terms of someone "who is capable of being depressed."[138] Like Klein's idea of the depressive position, Winnicott's notion here is potentially misleading. Depressive capability must be distinguished from outright depression or melancholia, which are typified by an absence of affect, withdrawal from the world, and a disregard for the self (as Freud put it, in mourning the world temporarily becomes "poor and empty" whereas in melancholia "it is the ego itself").[139] By contrast, the person capable of being depressed can sustain the stresses and strains within internal and external realities, and this ability serves as a hedge against depression or a debilitating melancholia. As Winnicott puts it, this capability implies that the individual can take "full responsibility for *all* feelings and ideas that belong to being alive."[140] Integrated egos are more capable of "find[ing] the whole conflict within the self as well as being able to see the whole conflict outside the self, in external (shared) reality."[141] In Klein's terms, the capacity for depressive functioning mitigates the temptations toward paranoid-schizoid defenses and allows for the clarification of and engagement with the conflicts that exist within and between selves.

Winnicott's work also shows how integration of the ego is a social project.

Winnicott argued that cultural symbols, discourses, and spaces were an important part of psychic life, as the latter's stability is ultimately inseparable from its environmental surroundings. At the root of this claim is Winnicott's idea of "potential space." Potential spaces are relational sites "between reality and fantasy, me and not-me, symbol and symbolized . . . each pole creating, preserving, and negating its opposite."[142] The idea is that these spaces are jointly created by the efforts of those who enter them; the space becomes a medium of interaction that is qualitatively different from the expectations that the individuals bring into the space. In other words, individuals create potential spaces, but these spaces exceed the sum of individual inputs and generate new and perhaps surprising forms of interaction. In potential spaces, individuals are both joined and separated— neither merged nor absolutely independent—allowing room for interactions that can mitigate the defenses of denial, splitting, and idealization. Examples of potential space include not only Winnicott's famous example of the transitional object but also the space of analysis and areas of cultural experience.[143] In this respect, the idea of potential space draws attention away from Klein's (supposed) focus on internal dramas and toward the interactions between self and other, ingroup and out-group, friend and stranger. Bonnie Honig, for instance, has used Winnicott's idea of potential spaces to theorize the political and cultural conditions conducive to a more generous immigration policy and to less dogmatic forms of cultural and national identity.[144] Following Winnicott, Honig has suggested that "there are institutional and cultural conditions for the proper work of mourning," and that political action requires and can actively seek to create these spaces and practices of mourning.[145] Potential spaces simultaneously testify to and help to cultivate a capacity for "depressive" social identities, in which clear distinctions between inside and outside are replaced by a more muddled, ambivalent picture of self, other, and world.[146]

Potential spaces, in effect, provide social breathing room; they are "the space in which we are alive as human beings, as opposed to being simply reflexively reactive beings."[147] Potential spaces enable the recognition of the ambivalence and wholeness of self and other, by relieving the pressures of idealization and persecution and allowing for creative engagement between self and the world. What gives these spaces their potential for generating creative or exploratory engagement is the way that subjects mutually experience the space as "not-me," as "outside magical control."[148] The meaning of the space, in effect, is built up through this mutual recognition of ambivalence—it unfolds from the simultaneous presence of multiple powers within a space that is beyond any individual's omnipotent control. The paranoid-schizoid position requires rigid and clearly defined spaces where the answer to the question "Who is in charge here?" can be easily discovered.

Spaces reveal their potential when they erode the need for this question through a gradual awareness that the different inhabitants of the space are mutually accountable and that no one is in charge. On this realization, the space between selves becomes a more plastic medium of communication and discovery.[149]

Political spaces and institutions can be seen as potential spaces that may weaken (or, conversely, intensify) the defenses inherent to the paranoid-schizoid position.[150] In other words, we can use Winnicott's ideas to identify and cultivate social settings in which democratic forms of agency might appear. Importantly, this does not presume the possibility of social consensus or the final overcoming of social conflicts. Nothing in Klein or Winnicott suggests that the macrodramas of reconciliation are reducible to the microdramas of self and other, or that integrated selves will not find reason to disagree or even violently clash with each other. As Winnicott colorfully puts it, integrated (or what he calls "democratic") selves are not incapable of antagonism, but "they have doubts . . . they are slow in getting the gun in hand and in pulling the trigger. In fact, they miss the bus to the front line."[151] Psychological developmental possibilities aside, however, collective life will still be marked by tensions and conflicts that may often tilt into violence. But object relations psychoanalysis does clearly indicate spaces and practices whereby the psychic work of integration and the social work of recognition and repair can mutually support one another.

I propose that we see Klein's ideas of the depressive position and its concurrent work of mourning, along with the good object and Winnicott's idea of potential space, as the kernel of social-political theory of mourning suitable for complex, pluralistic societies ostensibly committed to democratic ideals and practices. Klein saw the overcoming of paranoid-schizoid defenses as the basis of a more tolerant and generous attitude toward the fractiousness and complexity of self and other. In using Klein's ideas for political analysis, I am arguing that a similar process of facing down the complexity of social traumas can become the basis for a democratic mode of mourning that exceeds a deaf politics of endless agonism while also avoiding the amnesia of consensualism. For Klein, the work of mourning does not erase the conflicts within the self or between self and other; instead, mourning is a repeated process of clarifying and acknowledging these conflicts without the consolations of paranoid-schizoid defenses that simultaneously enshrine our innocence and the others' guilt. Yet this work of clarifying conflict is joined to a work of seeking and granting understanding qua social recognition. In other words, Klein's theory of mourning helps us to acknowledge the coexistence of agonism and consensualism, without reducing our aspirations for political life to either of these moments.

Central to the ongoing labor of mourning, as described earlier, is a practice with ambivalence, both within the self and within "whole" others. As the philosopher

David Wong has argued, ambivalence destabilizes confident moral judgments and shakes internal feelings of unique rightness or superiority.[152] Consequently, the experience of ambivalence can inspire a desire for mediation—for a cooperative search for new terms amidst an acknowledgement of multiple presences and powers.[153] Ambivalence can turn overinterpreted and overdetermined social spaces into potential spaces and cultivate depressive forms of agency as so many democratic ripple effects.

In sum, the work of object relations psychoanalysis provides a sharp diagnostic tool for describing the pathologies that shadow agonist and consensualist approaches to the politics of mourning. Klein's psychological theory of mourning can illuminate the politics of grief by showing how the latter trades on and activates various defenses that operate as mechanisms of denial. Social defenses against trauma and social and political responses to trauma bear a reciprocal relationship to internal, psychic defenses and positions.[154] Even if social institutions are not reducible to psychological or internal dramas, affective-cognitive modes of processing circulate around and contribute to the operation of social and political structures.[155] Klein's theory of the paranoid-schizoid position, then, helps to conceptualize the interconnection between agonistic and consensualist responses to loss, insofar as they can each trigger a manic politics in which the complexity of self and other is repressed and by which the mediating space of relational power is reduced to a zero-sum struggle for domination.

Klein's concepts of the depressive position and the good object, on the other hand, offer an alternative pathway for the politics of mourning. The depressive position marks the integration of conflicted passions and objects; it therefore occupies a middle position between amnesic merger and endless antagonism. Klein's idea of the good object emphasizes the importance of an idealizing commitment that, somewhat paradoxically, allows for the democratic work of de-idealization and relational agency. Winnicott's supplement to this story is the emphasis on the social and cultural spaces wherein this work of mourning could take place. I argue that the GTRC was both a potential space and a potentially good object, which made social recognition and repair more possible in Greensboro and in those places that might learn from its example.

Toward a Democratic Work of Mourning

The value of mourning as an interpretive discourse for social traumas of misrecognition is that it allows us to see agonistic grief-turned-grievance, consensualist rituals of memorialization, and civic efforts at working through public traumas as related elements within a broader struggle of what I am calling the democratic work of mourning. From within this framework, we can appreciate the ways in which agonism and consensualism mirror each other insofar as they each potentially activate defenses and cognitive-affective schemas that are problematic for democratic politics. And while the juxtaposition of agonism's and consensualism's potential pathologies next to the promise of efforts such as the GTRC may seem to imply a dialectic by which these one-sided activities are subsumed within a higher-order practice, a Kleinian emphasis on mourning as an ongoing developmental challenge shows this juxtaposition to be less dialectical than dialogical. In this book my intention is to stage an encounter between these aspects of the democratic work of mourning to better understand their interconnections, points of tension, and generative possibilities. A theory of a democratic work of mourning helps us to put the struggle for just recognition and the struggle for meaning and narrative into a more constructive conversation with each other, alongside (but never fully subsumed *by*) a civic process of working through trauma that, in the wake of the Greensboro Truth and Reconciliation Commission, could potentially take on a more prominent institutional form. In fact, my argument is that agonism and consensualism must *both* enliven public sites of memorialization and mourning in order to transform these sites into *potential* spaces. The pursuit of potential spaces can help citizens better engage each other beyond the static heuristics that often typify social and political interactions. Agonism and consensualism can each support manic forms of agency, in which political subjects give themselves over to omnipotent fantasies of a polity stripped of their opponents. Yet agonism and consensualism can also be seen as necessary components of a broader, democratic work of mourning and its corresponding images of acknowledgement and agency.

In part what I aim to do with this project is to shift the conversation within political theory about public mourning to the *means* and *meaning* of working through loss and trauma—the procedures and the forms by which mourning might support and enliven democratic agency. However, the question of *what* is mourned cannot be entirely avoided. To give the answer, "social trauma," is of course to invite additional questions about the meaning of that term.[156] In the past decades, trauma has become a widely used concept within political and social theory, but the particular content of traumatic experiences is often left unspecified.[157] Trauma is said to be a rupture of the expected order of things, a tear in the fabric of social norms or personal narratives.[158] Yet this definition seems both too broad and too narrow to cover the experiences of loss, suffering, and struggle represented within Greensboro's layered politics of mourning. For the damages of racism and official segregation cannot be exhausted by the idea of trauma, given that the social context of pre–civil rights Greensboro was characterized by norms of inequality, deference, and separation. And the Greensboro

Massacre does not reveal a reparable tear in social narratives or etiquettes so much as it reveals an ongoing struggle over those narratives. Therefore, as outlined earlier, I propose that we see social traumas in terms of an ongoing struggle for recognition, where losses and injustices can be seen as instances of misrecognition or nonrecognition.[159] For Axel Honneth, the struggle for recognition since the onset of modernity assumes a telos of equal legal respect, the denial of which necessarily provokes feelings of disrespect that can in turn become the basis for social struggle. Honneth, in short, assumes that indifference to misrecognition is impossible when basic rights are withheld or denied. Misrecognition therefore better captures the experiences of oppression within social orders where norms of deference and inequality are upheld because those norms are in violation of the ideals of recognition that increasingly shape social expectations and desires. Moreover, the concept for recognition and its absence helps to unpack both the CWP's resistant, militant politics both before and after the Greensboro Massacre and the broader struggle to articulate social narratives that reflect and reinforce consensual norms.[160] The search for consensualist norms fits into this broader process of recognition because it represents the background orders of articulation within which citizens and communities understand and contest the meaning of collective life and the significance of public events. Yet the CWP's efforts to challenge or overturn these semantic and symbolic arrangements shows that background civic narratives are always contested and essentially open. In other words, to approach public trauma in terms of a struggle for recognition encompasses both background recognition contexts within which we evaluate our lives and the agonistic struggle over the shape of those contexts themselves.

Misrecognition can also be read from within the Kleinian story of the paranoid-schizoid position and its associated defenses by which our perceptions of internal and external conflicts are split off, denied, or filtered through a consolatory framework of friend/enemy. Therefore, misrecognition can speak not only to experiences of violence or oppression but also to the potential pathologies attendant to the full range of the politics of mourning. In referring to public traumas as moments of misrecognition, then, I am also referring to recognition in terms of (a) an agonistic struggle over the kinds of losses that are socially recognized or honored, (b) the narratives and civic etiquettes that (ideally) embody norms of recognition and mutual respect, and (c) the psychological habits of denial and overcoming that interact with and affect both (a) and (b).

The use of object relations psychoanalysis helps to focus the conversation on the ongoing work of mourning within a democratic society—on how social episodes of misrecognition are (or can be) taken up within civic institutions or practices. Rooted in Klein's concepts of the depressive position and the good object, and inspired by Winnicott's description of potential spaces, I argue that the democratic work of mourning should be characterized by inclusive dialogue and deliberation, cooperative civic action, and broad-scale participation within rituals of memorialization. Inclusive dialogue is vital because, following Klein, only the recognition of concrete, whole others can effectively dispel the fantasies and habits of misrecognition that plague interpersonal and social life. Social contact and conversation across social divides are necessary, then, to erode stereotypes and the affective-cognitive schemas that hold those stereotypes in place.[161]

Cooperative public action can further erode these schemas, but more importantly it can cultivate a depressive understanding of agency in which power is fluid and emerges from multiple sites. Depressive modes of agency turn citizens toward the difficult work of persuasion and cooperation, and—as Sedgwick argues—the possibilities of relative empowerment and disempowerment. Moreover, broad-scale participation in rituals of memorialization or public mourning could shift those rituals from the search for (fantastical) univocal consensus toward the struggle for a more fractious coherence because the mere presence of polyphony means that negotiations over the meaning and reach of democratic norms cannot be too hastily foreclosed. All of these aspects of a democratic work of mourning were visible in the efforts and aftermath of the GTRC, and they serve as the baseline for civic innovations in how communities might mourn their past and improve their present.

There are both sound psychological and political reasons to pursue this inclusive, participatory, and active labor of mourning. Political psychologists emphasize the value of integrated dialogue groups as a means of establishing social trust in the wake of mass violence or devastation. Dialogic contact and engagement can erode both stereotypical judgments and fantasies of omnipotence, which often stand in the way of mutualistic social relationships.[162] And while contact and dialogue are crucial, the democratic work of mourning goes beyond these efforts to encourage episodes of cooperative public action through which citizens can craft rejoinders to legacies of misrecognition and contribute to the rites of and responses to public mourning.[163] Once again, I refer to these concrete actions as democratic ripple effects that can, and often do, follow from efforts to create public dialogue about social traumas of misrecognition. Episodes of cooperative public action will not, of course, magically transcend social differences or conflicts, but these efforts can clarify conflicts, legitimate social differences, and create social space for citizens to address issues of misrecognition in their communities. For instance, in the wake of the Greensboro Truth and Reconciliation Commission, new grassroots movements for social change emerged within the city, ranging from a minimum wage campaign to a cross-racial youth violence group to a local economic development group.[164] The GTRC, then, not only provided a space for the public examination of the Greensboro Massacre, but it situated Greensboro citizens within a potential space that helped to generate communication about and action on the conflicts within the city.

I return to the GTRC and its aftermath in chapter 5. In between, I explore some of the pathologies and possibilities attendant to agonistic and consensualist modes of public mourning, and I begin to sketch out the idea of a democratic work of mourning that leans on but is irreducible to either of these modes. Once again, Melanie Klein is a crucial interlocutor within this conversation. Klein's theory of the good object and the importance of understanding (both of self and other) at the root of intersubjective life provide support for the broader theory of recognition within which, I argue, the conversation about social mourning should be situated. Yet Klein's emphasis on the positions of psychic life and the ineliminable conflicts within and between selves reminds us of the potential pathologies and inherent limitations within this very struggle for recognition as it has been articulated by Honneth and others.[165] As Meira Likierman has argued, Klein's work is characterized by parallel moral and tragic narratives.[166] While the former centers around Klein's emphasis on understanding and reparation, the latter emphasizes our penchant for misrecognition and the snares of idealization, demonization, and omnipotence in which we periodically find ourselves. I argue that it is the intertwinement and simultaneity of these narratives that makes Klein such a fitting interlocutor for political theorists and everyday citizens concerned with the struggles of memory and mourning. Keeping both of these narratives in view can help us to diagnose the excesses and potentials attendant to the ongoing politics of mourning, while orienting this politics toward potential spaces and practices that might make our democratic life more livable.

TO JOIN IN HATE

Antigone and the Agonistic Politics of Mourning

It is my nature to join in love, not hate.

—Antigone

**I'm trying to love my neighbor, and do good unto others
But, oh mother, things ain't going well.**

—Bob Dylan, "Ain't Talking"

In scanning the history of mourning's public expression and political appropriations, we see that the politics of mourning are both mobile—they move across the political spectrum and across cultural contexts—and historically variable.[1] Nevertheless, certain images and ideas are so frequently associated with the political expression of mourning that they have come to dominate the interpretive field. This field, in effect, is prepopulated by figures that shape expectations of what the politics of mourning looks like, the kinds of actions it involves, and the affective registers through which it is filtered. In this chapter and chapter 3, I explore these figures and the interpretive screens that accompany them. I argue that these screens cannot adequately account for the promise or potential of the Greensboro Truth and Reconciliation Commission, and hence they are insufficient for theorizing a democratic work of mourning. Still, the persistent appearance and reappearance of these figures requires that we view them less as replaceable parts than as periodically occurring positions in which we will occasionally, inescapably, find ourselves.

Mourning begins in grief, but the politics of mourning often stem from grief's connection with anger or rage. Anger is the force that turns grief out into the public in ways that disrupt or contest forms of misrecognition or other sources of social trauma. Recall, for instance, the Greensboro Communist Worker Party's admonition to "Turn Grief into Strength! Avenge the CWP 5!" The politics of mourning often manifest as defiant protests against the established order, ranging from civil rights mobilizations following the funeral of Medgar Evers to the persistent resistance of the Madres de Plaza de Mayo in Argentina to the organized "die-ins" of AIDS activists in the 1980s.[2]

If anger is the dominant affective marker of mourning's politics, perhaps no figure better encapsulates this fact than that of Antigone, the Sophoclean heroine who has haunted political theory and practice for centuries. Antigone exemplifies and represents a resistant counterpolitics of grief, by which the aggrieved challenge the cultural and political orders that have either caused their suffering or have compounded their injuries through misrecognition, social stigma, or wounding silence.[3] Antigone's image and her narrative of resistance have been repeatedly deployed by artists and activists in a variety of conflicted contexts, ranging from Argentina after its "dirty war" to the Jenin Refugee Camp in the West Bank.[4] Recent performances of Sophocles's play have served as occasions for reflection and political mobilization in countries as diverse as Ireland, India, Taiwan, Turkey, Canada, and Poland.[5] In sum, Antigone has become the model activist mourner—an inspiration for those who would challenge their conditions of marginalization, oppression, or social erasure.

In this chapter, I unpack the intimate connection between mourning and activist politics of (violent and nonviolent) direct action (Section I), in part by examining recent appropriations of Antigone within agonist political theory (Section II). Insofar as mourning is approached under the image of resistant, Antigone-like voices, it fits snugly within an agonistic framework for political life. Although agonism is a diverse gathering of different voices, on the whole agonists advance a view of politics as a matter of endless contestation without the prospect of final settlement or consensus. Agonists do not necessarily romanticize conflict nor neglect the possibility of extreme violence, but their goal is not to *resolve* political antagonisms so much to *shift* them toward a less violent, if still contentious, agonism.[6] Agonists pitch their narrative of struggle and contestation against deliberative or consensualist approaches that—they argue—misrepresent politics through an emphasis on agreement or mutual understanding. Antigone's strong-necked resistance to Creon provides inspiration for activists' agonistic struggle, and the incommensurability of the struggle between Antigone and Creon provides agonist political theorists with evidence of the perpetual conflict that they insist resides at the root of collective life. As Bonnie Honig has noted, "the *agon* between Antigone and Creon is probably for most political theorists the template for what is meant by agonism."[7]

However, as I will argue, the agonist appropriation of Antigone risks losing touch with the complexity of her mourning claims and the complexity of mourning itself. In the third section of this chapter, I try to restore some of this complexity by reading Antigone from the perspective of Melanie Klein's theory of mourning and what I have defined as the democratic work of mourning in chapter 1.

By situating Antigone and agonism within this framework, I argue that the democratic work of mourning does not replace or supplant activist or agonistic contestation, but that it can filter this form of politics through awareness of ambivalence and the "agency" of Klein's depressive position.[8] Antigone herself passes through this filter and assumes (albeit briefly) this agency. Moving out from Antigone's example, I argue that the political theory and practice of AIDS activist Douglas Crimp helps us to see how activist anger, when connected with depressive agency, becomes a democratic form of anger that opens the spaces and practices that make this anger more generative of social change. Antigone's (or agonism's) anger can never be fully transcended—and certainly not by theoretical fiat—but Klein's theory of mourning gives us reason to question agonist political narratives that put anger or disagreement at the root of political life. By situating Antigone/agonism within a more encompassing theory of the democratic work of mourning, we can better approach complex objects and practices of mourning such as the Greensboro Truth and Reconciliation Commission, which, as chapter 1 argued, cannot be reduced to an agonistic story without remainder.

Antigone, Anger, Agonism

As Bonnie Honig has argued, our contemporary political imagination has been irrevocably shaped and disciplined by the image of Antigone, and this assertion is especially true when the subject of analysis is the political relevance of grief or mourning.[9] Antigone has come to represent a politics of mourning in which the bereaved mobilize on the basis of shared grief in order to press their claims into the public sphere. Sophocles's heroine also captures the penchant for mourning to edge into militancy and for the grief associated with injustice and trauma to be focused into a political rage that challenges the prevailing order of things. In *Antigone*, the eponymous protagonist violates the political order's norms of propriety through both her actions and her inflammatory rhetoric. Antigone's resistance has been alternately coded as a defense of the prerogatives of the private household, an articulation of aristocratic codes of honor, an antihumanist refusal of the symbolic order, and a complex form of immanent critique.[10] Although the meaning of Antigone's resistance is contested, the fact of her *resistance* seems relatively clear, and Sophocles's play marks how grief over injustice can morph into a political weapon with deadly consequences.

Antigone remains a generative interlocutor for political theory and practice in part because her situation, broadly understood, is incessantly repeated within political communities.[11] Across the political spectrum, across cultural traditions, and across centuries, grief has mobilized public actions in ways that invoke the conflagration between Antigone and Creon. From the Madres de Plaza de Mayo in Argentina, to the AIDS Coalition to Unleash Power (ACT UP) activists during the height of the AIDS crisis, to the antiwar activist Cindy Sheehan during the Iraq war (2003–2011), grief over unrecognized losses has galvanized struggles to challenge the status quo. These struggles seem to operate—and are often narrated—beneath the long shadow cast by Sophocles's conflicted character. As if repeating the trauma of Antigone's and Creon's agon, these eruptions of public grieving are typified by a confrontational style of protest that fashions alternative political spaces from which to gather supporters and criticize the actions of the state.

In these moments, mourning and mobilization collapse together. Political expressions of grief overturn the assumption behind the labor activist Joe Hill's famous last words ("Don't mourn, organize!") because mourning, far from being a narcissistic absorption with injury, becomes a powerful means of organizing resistance. Whereas the AIDS activist Larry Kramer echoed Hill when he chastised gay men in the 1980s for an indulgent focus on grief at the expense of radical action, Douglas Crimp responded that, for many gay men, political activism was not supplanted by mourning but grew from it.[12] Militancy and mourning were synced together for Crimp because the legitimacy of homosexual grief was disavowed by the broader culture. Cultural refusals of acknowledgment intensified suffering and provided additional fuel for militant political action, just as Creon's refusal to acknowledge Antigone's responsibilities to Polyneices sparked the conflagration at Thebes.

With his discussion of how social stigma "savaged" homosexuals during their most intense "hour[s] of loss," Crimp provides keen insight into the connection between grief and public acts of resistant protest. The traumas surrounding the AIDS crisis—ranging from a proliferating infection rate, rapid declines in health and the disturbing deaths of friends and loved ones, and the deep uncertainty and fear surrounding the causes of infection and means of protection—were impoverishing and devastating. Yet these losses were intensified by what Crimp describes as American society's "ruthless interference with our bereavement." The cold indifference of those unaffected by AIDS, the cruel persecutions of state and national administrations, and the prevailing sense of stigma attached to homosexual desire added up to a felt sense that homosexuals were robbed of social standing through a "violence of silence and omission" that was "almost as impossible to endure as the violence of unleashed hatred and outright murder." The wounding or heavy silence of social non- or misrecognition, Crimp argued, "desecrates the memories of our dead," and as a result "we rise in anger to vindicate them."[13] Nonrecognition, then, provides an important motivational link between grief and activist mourning. It also places Crimp's reflections on mourning beneath the long shadow cast by *Antigone*.[14] For Antigone, the pain of her loss was intensified by

Creon's proclamation to leave Polyneices's body unburied. Creon's savage interference with Antigone's bereavement is what seems to have triggered her resistance, because "to leave the dead man, my mother's son, dead and unburied, that would have been real pain." (468). Crimp echoes Antigone, then, when he argues that the violence of social erasure or desecration doubles the pain of loss and, in turn, inspires acts of vindication.

Crimp's essay provides another clue to understanding why grief can morph into political grievance and activism. Strong identification with the suffering and the departed can cultivate a powerful sense of guilt among the healthy and the surviving, and this guilt—both expressed or unconscious—in turn feeds activist anger. As Crimp puts it, the painful feelings associated with socially nonrecognized losses are "exacerbated" by "secret wishes, during our lovers' and friends' protracted illnesses, that they would just die and let us get on with our lives." Survivors' guilt is then faced down, Crimp argues, through the commitment to publicly "uphold . . . the memories of our lost friends and lovers." Yet this commitment takes the same form as the reaction to desecration; it "impose[s] the same demand: resist!"[15] Militancy arises not only from social interference with mourning but "from conscious conflicts *within* mourning itself"—namely, the struggle to work through the Janus-faced obligations to the dead and to those who survive (including the self). For ACT UP activists such as Crimp, then, militancy springs from the painful erasures of social stigma and from what we could call a survivors' commitment (triggered by intense feelings of guilt) to honor the dead through the agency of the living. In these ways, guilt at having survived helps turn felt grief into an angry, activist politics of mourning. If the ambivalent feelings of sadness and relief, terror and triumph, cannot be consciously experienced or worked through, then the lost object is internalized alongside an overwhelming sense of guilt, which intensifies militant resistance in that object's name.

At a different point of the political spectrum—but within a similar register of grief qua grievance—many pro-life activists have described their form of direct action as a process of mourning and coping with death.[16] In such cases, the mourning is both retrospective and prospective—aborted fetuses are often given names, "baptisms," and "funerals," and the threat of imminent death galvanizes protests at abortion clinics and family planning centers. For many of these activists, "rescue" provides "a format for trying to fight against death."[17] Similar in style, if not substance, AIDS and pro-life activists have each sought to mobilize supporters through a shared sense of vulnerability and outrage, fueled by insistent claims that the larger culture was both indifferent toward their suffering and hostile toward their cause. Each, then, trades on themes of desecration and survivor guilt in order to turn grief into political action. Similarly, for Antigone, the compulsion to act was driven by a commitment to the dead, internalized object of Polyneices, reinforced by the public denial of her loss. Above all else, she claims, "I will not be false to him" (47), despite Theban indifference or hostility.

Feelings of nonrecognition and the Janus-faced nature of survivors' guilt, some argue, are intensified through connections to the liminal experience of death and grief. For Gail Holst-Warhaft, grief offers a "unique opportunity for social mobilization and political action" because "grief is probably the most powerful emotion we ever feel."[18] While anthropologists have challenged the universality of grief as a deeply emotional experience, the eruptive and urgent power of grief has been noted across a variety of cultural traditions.[19] Grief's passion, according to Holst-Warhaft, is excessive and ecstatic; it carries us "to the edge of madness."[20] At this edge, grief and anger collapse together in ways that spark powerful resistance. The power of mourning, whether stemming from named violations or from a sense of survivor's commitment, rests on the energy created by what Holst-Warhaft calls the "unity of shared rage."[21] The unity of shared rage fashions solidarity out of sorrow and channels mutual grief into public grievance. It is what allowed the Madres de Plaza de Mayo in Argentina to form an effective grassroots organization despite threats and intimidation. Transforming their "anguish into action," the Madres fashioned an organization that gathered together their individual sufferings into a potent political force.[22] They overcame the enforced silence over the disappearances and "forged a space in political vocabulary and hence in political consciousness."[23] Shared grief and rage amplified individual suffering into an effective and affectively charged public voice that disrupted and challenged the Argentine junta's ability to act with impunity.

Nicole Loraux has also noted the penchant for grief to turn into political grievance—and for mourning to manifest itself as political mobilization. Similar to Holst-Warhaft, Loraux argues that grief can be transformed into a form of "defiance" and "memory-wrath" because grief "does not forget and feeds on itself."[24] Comparing the wrath of aggrieved mothers to the anger of Achilles, Loraux notes how the Greeks of classical Athens were both fascinated by and wary of the strange power of grief. As she puts it, excessive mourning was "a threat to be contained, but also to be fantasized about."[25] This ambivalence shines forth in the portrayal not only of Antigone but also of Electra, who embodies the power of a grief that feeds on itself until it can only be expressed as wrath and fury. Endlessly repeating her lament, Electra's grief/rage is "unmanageable" in its excess—an eruptive and urgent passion that insists on remembrance of Clytemnestra's deed over and against any efforts at forgiving or moving on.

Loraux contextualizes her reading of tragedy within the struggle over mourning rites and rituals in the ancient polis. In Athens of the sixth and fifth centuries BCE, there was an ongoing struggle to discipline and disrupt archaic forms of public mourning, which were typified by passionate and violent actions that often contributed to ongoing blood feuds between warring clans.[26] In the sixth century, the Athenian lawgiver Solon famously prohibited certain traditional lamentation practices such as the laceration of the face and body; he also decreased the number of mourners who could be present for the funeral and its procession and forbade the performance of lamentations in any place outside of the household or the cemetery.[27] Despite these prohibitions, however, for Loraux the portrayal of the dangerous passion of grief within Greek tragedy betrayed a persistent anxiety about grief's power that Solon's edicts had clearly failed to assuage. Portrayals of excessive grief such as Antigone's and Electra's demonstrated that the conflict over mourning was never fully settled in the Athenian polis.[28]

Between Holst-Warhaft and Loraux, we can detect two varieties of agonistic mourning: *agonism as response* and *agonism as ground*. For Holst-Warhaft, the unity of shared rage stems from experiences of disrespect or desecration. Feeding off the intense power of grief, activists cultivate solidarity and mobilize in ways that challenge or disrupt the circuitry of violence or nonrecognition that intensifies social trauma.[29] The angry, activist reply—pitched in the discourse and often the iconography of mourning—is a *response* to the conditions of misrecognition or trauma within which the bereaved find themselves. For Loraux, on the other hand, the excessive passion of grief provides testimony to the perpetual conflict and discord at the root of common life. Grief's unmanageable excess reflects a deep source of conflict that is in constant tension with the polis's desire for order. Tragedy, as a "genre in conflict," exemplified this tension because, while it took place within the context of a civic festival that aimed in part at reinforcing the boundaries of political membership, it also gave voice to the "noncivic" passion of excessive grief. The mourning represented in tragedy indexes not merely a temporary unity of rage that can challenge the political status quo but also an endless agonistic conflict where, *pace* Heraclitus, "struggle (*eris*) is inseparable from justice (*dikê*) and discord is the rule."[30]

Loraux, then, locates "another politics" at the crossroads of the passionate "forever" of grief and the organizing force of the polis. This other form of politics is "no longer based on consensus and living together" but on what Loraux calls the "bond of division."[31] The bond of division indexes a foundational antagonism at the root of all political orders. As Loraux puts it, the "civil war" that is "congenital to the city" is the only thing truly "held in common."[32] The mourning represented in tragedy, on Loraux's reading, reveals an internal division that no performed act—from passionate lament to civic rites to tragic festival—can eliminate.

The agonism of Antigone-style mourning, then, persists on two levels. Crimp (along with pro-life advocates) sees an occasion for militant political activism within the conflict between felt grief and an indifferent or hostile culture that surrounds and intensifies this grief. In their responses to named instances of misrecognition or desecration, these actors challenge hegemonic norms that disavow their lives and losses. Similarly, Holst-Warhaft sees grief as an easily manipulable resource for agonistic politics, as a potent "cue for passion."[33] Mourning is reliably political because the doubled grief of loss and misrecognition inspires rage that can be effectively channeled into action.

Loraux acknowledges this level of mourning's agonism but goes further. She locates within tragedy a portrayal of (atemporal) grief that reveals an irresolvable internal conflict within every community. For Loraux, Electra's passionate mourning—which claims eternity as its temporality—restages a bond of division that cannot be the source of a consensus because it is every agreement's hidden scandal. For Loraux, the ancient polis—in fact, every political order—is founded in conflict, which remains "an innate force" despite occasional fantasies of unity.[34]

How should we approach this suturing between an affectively charged, activist politics of mourning and the two levels of agonism—as response and as ground? On the one hand, it is important to note that the activist anger associated with shared grief or rage often threatens to re-create, rather than to interrupt, the circuitry of violence or nonrecognition that it aims to challenge. The justifiable need to register pain and loss can quickly morph into the need to punish persecutors, leading to possibility that, in Mahmoud Mamdani's words, victims become killers.[35] Mamdani refers to this connection between a sense of loss and a resentful need to punish others within the context of pregenocide Rwanda, yet similar cases abound from diverse contexts such as Northern Ireland to Palestine/Israel. Each of these cases shows the dangerous edge of agonism as response—the tendency, as it were, for agonism to slide into violent antagonism, via the resentful search for scapegoats on which one's suffering can be discharged. As Holst-Warhaft puts it, "it is a fine line between channeling grief for the benefit of the oppressed and unleashing the violent anger of suffering."[36]

On the other hand, to deny or to discipline the rage associated with social nonrecognition or violent trauma is also not without problems. As many have argued, activist anger has often been unjustly pathologized or stigmatized by cultural norms (such as "civility") that serve to reinforce oppression or practices of marginalization. Hence for bell hooks, "it is humanizing" to rage against oppression.[37] If we understand or approach rage from the perspective of the powerless, rather from the perspective of the social order that is being called to account, then we can see anger as an essential strategy for the achievement of social voice and presence. What hooks refers to as "killing rage" is a form of psychic "ammunition" for the colonized or oppressed; it nurtures the possibility of an active politics of refusal and provides space for social hope.[38] The killing rage drawn from shared experiences of social humiliation or stigma can open up new political horizons that have been foreclosed on by the status quo. Without these expressions of rage, the circuitry of social misrecognition can go unchallenged and undisturbed. Rage, in short, is a necessary precondition for the expression of political subjectivity for those who have been socially erased or marginalized. As Honneth has argued, subjects are ultimately incapable of indifference to the violation of respect insofar as it compromises needs for basic self-esteem and a sense of social standing. James Baldwin referred to this lack of indifference to experiences of disrespect as the "rage of the disesteemed," which according to Baldwin is "absolutely inevitable" in contexts of social nonrecognition and is "one of the things that makes history."[39]

Nevertheless, the dangers surrounding "killing rage" of the disesteemed, including the possibilities that justified anger will turn into the resentful search for scapegoats, or that rage will slip into a cycle of retribution, require sensitivity to the complex demands attendant to the political expression of grief. On this point, Klein's account proves essential because Klein gives us a vantage point onto the interactions between social experiences of, and psychic defenses against, grief.

As described in chapter 1, Klein argues that experiences of loss give rise to divergent responses. In the paranoid-schizoid position, mourning is forestalled as internal and external stresses and strains are projected out and sutured onto a one-sided persecutory other. Through mechanisms of splitting, idealization, and demonization, the ego defends itself against the pain of loss or nonrecognition. Rage directed at the persecutory other, then, can take the place of mourning. This was one of Crimp's insights, who warned fellow activists that the justified rage against an indifferent or hostile culture could also function as a form of defense or "disavowal," which by "making all violence external" fails to "acknowledge our ambivalence."[40] For Crimp, angry, passionate activism was warranted, but it also was a potential "means of dangerous denial."[41] In this respect Crimp echoed the insights of Klein, who noted how the "intensely moral and exacting" nature of paranoid-schizoid defenses resulted in a split perceptual-affective experience of the world, which is subsequently divided into "extremely bad and extremely perfect objects."[42] These defenses protect the ego against the dislocating force of loss, but only at the expense of the "relentless" and "extremely cruel demands" of the idealized, internalized object.[43]

Eve Sedgwick provides an explicit bridge from the theory of Klein to agonistic activism. As Sedgwick puts it, the "propulsive energy of activist justification . . . tends to be structured very much in a paranoid-schizoid fashion," including tendencies toward "scapegoating, purism, and schism."[44] Political struggles are often rhetorically and affectively framed in ways that activate what Klein saw as the defenses against mourning, which serve to freeze self and other into one-sided caricatures engaged in a melodramatic struggle of good versus evil. An agonistic politics of mourning, then, fulfills its own prophecy about the intimate connection between conflict and political communities. It incessantly repeats the conflict while citing discord as its ground. Yet an agonistic politics of mourning is self-defeating insofar as it presumes a structurally hostile audience that can only be engaged through a confrontational and militant form of direct action because its dominant normative practices contribute to the suffering that inspires resistance. In this way, activist anger risks sliding from a struggle to acknowledge wounds into a form of "wounded identity" that only mimics what it struggles against.[45] Agonistic mourning challenges the boundaries and coherence of the political order, but it can also reify and mimic this (fantasy-imbued) order through the performance of its own dogmatic claims. Every Antigone seemingly requires, if he or she does not actively morph into, a Creon. At its most extreme edge (Loraux's "bond of division"), agonism's claims actually dissolve *as claims* and persist only as reminders of perpetual discord, strife, and grief. At this level, mourning as agonism fulfills the literal meaning (or curse?) of Antigone, whose name translates as "in the place of birth or generation." Agonism cannot generate anything beyond stale repetitions of negation or resistance. The absolute, guilt-ridden commitment to the internalized object collapses together *eris* and *dikê*—strife and justice.

With the idea of the depressive position, however, Klein describes a form of mourning that avoids the pathologies attendant to a purely agonistic politics of grief. The defenses against mourning testified to by Crimp and Sedgwick—the tendencies toward splitting, idealization, and demonization, the "baleful circuit" of resentment,[46] and the projection or expulsion of the stresses and strains of loss or trauma—are each mitigated by the work of mourning that takes place within the depressive position. The depressive position is the space from which the individual can repair their (internal and external) connections with others. For Klein, loss or trauma disrupts not only the individual's experience with the external world (which, following Freud, feels cold and barren following a loss) but also the internal "assembly" of objects and affects that constitute the inner side of experience. Mourning involves a doubled labor of repairing the world—reanimating the internal space populated by multiple, whole internal objects while renewing links to the external world. Essential to this labor is recognition of the "wholeness" or multisidedness of our objects of attachment. In other words, not until the ambivalence of self and other is faced down and acknowledged can the defenses of the paranoid-schizoid position—and the "intensely moral" and persecutory guilt attendant to that position—be mitigated or overcome.[47]

Klein's theory is a subtle but ultimately significant revision of Freud's account of mourning, which focused on the conflict between an ego that is reluctant to forsake its libidinal investments in the lost object and the harsh, cold truth bespoken by the reality principle, which serves as a perpetual reminder of the object's absence and the need for reattachment. Unlike Freud, Klein does not lay strong emphasis on the process of *detachment*. Instead she focuses on the different ways in which a relationship to the internal object is maintained—either through the intense, persecutory circuitry of the paranoid-schizoid position, under which the object assumes an outsized and cruel presence within the psyche (akin to Freud's account of melancholia, in which the "shadow of the object falls upon the ego"), or through the depressive position, in which the demands of the internalized object are intermixed with the demands of other, whole objects of attachment—both living and departed. The depressive position bridges the stark "cleavage between idealized and persecutory objects" in ways such that the "fantastic objects lose in strength."[48] The depressive position acts as a perceptual-affective filter that processes internal and external relationships through an awareness of ambivalence and wholeness.

How does the depressive position interact with the affects of rage or anger? For Klein, the depressive position does not defeat or transcend these affects—any more than it defeats or transcends grief—but it marks the filtering of anger through the sieve of whole object relations. Anger is no longer manically focused on the caricatured objects of the paranoid-schizoid position; instead it is refracted through the prism of depressive awareness by which the conflicts within and between selves can be more accurately perceived and worked through. The depressive position, then, represents less the *defeat* of rage than the *integration* of rage with what Winnicott called the "capacity to become depressed." By contrast, in the words of Crimp, a failure of integration is to "make . . . all violence external" and to fail to comprehend how rage can function as a dangerous and self-defeating "mechanism of our disavowal."[49]

For Klein, the depressive position is the basis for an affirmative and constructive response to loss or trauma, though these responses will also always be marked by an essential tragedy. By acknowledging the complexity and ambivalence of our objects of attachment and by facing down our aggression and vulnerability—rather than anxiously projecting out unsafe affects into idealized or demonized others—desecration can be challenged outside the consoling defenses of the paranoid-schizoid position. By these means, survivor's guilt can be acknowledged and worked through, without succumbing to the overwhelming cruelty of persecutory forms of guilt. This marks the achievement of what Sedgwick calls the "agency" of the depressive position, which comes from the acknowledgment that one "can be relatively empowered or disempowered without annihilating someone else or being annihilated."[50] The agency of the depressive position can be contrasted to the agency of the paranoid-schizoid position, which, through defenses of omnipotence and denial, sees agency in zero-sum terms of absolute triumph or utter annihilation.

Klein does not say the last word on the connection between anger, activism, and mourning—if only because she was not sensitive to the ways in which the external stresses and strains of trauma are unevenly distributed across social space.[51] Because violent trauma and social nonrecognition have historically tracked along racial, class, and gender markers, a political or social theory of mourning must not only understand the psychic vicissitudes of activism qua defense but also appreciate the social defensibility of activist anger as a response to the experiences of exclusion or oppression. hooks's argument is compelling—rage in response to desecration can be liberating and humanizing because this "killing rage" might be the only means of breaking through layers of social indifference or active oppression in ways that allow subjects to assert their claims for standing and recognition. What is missing from an agonistic defense of rage, however, is an appreciation of how anger and rage, because they can *take the place* of mourning, can repeat, rather than disrupt or challenge, patterns of social erasure or misrecognition. In other words, a social theory of mourning that is missing an account of the psychic positions of grief—and the defenses against mourning—is as inadequate as a purely psychological approach that reduces all public manifestations of activist rage to defenses against internal turmoil.

Although Klein stopped short of a political theory of mourning, her claims about the positions have immanent social and political content. For Klein, the achievement (always unsteady and fragile) of the depressive position depends on the experience of "mutual sorrow and sympathy" within external relationships.[52] Correspondingly, the baleful circuits of resentment, punishment, and cruelty of the paranoid-schizoid position reflect and are reinforced by social experiences of marginalization or misrecognition. In other words, the individual labor of mourning and the social work of recognition are deeply dependent on one another; in fact, it is impossible to even speak of one in isolation from the other.[53] If Crimp, Sedgwick, and Klein are correct, then the angry work of political activism and the work of mourning are not diametrically opposed but are in desperate need of one another. What remains to be sketched, however, is an argument that connects the agency of the depressive position with an effective activist politics. In the next two sections of this chapter, I create some space for this argument through a return to the haunting, mournful figure of Antigone.

Antigone and Agonist Political Theory

The connections between anger, grief, and an agonistic mode of politics can be further teased out through a reading of recent appropriations of Antigone within political theory. Judith Butler, for instance, has repeatedly turned to Antigone in order to theorize the connection between mourning and a critical, left politics. In these writings, Butler has reflected both levels of mourning's agonism. Namely, Butler has used Antigone to describe a disruptive mode of political resistance that is sparked by the struggle between disavowed desire and cultural forces of prohibition; yet Butler, like Loraux, also sees the conflict between Antigone and Creon as an instantiation of the inherently contested and conflicted nature of politics itself. Butler, then, oscillates between different levels of agonism: she invokes Antigone to describe a concrete politics of resistance, but Antigone's claims also point beyond a politics of recognition toward "the limits of representation and representability."[54]

Butler's interest in mourning and melancholia traces back to her influential theory of gender constructivism.[55] In this work, Butler wrote about "aborted" or "foreclosed" mourning surrounding homosexual desire.[56] Because this desire faced social stigma, homosexual losses could not be registered or acknowledged. The "absence of cultural conventions for avowing the loss of homosexual love" amounted to a "preemption of grief."[57] Drawing on Freud's account of character formation through gender consolidation, Butler argued that a foundational repudiation of same-sex desire inaugurated the gendered subject. In this way, the child internalizes, as "an interior moral directive," a prohibition resulting from social taboo.[58] By accepting this directive, the heretofore loose or anarchic desire of the young child is channeled according to the dictates of cultural prejudice, and the loss that occurs at this moment cannot thereafter be consciously acknowledged or mourned. The loss, denied as such, becomes unspeakable.

In her later work, Butler generalized from the melancholia of gender norms to describe a series of concrete political and cultural prohibitions that have shaped which losses can be properly mourned and which, on the other hand, are passed over in silence. These cultural refusals of mourning included, for instance, the losses due to AIDS, the deaths caused by the prosecution of the so-called war on terror, and the inability to recognize or mourn for those caught up in U.S. practices of indefinite detention and torture.[59] In all of this work, Butler has drawn attention to the paucity of available means for the public expression of certain losses and the inability of the marginalized to make their grief visible because their losses are prohibited by social stigma. As Butler argued, the losses from AIDS could not rise above the stigma attached to homosexual desire, just as the deaths of foreign civilians caught up in the global war on terror had difficulty breaking through the dominant frames of the conflict. In these instances, melancholia is less a psychological pathology than a political and cultural phenomenon. As Butler put it, "where there is no public recognition or discourse through which such [losses] might be named and mourned, then melancholia takes on cultural dimensions."[60] The prohibition of public mourning doubles the trauma of loss.

To confront these cultural prohibitions, Butler focuses on the discursive frames by which experience is organized in mediated culture. As she puts it, "a frame for understanding violence emerges in tandem with the experience, and that frame works . . . to preclude certain kinds of questions."[61] For instance, in describing the dominant response to September 11, Butler laments the delegitimization of efforts to contextualize the terrorists' actions in a history of U.S. foreign intervention, or in global patterns of poverty and religiosity, as rationalizations for the attacks or blaming the victim. Instead, media coverage focused on the attackers' personal histories and on shadowy Al Qaeda "masterminds" like Osama bin Laden. On Butler's understanding, this was largely an effort to make sense of the events by situating them within a recognizable frame of subjective agency and charismatic leadership. As she puts it, "isolating the individuals involved absolves us of the necessity of coming up with a broader explanation for events."[62] Moreover, public commemorations of these events are typified by a "monumental" style of mourning that short-circuits critical reflection on these losses.[63] At these moments, critical modes of questioning are drowned out and overwhelmed by rituals of "spectacular public grief."[64]

Recognition of the limited framing of loss and the monumental performances of mourning that perpetuate denials inspired Butler to assert a disruptive politics of grief as the means of resignifying the "conditions of grievability."[65] It is here that Butler turns to Antigone. Antigone represents the possibility of refusing the hegemonic orders of intelligibility by which grief is apportioned out. She does so by revealing what Butler calls the "aberrant temporality of the norm," or its dependence on sustained performances that are never guaranteed.[66] Creon's edict outlawing mourning rites for Polyneices functions only insofar as it is taken up and repeated by the Theban subjects. Antigone's insistent refusal to recognize Creon's law gives momentum to growing doubts within the city, first voiced in the play by Haemon and later echoed by the chorus of Theban elders. Ultimately, Antigone sparks a political conflagration by refusing the frame that organizes the city's grief.

For Butler, Antigone's predicament offers an allegory about similar crises in our time. As she puts it, "Antigone refuses to obey any law that refuses public recognition of her loss, and in this way prefigures the situation that those with publicly ungrievable losses—from AIDS, for instance—know too well."[67] By her actions Antigone hints at the possibility that subjects might resist and reconfigure the discursive norms that bind them. Antigone's particular claims over the body of her fallen brother ultimately force a polis-wide recognition of the law's inherent instability. Antigone troubles the distinctions over who can speak in public and over which losses could or should be mourned.

Antigone's agonism, for Butler, is one both of response and of ground. On the one hand, Antigone's claim is concrete and political. She insists on a proper burial for Polyneices against the dictates of Creon. In this respect, she "speaks in the name of politics and the law," and her resistance is made from within that language and as a reaction to an abuse of power.[68] However, for Butler, Antigone's claims also point beyond the "question of representation" to "somewhere else . . . to that political possibility that emerges when the limits to representation and representability are exposed."[69] Antigone gives voice to a limit that is "internal to normative construction itself."[70] The power of Antigone's claim is that it demonstrates an inherent instability within discursive subjugation.[71] The norm or prohibition that structures subjectivity never fully determines the subject because "the 'subject' created is not for that reason fixed in place: it becomes the occasion for a further making . . . a subject only remains a subject through a reiteration or rearticulation of itself as a subject, and this dependency of the subject on repetition for coherence may constitute that subject's incoherence."[72]

Hence, for Butler, Antigone's grief is not exemplary because it attempts to create more public space for the working through of traumatic loss or to slowly bend the norms and codes of speech. Instead, Antigone is exemplary because she signals the "scandal" by "which the unspeakable . . . makes itself heard through borrowing and exploiting the very terms that are meant to enforce its silence."[73] Antigone's speech acts are, as literal claims, irrelevant; instead what is significant is the way in which her speech leads to a "fatality [that] exceeds her life and enters the discourse of intelligibility as its own promising fatality, the social form of its aberrant, unprecedented future."[74]

However, Butler's attempt to link the praxis of disruption with more comprehensive agonistic claims is not without costs. In the particular case of Antigone, it serves to push her concrete claims, and her acts of mourning, outside of the polis (a replication, in effect, of Creon's prohibition). Butler elevates Antigone's acts of grieving into a paradigmatic politics of disruption, yet in this elevation Antigone's recorded laments seem to lose the texture and ambivalence that comes from their location within codes of speech and public interaction. That these norms sought to exclude the rights of the claimant to speak is surely relevant to any reading of the play, but also relevant is Sophocles' inversion of these norms and Antigone's discursive success in undermining Creon's claims for legitimacy and, even, in altering the Theban codes of speech surrounding grief. It is worth recalling that Antigone's first actual laments in the play are not directed at her brother but at the polis and her fellow Thebans: "My City! Rich citizens of my city! . . . I would still have you as my witnesses" (line 842). Even more important and remarkable is the effect that Antigone's efforts have on how the citizens of Thebes view the traditional codes surrounding lamentation and speech. Toward the end of the drama, when Eurydice learns of the death of her son Haemon, she retreats into the home in order—we soon discover—to commit suicide. In the wake of her departure, the leader of the chorus and the messenger begin to question the wisdom of domestic "repression" surrounding grief (1250). As the chorus leader puts it, "a silence so extreme is as dangerous as a flood of silly tears" (1248). The messenger concurs, "You are right: in an excess of silence, too, there may be trouble" (1256). The agon between Antigone and Creon is hardly an ideal speech situation, but it does appear to have yielded public reflection on the norms by which life at Thebes was organized.

Butler's reading of Antigone obscures this ambiguity. Despite Butler's acknowledgment that Antigone is "trying to grieve, to grieve publicly," she avers that these "loud proclamations of grief presuppose a domain of the ungrievable."[75] Unsatisfied with a diagnosis of Thebes' political melancholia, manifested by Creon's dictatorial prohibition of discursive contestation surrounding the death of Polyneices, Butler insists on a register of unknowable conflict perpetually beyond our discursive grasp. As a result, Butler interprets Antigone's public mourning less as a representable claim within a concrete community than as an irruptive force that reveals the limits of representation, sovereignty, and the law.[76] Butler's insistence on reading Antigone's claim as an "impossible" form of mourning, then, ultimately obscures the complex texture of Antigone's claims and their partial success. As a result, mourning as a political practice becomes abstracted from the social contexts within which losses are described, contested, and redescribed.[77] Anger becomes detached from desecration, nonrecognition, and survivors' commitment, and it becomes, *pace* Loraux, a reminder of endless discord at the root of political and interpersonal life. Anger feeds on itself, losing touch with the broader world and the complex, ambivalent objects within that world.

These points against Butler's reading of Antigone are reinforced by Bonnie Honig's interpretation of Butler in the context of Honig's own agonist reappropriation of Antigone. For Honig, it is important not to abstract Antigone's claims— as Butler does—such that they become elevated into paradigmatic expressions of vulnerability or performativity. Rather, interpreters of Antigone should embed her laments within their original context of articulation before using this (resituated) Antigone to reflect on one's own political situation. Like Butler, Honig wants to reflect on contemporary politics through the story of Antigone; in fact, as previously mentioned, she argues that doing without Antigone "is not something we are free to do," any more than Oedipus could flee his fate by leaving Corinth.[78] But without an effort to situate Antigone's claims within the politics of ancient Athens, Honig argues that Antigone's story is reduced to free-floating ethical abstractions about filial duty or postpolitical exhortations about universal vulnerability. As a side effect of this abstraction, Antigone becomes a merely reactive figure whose actions are framed as disobedience, dissidence, or refusal. Yet to identify Antigone's political choices in terms of disobedience is to fall for "hegemony's tactic," by describing actions from the vantage point of the established order. If we focus on what Antigone says "no" to, we obscure the alternative political order to which she wants to say "yes." Honig's interpretive efforts seek to rescue Antigone from sentimentalist discourses that see her as a loving sister forced into disobedience by an unjust political order, or critical discourses that focus on Antigone's strangeness or lack of fit, and to focus on Antigone as a vibrant political actor, representing a viable alternative from within the given order of things.

To better see Antigone as a yes-saying figure of action, Honig revivifies the ancient Athenian struggle over competing political orders that formed the background within which Sophocles wrote his play. For Honig, *Antigone* stages a struggle between different "economies" of mourning, relating to classical Athens' struggle over burial procedures and mourning rites. Sophocles's play involves a struggle between a displaced Homeric style of individualized grief (represented by Antigone) and a democratic style of mourning that seeks to tightly regulate funerary practices in order to glorify the polis itself (represented by Creon).[79] Creon's edict forbidding the burial of Polyneices demonstrates how an aristocratic style of lamentation focusing on individual achievement and suffering was being supplanted by the city's anonymization of the dead—which was given its classical form, a decade after the play's first performance, in Pericles's oration.

By resituating Antigone's story, Honig hopes to resituate the politics of grief within a more encompassing, agonistic "politics of enmity." For Honig, the fight over grievable life is merely a "synecdoche" of the broader political struggle by which plural and contending wills perpetually clash.[80] The body of Polyneices, then, is less the sole cause of the conflict and more of a pretext for a broader power struggle in Thebes (itself a thinly veiled representation for ongoing power struggles in Athens). For Honig, by focusing less on Antigone's natal politics, and more on her reactive laments, political theorists and actors risk advancing either an apolitical humanism (what Honig calls "mortalist humanism") or a constrained politics of lamentation that freezes actors within a "bad script" of the woeful, grieving sister/mother.[81] Political action is reduced and misplaced by the frame of grievability, so despite the "grief that in our politics we . . . do so much to generate,"[82] political theorists and activists have to exceed the lamentation of power and its excesses and search for ways to claim power. For Honig, Antigone can be a model for this form of politics, if we rescue her from the framework of the model mourner as offered by Butler and others.

As noted by Honig, Butler's appropriations of Antigone have shifted over time, from a focus on the Sophoclean heroine's resistance to the state toward an ethical universalism that focuses on humans' "equal grievability." According to Honig, however, with this second move Butler risks joining those—such as Jean Elshtain—who sentimentalize Antigone and the political actors who invoke her (such as the Madres de Plaza de Mayo). By sentimentalizing Antigone as a model mourner, Butler betrays her earlier (agonistic) argument, which emphasized how Antigone's irreducible impropriety serves to throw gender and familial norms into crisis. Moreover, Butler and other mortalist humanists, in order to fit Antigone in the straitjacket of universal lamentation, divest her of her "politicality—sometimes ugly, violent, difficult."[83] Yet the projection of politicality and sovereignty onto another space is to supplant political struggle over power with an ethical lamentation of power's excesses.[84] If mourning is reified as a pre- or postpolitical exercise by which claims for universal vulnerability are addressed to power, rather than being seen as an intervention within the clash of wills by which power is claimed, then perhaps, Honig argues, we ought to resist the framework of lamentation and its depoliticizing traps. Both the rhetoric and the practices of mourning might be inappropriate for political actors insofar as the former are compromised by apolitical overtones.

In a second attempt to resituate Antigone's claims within their broader political context, Honig sketches out what it might mean to resist the seduction of a lamentation framework.[85] In this essay, Honig describes what she refers to as Antigone's "complex politicality," which has been obscured by readings such as Butler's that see Antigone as the model mourner while abstracting her claims from their original context of enunciation. Honig bases this reading on a subtle interpretation of Antigone's final speech, in which she claims that it was only a brother—not a husband or a child or a parent—that could have inspired her acts of resistance. The speech has been interpreted, both sympathetically and critically, as revealing Antigone's horrifying excess.[86] Yet for Honig, this speech, read in its original context, "makes political sense."[87] Within the speech, Antigone makes a complex political argument through "parody, mimicry, and citation," which puts "Creon on trial."[88] Antigone parodies Athenian funeral oratory by focusing on the irreplaceability of her lost brother; she mimics Creon by implying that it is she—and not Haemon—who has the ability to find other lovers; and she cites Herodotus's story about Darius and Intraphrenes's wife in order to (implicitly) chastise Creon for a failure to govern properly. For Honig, Antigone's layered claims are obscured when interpreters focus only on her laments; her laments are excessive but they also exceed lament to claim a political "place from which to be heard."[89] By putting the speech into its political context, Honig shows that Antigone's story is one not only of lamentation but also of natality and pleasure—not only the "mere life" of mourning but also the "more life" of action.[90]

Antigone's layered political claims, with their mixture of lament, parody, mimicry, resistance, pain, and pleasure can offer "a still powerful solicitation to contemporary audiences to see grief and lamentation in political not ethical terms."[91] To claim Antigone, then, is to reclaim her politics and her anger, while deprivileging or, rather, *contextualizing* her grief within the more encompassing clash of wills that is agonistic politics. If Antigone is restored as a political actor—rather than being reduced to a model mourner—then we can see the task of politics more clearly as the contestation for power rather than the lamentation over power's excesses. Moving out from the example of Antigone, Honig counsels a similar move with regard to the contemporary politics of mourning—to see struggles over the recognition of grief and loss as instances of the larger, endless struggle over power that constitutes political life, that is, to put lamentations of "mere life" into conversation with activist struggles for "more life." Because grief—while generative of solidarity and energy for action—can drain or absorb the "more life" of politics, Honig argues that we must counterbalance the politics of mourning with practices that celebrate natality and agency.

Honig turns to the figure of Crimp in order to locate a natal praxis of struggle that, while acknowledging the importance of mourning, also does more than mourn. Unlike Butler and other ethical antistatists, Crimp and ACT UP had an ambivalent relationship to the state that went beyond pure opposition. Honig refers to this as Crimp's and ACT UP's "demanding, agonistic enlistment of the state," which combined a protest politics that could "shout out or make visible emotions and actions cast as transgressive" with a civic demand that the state fulfill its responsibilities.[92] As such, it worked at the intervals not only *between* the state, the scientific community, and the gay community but also *within* these communities—looking for irregularities and leverage points rather than assuming uniformity and absolute coherence. For example, Honig describes how activists undertook their own detailed research into the virus in order to be more conversant with the scientific community, which in turn allowed for a combination of insider and outsider tactics that "worked one model of good research against another."[93] This complex, intersectional work combined mourning's "mere life" and militancy's "more life" in ways that were "adamantly life-affirming: mobilizing, militant, passionate, and erotic—natal, angry, and funny."[94]

Ultimately, however, if Crimp and ACT UP represent a complex political practice, then for Honig the most important signpost for this practice seems to be the "rage and righteous anger" that drives and feeds "political protest, activism, self-organization, and communal self-care."[95] It is Crimp's refusal to relinquish the power of shared grief/rage, or to subsume it entirely within a sentimentalist discourse of mourning, that makes his natal, erotic, and mortalist politics so appealing for Honig. However, as we have previously discussed, Crimp was also sensitive, in ways that Honig does not dwell on, to how rage and righteous anger can act as defenses and modes of disavowal that prevent activists from acknowledging their own imperfections and ambivalence.[96] As Crimp puts it in "Mourning and Militancy," the tendency to make "all violence external" is to "fail to confront ourselves, to acknowledge our ambivalence."[97] While careful not to fall into a pathologizing discourse that he ultimately hopes to unravel, Crimp argues that AIDS activists also have to "comprehend that our misery is also self-inflicted . . . it is not only New York City's collapsing healthcare system and its sinister health commissioner that affect our fate."[98] When Crimp advocates for a fraught interaction between mourning and militancy, it is this acceptance of ambivalence and self-inflicted wounds that seems foremost in his mind, and this is a possible articulation of the politics of mourning that Honig has not yet seriously entertained.

Crimp's approach to mourning is layered in ways similar to Antigone's dirge. Within "Mourning and Militancy," there are two distinct conceptions of mourning and the intimation of a third. The first explains the "internal opposition of activism and mourning" by reflecting on the "absorbing" or privatizing nature of grief. The second conception of mourning reconnects grief to activism because the "violence of silence and omission" interferes with the ability to grieve and give rise to a militant response. Crimp derives both of these approaches from Freud's account of mourning in "Mourning and Melancholia," where the work of mourning proceeds through hypercathection and substitution of the lost object (an "absorbing" process) unless it is "inadvisably" interfered with or aborted (desecration). From within these terms, grief and mourning offer either a retreat from the life of political action or instigation to militant resistance born from social melancholia and disavowal.[99]

Yet within this essay Crimp moves toward a different articulation of grief that we could fairly call Kleinian. In doing so, he ties mourning explicitly to the acknowledgment of constitutive ambivalence along with "our terror, our guilt, and our profound sadness." Mourning is not reducible to either an absorbing or privatizing process of working through, or to a resistance born of social misrecognition. Mourning must also be seen as an ongoing challenge of acknowledging ambivalence within the self and within the broader social world and of working through the losses (of absolute moral certainty, of convenient scapegoats, of an omnipotent "killing rage") that accompany such acts of recognition. I would argue that it is *this* idea of mourning that, when crossed with militancy born of disavowal, produces the complex agonistic statism of ACT UP.

Instead of finding Loraux's bond of division or Honig's complex (but ultimately agonistic) politicality at this crossroads of militancy and mourning, we encounter a vision of politics as a complex mixture of consensus and disruption, community and difference, bonds of attachment and aggressive acts of separation. Instead of rejecting either the search for coherence and meaning or the task of disruption, Crimp turns the ambivalent crossroads between agonism and consensualism into a productive resource for interpersonal and political life. In doing so, he acknowledges not only the crossroads of political action that require a flexible and open strategy but also an internal crossroads. Using Freud's idea of the death drive, Crimps calls for a confrontation with our native aggression and negativity. He argues that only by making this negativity conscious and avoiding the temptation to project it onto easily hated external sources can activists combine their rage with their (often unacknowledged) "terror . . . guilt, and . . . profound sadness" in order to generate a politics that avoids replicating the violence they are resisting.

In staking a claim to the natalist politics of ACT UP, Honig overplays Crimp's rage and downplays his calls for ambivalence and guilt. Honig accepts Crimp's accents on mourning mainly because they are tied to an angry and natal activism; on the whole, she seems increasingly leery of conceptualizing politics in terms of mourning. Yet Crimp seems to imply that mourning is not merely a mortalist supplement to activist militancy but that which makes militancy effective. This hints at an approach to mourning that goes beyond antipolitical humanism, passive apolitical withdrawal, or defensive and melancholic resistance. It resembles nothing so much as the image of agency offered by the depressive position, with the understanding of collaborative power sharing.

In this light, Crimp's appreciation of the complex work of mourning—and its interdependency with militant anger—offers an alternative trajectory for the politics of mourning. In the next section of this chapter, I will describe this trajectory from within the action of *Antigone*, where we can detect—despite all the interpretive layers that may block our view—the agency of Klein's depressive position and what I will refer to as "democratic anger." Antigone may yet be a model mourner, but less in the way that her angry resistance writes the script for contemporary agonistic politics and more for the way that her (momentary) obtainment of depressive agency can help us to rewrite this script in ways that erode habits of nonrecognition and cultivate civic relationships in the wake of social traumas.

Antigone's Claims Reclaimed: Democratic Anger and Depressive Agency

How we tell the story of Antigone matters because, as Honig reminds us, we tell our own stories partly in her shadow. I have argued that the agonistic framing for Antigone's actions is inadequate, insofar as it privileges either Antigone's outsider status as opposed to her embeddedness (Butler) or her anger at the expense of her mourning (Honig). It is better, I will argue, to see Antigone *in transition*—to see her in-between the competing logics of an endless agonistic clash of wills and consensualist humanism. If we see Antigone as herself unsettled or in process, we can revivify the ongoing and endless democratic work of mourning that Klein and Crimp—each in their own way—help us to imagine.

However, given the dense layers of interpretation and appropriation that cover Antigone's tomb, is it even possible to see Antigone as an *unsettled* figure? Honig argues that Antigone has become so sanctified and sentimentalized that she is unavailable as a resource for a political actor like Crimp, who frames his own combination of mourning and militancy in different terms. In part for this reason, Honig advises political theorists and actors to resist the lamentation frame, by de-sanctifying Antigone and recontextualizing her laments within a broader political struggle. Once this rescue mission is completed, then an activist like Crimp could be seen as an Antigonean figure whose politics of mourning is less a lamentation of power than a strategy for claiming power.

But there is another way of thinking about the politics of mourning, where mourning is the endless practice of facing down the ambivalence of self and other by restoring wholeness to our objects of attachment, in part by cultivating and occupying the spaces and relational forms that allow us to reclaim the full range of emotions and ideas that belong to being alive. This is not a private labor, but an intersubjective and social struggle for what Klein and Winnicott both call "integration." Building from the groundwork provided by object relations psychoanalysis, the democratic theory of mourning looks for the spaces, settings, and relational practices that support the work of integration through dialogic and collaborative encounters between whole, ambivalent objects amid the search and struggle for a livable democratic order. The democratic work of mourning does not transcend an angry, agonistic politics, but it orients this politics to a higher-order practice of democracy in which neither agreement nor disagreement can be ruled out of bounds, and in which conflict and settlement are seen as live possibilities on the risky terrain of the political.

How can a revised account of Antigone support this work? So many interpreters of Antigone have focused on her identity—as sister, as civil disobedient, as an insistent voice of mourning, as the daughter of Oedipus—or on the impossibility of her identity—her impurity that bedevils gender and familial norms, her hideous antihumanist excess that casts the entire symbolic order into crisis. But often left unacknowledged is Antigone's ambivalence—her multisidedness that, despite her apparent dogmatism, marks her as a figure in transition. If Antigone can be reenvisioned as an ambivalent actor, then her militancy and her mourning might be seen as constitutive components of a depressive form of political agency. By listening for Antigone's ambivalence, we can also locate her democratic anger at the structures of misrecognition within Thebes. This anger can be situated within an ongoing struggle for integration at the intersection between the equally fractious spaces of the polis and the psyche.

Like many other interpreters of *Antigone*, I focus primarily on her enigmatic speech that ends with the claim that only a brother's death—not a husband's, nor a child's—could have inspired her actions. This speech has been interpreted, by Jacques Lacan and others, as the culminating moment of Antigone's autonomy—in which she advances an entirely different order that overturns the hold of symbolic and cultural norms.[100] As discussed earlier, it has also been read by Honig as an expression of Antigone's complex, layered political claims that cite and challenge the order of things at Thebes (or Athens). For Honig, then, the speech is the culmination of the clash of wills and political orders represented by Creon and Antigone. Yet there are moments within Antigone's final speech that show it to be less a culmination than an incomplete and unstable act of transition—away from the persecutory guilt and melancholic identification that mark her first appearances in the play and toward the riskier terrain of depressive agency.

To see this shift, we must look back to these first appearances and place them within the light of Klein's "positional" theory of mourning. For Klein, paranoid-schizoid defenses against grief manifest themselves as a slavish attachment to the lost object, which, under the pressure of idealization, has become "extremely perfect."[101] To admit the imperfection of the internalized object would be a form of betrayal, so the ego is forced into a form of "slavery" in which the "extremely cruel demands and admonitions of its loved object . . . become installed within the ego."[102] The idealized object demands absolute fidelity; other objects of attachment fade in comparison, if they are not split off entirely as "extremely bad" objects who threaten the position of the internalized perfect other. The ego becomes "prey to contradictory and impossible claims from within, a condition which is felt as a bad conscience."[103] Love and hatred are split off from one another—love is attached to the internal perfect object, and hatred is projected out onto those who would threaten this bond (or bondage).

When Antigone first comes onto the stage, she appears to be in the thrall of a persecutory commitment to her dead brother Polyneices. Despite Creon's edict that Polyneices's body should go unmourned, Antigone claims that she "will not prove false to him" (40) and will not be kept "from my own" (48). Her sister, Ismene, grows concerned about Antigone's "dark thoughts" and argues that they should yield to the authorities rather than risk a suicidal transgression. Antigone, however, is unpersuaded. Ismene's refusal becomes an inexcusable betrayal ("I would not urge you now; nor if you wanted to act would I be glad to have you with me"), and Antigone would prefer to be buried alongside her dead brother than to fail in her duties to his memory ("I shall lie by his side"). Antigone seems captivated by an idealized image of Polyneices. Despite the latter's recent violent assault on Thebes, Antigone feels compelled to "love . . . him as he loved me" (74). She knows that her actions—even if they scandalize the city, will please "those I should please most" (89). When Ismene pleads that Antigone is in "love with the impossible," it drives a further wedge between them. The pressure of the idealization forces Antigone into a furious rejection of her sister: "If you talk like this I will loathe you, and you will be adjudged an enemy" (93). Antigone draws a clear, sharp line between "noble" and "base" actions and asserts that she, unlike her sister, will not prove false to her noble birth. She then omnipotently assumes the burden of her burial duty, which she describes—tellingly—as a "terror" (95).

Later, once her actions have been discovered and she has been confronted by Creon, Antigone intensifies her defenses of splitting and idealization, isolating not only the noble from the base but also splitting off her guilt and hatred onto others. She maintains that her actions are blameless ("there is nothing shameful in honoring my brother" [512]) while denying the hatefulness she has just expressed toward Ismene and Creon: "It is my nature to join in love, not hate" (525). She once again denies her sister ("I will have none of your partnership") along with all other objects of attachment aside from Polyneices. In doing so, however, Antigone does more than deny the counsel of false friends; she also denies filial obligations that fall outside the singular commitment to her brother. She also denies *herself*—she denies her hatred ("I . . . join in love, not hate") even as she expresses it ("I will loathe you").

From the light of Klein's account of the paranoid-schizoid position, Antigone's actions make a perverse kind of sense. As a defense against loss (of her brothers) and guilt (perhaps her relief that Polyneices did not triumph?), Antigone is in the persecutory thrall of her idealized object, splitting not only the social world but her very self into extremely perfect and safely hated pieces. The stunning dissonance between her claim to join "in love" and the venom and loathing she directs toward her still-living attachments is explained by a split between a good and a bad Antigone, matching the split between good and bad siblings and lovers (note the incestuous longing for Polyneices and the blithe disregard of Haemon). Forsaking all living attachments, Antigone cuts a figure of autonomy, but in reality she is under the sway of a melancholic, unyielding law guarded over by the idealized Polyneices. The latter is stripped of ambivalence, and Antigone splits herself—her nobility from her impurity, her love from her hate—and all of Thebes into hermetically sealed camps of the pure and the corrupted.

But this is not the end of Antigone's story. In her final appearance on stage, Antigone—while maintaining that her actions were just—appears to overcome her defenses of idealization and splitting and to move from a paranoid-schizoid position of persecutory "terror" toward a depressive awareness of the consequences of her actions. Recall that for Klein the depressive position is marked by the appearance of the whole object, but this takes place in part through the appearance of other objects—that is, the internal world of the ego comes to be less dominated by the cruel, persecutory voice of the idealized object and becomes a multiplicitous assembly of fractious and many-sided objects. Mourning in the depressive position repairs the internal and external worlds of the subject by restoring their wholeness and multiplicity. As Sedgwick puts it, the threshold to the depressive position is "the simple, foundational, authentically very difficult understanding that good and bad tend to be inseparable at every level."[104] This realization marks the end of omnipotence, itself based on the splitting of the ego and its objects of attachment. For Klein, omnipotence eventually leads to the sadistic, cannibalistic destruction—in fantasy—of "the external world and . . . real people" through the zero-sum calculation of annihilation or absolute triumph. The depressive position marks the ability to recognize this destruction as a "disaster," and to make reparative connections within the self and to the world.[105] By identifying with multiple, whole objects, the ego forsakes omnipotence for a depressive agency in which others can—and inevitably must—take part. The perverse consolations of the paranoid-schizoid position—including the airtight distinctions between noble and base—are mitigated. As Thomas Ogden puts it, in the depressive position fantasies of "omnipotently annihilating one's rival . . . no longer provide a satisfactory solution to a problem in a human relationship."[106]

Where and how does Antigone transition toward a position of depressive agency? When Antigone makes her final appearance on the stage, her tone is markedly different than before. Until this moment, she had shown little care for her other objects of attachment—from Ismene to Haemon to the city of Thebes itself—while maintaining strict fidelity to the corpse of Polyneices. Yet at this moment, she laments her impending death and the sacrifices that it implies. She bemoans that she has "not lived the due term of my life" (895). She has "known nothing of the marriage songs, nor the chant that brings the bride to bed" (811–12). She recognizes and addresses the audience of Theben elders, imploring them to see "under what laws I make my way to my prison sealed like a tomb" (845). Instead of her manic, single-minded focus on Polyneices, she now bemoans not only her own fate but also the fate of Thebes and of her infamous parents. In effect, Thebes has been restored as an imperfect but still "good" object that licenses her disapproval of its current course. Relatedly, Antigone appears to overcome the defenses of idealization and demonization that have insulated her from the full range of her "painful . . . cares" (857). She cries, "What parents I was born of, God help me!" (865) and she implicates Polyneices in the tragic actions that have led to her death: "Brother, it was a luckless marriage you made, and dying killed my life" (870–71). Antigone has, through a work of mourning, repaired the connections to her internal and external worlds ("O my father's city, in Theban land" [840]). She acknowledges plural, whole objects along with the consequences of her actions, which, though they have won her "great renown," make her punishment akin to the "saddest of deaths" (825). Even though she maintains that it was for Polyneices alone that she would have acted—because "no brother's life would bloom for me again"—she does so while entertaining the ideas of motherhood and matrimony ("had I been a mother . . . if my husband were dead"). In other words, Antigone puts the obligation to her brother within the context of other relational possibilities, whereas before she had been exclusively concerned with the demands of her departed sibling. The idealized object (Polyneices) yields to the desired but disappointing good object (Thebes), which in turn repopulates the assembly of Antigone's internal and external worlds. She is reconnected to the world that she is, tragically, quickly to exit.

Antigone also obtains a depressive form of agency, insofar as she overcomes her omnipotent fantasies of autonomy and calls on the citizens of Thebes to acknowledge and to question the norms by which her grief has been criminalized. She asks them to "see what I suffer and who makes me suffer" (847), which invites the polis to reflect on its normative codes and political decisions. Antigone politicizes these decisions. Whereas the chorus responds to Antigone's laments that "the long-lived Fates" (929) shape individual and collective destiny, the agon between the messengers toward the end of the play shows that her intervention has turned the propriety or impropriety of public grief into a political question that cannot be solved through reference to the gods. In realizing a depressive form of agency, Antigone does not posit, omnipotently or autonomously, an alternative order of law, but she situates herself within the ongoing struggle over the orders of recognition at Thebes. In this (Kleinian) light, we can reenvision Antigone—not as a hero for mortalist humanists, or as a sanctified figure of pure resistance, but as a conflicted character embedded within a struggle both to mourn her dead brother and to live within a polis marked by relations of mutual recognition instead of social erasure.

The risk of reading *Antigone* in this light, of course, is that we commit the error of reading the action only through the psychological account of Klein's positions, instead of adjoining this account to a political narrative of resistance and integration. Antigone's "burying rage" may make perverse psychological sense if seen from within the paranoid-schizoid position, but by reading it in this frame, we might unjustly tether the politics of grief/rage to a normative ideal of depressive working through, which could pathologize and patronize Antigone's resistance. Yet this is a specious objection. Klein's account should not be seen as a strictly psychological story because she points not only to the individual, psychic labor of mourning but also to the structures of recognition that get this labor off the ground. Antigone's actions, then, make psychological and political sense insofar as they reflect her psychic struggle and the norms and *nomoi* by which her choice was forced and her persecution intensified.

A Kleinian account of Antigone's story, however, shows that the effectiveness of her protest and her attainment of depressive agency are coimplicated. We see this not only in the exchange between the messengers at the end of the play, but in the movement of the chorus itself. When Antigone first addresses Creon, at the height of her manic omnipotence, the chorus sings despairingly that "for those whose house has been shaken by God, there is never cessation of ruin . . . no generation frees another . . . there is no deliverance" (584–92). Yet in the final exchange between Antigone and the chorus, the latter speaks of afterlife and regeneration—including the "great renown" and "distinction and praise" that Antigone has won from death (835, 817). The chorus implies that Antigone—whose name, once again, means "antigeneration"—will live on. Despite being walled in a living tomb, she carries a seed of renown that can still flower, just as Danae, who was also held in a "tomb-like cell" nevertheless "kept, as guardian, the seed of Zeus" (945).

One should be careful, however, not to use Klein to exorcise the specter of Antigone's rage, which is an essential aspect of her story and the (ongoing) story of mourning's politics. While the play hints at the structures of recognition that might mitigate a persecutory and zero-sum politics, it is also a potent reminder of the perpetual misrecognitions and conflicts to which we are prone. Yet these conflicts cannot serve as an effective ground for an agonistic politics—any more than the moments of recognition can license a nontragic consensualism. The ground—*Antigone's ground*—rather, is the risky terrain where conflict and recognition play it out, where the search for justified and justifiable political order(s) is bedeviled but never fully derailed by the native fractiousness within and between psyches. Klein saw this as the interplay between the death and life instincts, but these instincts interact with the uneven experiences of care and neglect, respect and desecration, in which we perpetually find ourselves. For Klein, the best response to this situation was a depressive awareness of complexity and ambivalence that keeps love and integration as live possibilities amid the baleful circuits of hatred and misrecognition to which we are tragically susceptible. Antigone—albeit briefly—seems to achieve such awareness, which can serve as a model for how we might understand and practice a democratic politics of mourning in our own time.

Conclusion: Antigone and the Democratic Work of Mourning

The connection between anger and public expressions of mourning has a long history and a lively present. Under the image of the resistant, mournful Antigone, political theorists have defended an agonistic approach to public life and activists have performed inspiring acts of resistance. Yet this chapter has argued for a different approach to the politics of mourning, not by leaving Antigone behind, but by resituating her claims within Klein's account of mourning and within the broader struggle for integration on the risky terrain of the political.

For Klein, mourning is an ongoing developmental challenge, and an account of what Sedgwick calls the "agency" of the depressive position points toward relational dynamics and social spaces that might make democratic mourning a live possibility. Outside the story of Antigone, I have argued that the complex activism of Douglas Crimp and ACT UP provide an example of how depressive agency and democratic anger form crucial components of the democratic work of mourning. Crimp argues for a productive synergy between mourning and militancy, based on his awareness that militancy can be a self-defeating and self-denying form of defense and disavowal. Bonnie Honig also praises Crimp's marriage of mourning and militancy, but for Honig the most crucial aspect of Crimp's story is the "rage and righteous anger" that might inspire political theorists and activists to leave behind a lamentation framework and its largely apolitical (or postpolitical) resonances. Here, however, I am attempting see mourning less as lamentation and more in terms of the ongoing psychosocial challenge of integration facing democratic societies marked by dislocative traumas, desecrations, and misrecognitions.

Ironically, in her earlier work on mourning, Honig seemed closer to this position. There, in her reading of membership, identity, and immigration policies, Honig used Winnicott's idea of the transitional object to theorize the conditions for separation and complex attachment within both immigrant and receiver communities. The idea of a transitional object, for Honig, illuminated efforts to create an environment conducive to a more generous immigration policy and to less dogmatic forms of national identity.[107] Honig's reading of object relations psychoanalysis suggested that "there are institutional and cultural conditions for the proper work of mourning" and that political action requires and can actively seek to create these spaces and practices of mourning.[108]

Honig has shifted away from this politics of mourning because she is anxious of the postpolitical or ethical displacements inherent to the "bad script" of lamentation. However, in counseling a decentering of mourning in the interests of a broader, natal agonism, Honig may be too hastily quitting the politically generative territory of grief. Winnicott's idea of the transitional object (and his larger concept of potential space), along with the agency of Klein's depressive position, on the other hand, recontextualize mourning within the democratic struggle not only for disruption but for agreement, not only for hegemony but for recognition. Potential spaces and transitional objects are what allow us, *pace* Crimp, to "confront ourselves" and to acknowledge our ambivalence as a step toward more open, generative engagements with others. They point to an alternative practice of mourning that challenges the assumptions of agonism. Honig wants to supplement mourning with the "more life" of activism, not only to infuse political life with generative natality but also to ensure that, *pace* Crimp, the rage and righteous anger that feeds political protest will not be subsumed by an overindulgent focus on mortality. Yet Crimp's insight is that there is a form of mourning that does not sacrifice rage but educates it, that makes rage more realistic and reparative, and that does not postpone political action but makes possible collaborative forms of agency. This is the democratic work of mourning, as described here and developed further in chapters 3 through 5.

THE IMAGINARY CITY

Consensual Mourning from Pericles
to John Rawls

> We must now ask whether the eulogy actually addresses the real
> object to which it is supposedly dedicated . . . are the orators not
> praising an imaginary, or at least ideal, city, without tensions or
> factions? . . . they . . . transform democracy into a beautiful,
> harmonious whole.

—Nicole Loraux, *The Invention of Athens*

> People are always trying to fool themselves, for one reason or
> another. The trick is to know it. Everybody has a tendency to hold
> onto what you think you know. But life is always smashing you into
> pieces . . . you pick it up and start again. And in all that I think
> something else begins to happen, which is a kind of good-natured
> reconciliation, an awareness that everything is much vaster than
> you can imagine—much worse and much better.

—James Baldwin, 1980 interview

Antigone provides the figure for a style of mourning politics in which claims for recognition disrupt the disavowals and silences of the status quo. Unruly, mournful voices mobilize on the basis of shared grief in order to challenge the norms that have made their suffering unrecognizable or their lives impossible. Yet these insistent mourning voices circulate within, attempt to influence, and implicitly acknowledge a broader struggle of narration over the meaning of historical suffering and enduring traumas.[1] Here the most prominent voices are often the official discourses and rituals that seek to memorialize the past in ways that reinforce common or binding traditions within the polity.[2] To encapsulate public mourning, I propose to use the figure of Pericles because his famous oration (as described by Thucydides) provides the classical form of a civic funeral discourse. The funeral oration tradition, according to Nicole Loraux, "invented" the Athenian polis, by offering an exemplary image of the city and of its inhabitants as a means of constructing and performing civic identity.[3] The real subject matter of civic funereal discourse, then, is often less the particular bodies of the dead than the polis itself—the collective object consecrated by the fallen and idealized through fulsome praise of those who remain. The funeral oration form has been criticized from practically its point of origin. In Plato's *Menexenus*, for instance, Socrates implies that the funeral oration falsifies history and impairs political and moral judgment. Yet the basic tropes of the practice have persisted into the contemporary age.

In this chapter, I argue that a Periclean politics of mourning—like the Antigonean politics described in chapter 2—is shadowed by political-psychological dangers that must be understood if collectivities are to move toward more democratic forms of mourning. These dangers include an uncritical, patriotic attachment to the state and a befogged romanticism about its history and traditions. I argue that these political pathologies stem in part from psychological tendencies described by Melanie Klein. Civic discourses of mourning repeatedly trigger the defenses within what Klein called the paranoid-schizoid position—defenses such as omnipotence, denial, splitting, idealization, and demonization. These defenses reinforce cognitive-affective schemas and modes of agency that make it harder for citizens to address the complexities and conflicts inherent to public life.

The shadow of Pericles—just like the shadow of Antigone—persists within contemporary political theory as well as contemporary civic discourse and practice. The work of John Rawls, for instance, has been challenged from voices on the left in ways that echo Socrates's critique of Pericles. Famously, Charles Mills has argued that Rawlsian liberalism is typified by a "studied ignorance" and "amnesia" over the historical traumas surrounding racial stigma and misrecognition in the United States. Rawlsian theory, in Periclean fashion, obscures a conflicted past and leaves its readers unprepared for confronting the injustices that presently surround them.[4] Instead of falsifying history, á la Pericles, Rawls's brand of ideal theory simply occludes historical development from its argument, with the resulting amnesia supposedly providing a better means of deciding on the principles of justice that could guide public action. Yet for many of his critics, the amnesia of Rawlsian ideal theory amounts to a pernicious form of denial. According to Mills, Rawls leaves his readers cognitively and morally handicapped.[5] For some of his critics on the left, then, Rawls's political philosophy—while intended to educate and guide political judgment—desensitizes its audience to the ambivalences and injustices of the actually existing polity, just as Pericles's commemorative speech erases the complexity of the Athenian polis.[6]

In Simon Stow's view, Rawlsian ideal theory imitates a Periclean mode of mourning insofar as it trades on a consensualist vision of political life.[7] Consensualist political theories, in turn, give license to civic rituals and discourses that obscure the conflicts and injustices within the polity's past and present, focusing our attention away from the violence in our tradition, the messiness of social conflict, and the contingency of progress. The drive toward consensus—whether the vehicle is public funeral oratory or political philosophy—is pernicious insofar as it desensitizes its audience to historical and enduring traumas of misrecognition.

The conceptual approach of this project, drawing on object relations psychoanalysis, provides a vocabulary that extends and deepens this line of critique. In light of this approach, Rawls's original theory of justice can be seen as being characterized by paranoid-schizoid thinking insofar as its characteristic elements, such as the original position and public reason, reinforce defenses such as splitting and idealization.[8] There is more in common, then, between a Periclean politics of mourning and Rawlsian theory than an interest in social consensus. Each discourse reinforces cognitive-affective schemas that have significant costs and consequences for democratic societies marked by historical and enduring traumas. Consensualist social theory and the Periclean mode of public mourning are—as was the case with Antigone and agonism—precariously perched between democratic performance and pathology.

My argument in this chapter begins with a description of the Periclean mode of mourning and shows how it triggers paranoid-schizoid defenses that have significant consequences for public life. Periclean funeral orations operate as a demanding civic superego, which redirects attachment from unreliable objects toward an idealized image of the polity. Yet this redirection both reflects and reinforces social-psychological defenses against anxiety, and it serves to entrench a paranoid-schizoid politics in which self and other are flattened and falsified through an oscillation between idealization and demonization.

In the next section, I turn directly to the work of Rawls, detailing aspects of the critical race and agonist critiques against Rawls insofar as each echoes Socrates's critique of Pericles. I argue that Rawls's work is characterized by an anxiety over an absent civic superego that could secure a moral psychology of justice, a vacuum that is filled in his early work by the original position. His *Theory of Justice* (hereafter *Theory*) relies on a theory of moral psychology that is implicitly Kleinian and that is explicitly set against Freud's ontogenetic theory of justice (where justice stems from envy rather than benevolence or love). Yet because Rawls could not adequately explain the development of a passionate attachment to the principles of justice with the resources of his account of moral psychology, he devised a thought experiment that is functionally similar to a demanding, univocal (Freudian) superego. Rawls's original position—like the Periclean politics of mourning—suffers from what Nicole Loraux has called the "dream of unanimous assemblies"—a dangerous fantasy for democratic politics that betrays *Theory's* roots in the paranoid-schizoid position with its persecutory superego.[9]

Rawls seemingly acknowledges the overreach of *Theory* in his later work. In *Political Liberalism* (hereafter *Liberalism*), Rawls argues that the "fact of reasonable pluralism" required substantive visions of justice to undergo a trial of public reason rather than pressing their claims dogmatically in the public sphere. However, Rawls's Freudian move (or slip?) reappears in this later work. In *Liberalism*, Rawls's account of moral psychology retreats into the background in the name of a "political" (not metaphysical) theory of both justice and the self, yet the felt need for a superordinate mechanism of social order and self-control reappears within Rawls's idea of public reason. Rawls's Periclean politics retreats only slightly, then, from the substantive consensus of *Theory* to the "overlapping" consensus of *Liberalism*. But this move still betrays an unacknowledged nexus of paranoid-schizoid anxieties that gives license to an amnesic form of politics.

Consensualist theories of politics, then, risk sliding into the same pathologies as the Periclean politics of mourning. Yet this does not imply that we can leave behind what Paul Ricoeur has called the "dangerous game" of social consensus.[10] The challenge is not to reject Periclean mourning in the name of an agonistic alternative, but to work within the narratives surrounding historical and enduring traumas to create space for democratic dialogue and public action. Mourning rites and rituals can become *potential spaces* of democratic engagement in ways that mitigate, rather than enflame, paranoid-schizoid defenses. Toward this end, I argue that the dream of a civic superego as a *unanimous assembly* could be displaced by one of a (Kleinian) civic conscience as a *fractious assembly* of whole, ambivalent others. I refer to this in terms of the "democratic superego," which would be composed of a fuller range of voices in order to militate against the dreams of frictionless consensus or unanimous assemblies but which could still guide public discourse toward a fractious coherence or democratic wholeness.[11]

The democratic superego requires what we would call "viable others." Viable others, like the Kleinian good object, are shadowed by a touch of idealization that, paradoxically, makes possible the work of deidealization and that opens up spaces of dialogue and depressive agency. Viable others are "whole" individuals who bear and testify to the ambivalence of internal and external life. I argue that perceptual-affective reversals offer up viable others that could coalesce into a democratic superego qua fractious assembly. In particular, I show how reversals within Michelle Alexander's critique of the war on drugs have the potential to turn back paranoid-schizoid defenses. Similarly, what James Baldwin referred to as "poets" embody a practice of viable otherness that leads to what Baldwin referred to as "good natured reconciliation" and what Klein would call integration: an awareness "that things are much worse *and* much better" than we imagine.[12] Practices of viable otherness in everyday social contexts are insufficient but necessary pieces of the democratic work of mourning, and political theory committed to viable otherness is better positioned than Rawlsian ideal theory to move democratic politics toward a depressive position of democratic repair.

The Periclean Tradition of Public Mourning

Sociological accounts of mourning rituals emphasize the ways in which such rituals do not invoke an unchallenged and preexisting social consensus so much as they produce or perform this consensus, by channeling the emotions and energy surrounding grief into solidaristic attachments. Public mourning rituals exert a subtle moral pressure on participants. They provide a focusing or unifying interpretation of what has been lost and, at a deeper level, narrate a common tradition that provides the context of meaning in which the event(s) can be located.[13] The interest in a cohesive narrative explains why these rituals—while often characterized by wild swings from sadness to joy, or from violent rage to extreme passivity—are themselves governed by rigid norms of appropriate speech and action.[14] Durkheim was one of the first sociologists to emphasize the controlled ambiguity of mourning rituals, including the simultaneous presence of joyful rage and manic sadness.[15] For Durkheim, the ritual aims to dissolve these tensions by splitting the joy from the rage and discharging each affect onto separate representative fields. Collective affirmation of the passions causes joy to be "exalted and amplified by [the] reverberation from consciousness to consciousness," allowing the emotion to be "expressed outwardly in the form of exuberant and violent movements."[16] Passionate reverberation creates a collective "effervescence" that transitions love and attachment from the dead object onto the (enduring) group. Mourning, in fact, is a "duty imposed by the group" in order to fulfill this need for social resiliency and solidarity.[17]

The flipside of effervescently circulating solidarity is the splitting off and displacement of grief's pain and anger. Rage cannot be expressed at the substitute object of attachment—the solidarity group that endures—so it must be discharged onto what Durkheim calls the "subject *minoris resistentiae* (less able to resist)."[18] A flattened or emptied "stranger," who provides no resistance to the group's projective fantasies, must be identified or manufactured. Only the combination of selective identification and targeted abjection, according to Durkheim, can resolve mourning's "disabling effects."[19] As a result, "mourning is left behind, thanks to mourning itself."[20]

The discourse of funeral orations rests at the heart of these mourning rituals. Funeral orations, in both their classical and contemporary form, often present a cohesive and romanticized image of civic life that obscures the conflicts, complexity, and injustices within the polity. As Simon Stow has argued, the funeral oration tradition that runs back to Pericles generates "unquestioning" and "uncritical" attachment to the civic body.[21] In Sara Monoson's words, the funeral oration tradition illuminates the "political and personal virtues" toward which citizens should aspire.[22] It offers an idealized object of attachment that consoles the bereft through the affirmation of civic cohesion. More importantly, Periclean mourning articulates a broader context of meaning—the ongoing life of the political community—that sublimates felt grief and disruptive passions into civic identification and social coherence.

In Thucydides's *Peloponnesian War*, Pericles begins his oration by acknowledging both the propriety and the difficulty of the funeral oration as a form of public address. Although he recognizes his just duty to perform a panegyric for the fallen dead, he indicates the conflicted political terrain that inevitably shapes the speech's reception: "For it is hard to say the right thing when people barely agree as to the truth of it."[23] "Friends" within the audience—those "familiar with every fact" of the event—will find that not enough has been said. Yet those who are "strangers" may, out of envy, suspect exaggeration.[24] By this admission, Pericles indicates a conflicted or ambiguous starting point for his oration, a situation that the speech then attempts to resolve in order to, in Durkheim's words, reaffirm the "moral unity and cohesion" of the polis.[25] Pericles goes on to craft a coherent Athenian political tradition by drawing lines of continuity between the polis's virtuous and steadfast ancestors, its democratic constitution, the liberality of its daily life, and its success as an imperial power. Within this performance, the initial fractiousness and complexity of the listening audience is reduced by their common allegiance to a superordinate political tradition, a kind of civic superego that redirects particular passions and overcomes the fractiousness that he had initially seemed to acknowledge. As Pericles puts it, the democratic freedom of the Athenian constitution and the freedom in its daily life do "not make us lawless as citizens" because "fear . . . our chief safeguard, teach[es] us to obey the magistrates and the laws."[26]

According to Freud, the superego is built up within the post-Oedipal child through repeated identifications with his or her objects of attachment, filtered through the conscious and unconscious struggles between aggression, love, guilt, and fear. Pericles invokes a similar process as he counsels his listeners to become "like lovers" to the city-state, to "feed your eyes upon her from day to day."[27] Only through these repeated acts of identification can the citizens "realize the power of Athens."[28] Tellingly, the power of Athens is outsized; in Pericles's formulation, the city-state is an omnipotent actor that has "forced every sea and land to be the highway of our daring" and has left "everywhere . . . imperishable monuments behind us."[29] Disregarding—or dissolving—the envy that might suspect exaggeration, Pericles even rejects the idea that the Athenian polis requires a storyteller:

"We need no more, not a Homer to sing our praises nor any other poet. . . ."[30] By this move, Pericles obscures the narrative effects of his own speech, which is absorbed into the omnipotent and self-storying polis. Omnipotence, moreover, is paired with idealization. The faults of the Athenian citizens are erased by their public sacrifice: "Steadfastness in his country's battles should be as a cloak to cover man's imperfections . . . the good action has blotted out the bad."[31] Athenians are sanctified by death in the polis's name, and the polis is sanctified through the course of the mourning ritual's performance.

The funeral oration form, however, met with criticism at practically its point of origin. Plato's dialogue *Menexenus*, for instance, appears to be a scathing critique of Pericles and the funeral oration tradition, articulated in the guise of a sarcastic performance of a similar speech. The dialogue consists of two parts. In the first, Socrates openly criticizes the rhetorical tropes of the funeral oration tradition, describing it as a pro forma performance full of embellishment and distortions.[32] The "elaborate speech" idealizes the dead, even if "he who is praised may not have been good for much" (234a). Idealization affects not only the audience's memory of the dead but also, Socrates claims, damages their faculties of moral-political perception. Embellished rhetoric "steal[s] away our souls" and impairs the listener's judgment (234b). As Socrates puts it, "I feel quite elevated by their laudations . . . this consciousness of dignity lasts me more than three days, and not until the fourth or fifth day do I come to my senses and know where I am—in the meantime, I have been living in the Islands of the Blessed" (234c). Socrates seems to be describing the feeling of "effervescence" that Durkheim saw as a constitutive element of public funeral rituals. The oration powerfully affects Socrates's perceptual-affective connection to the world. The speech imbues the polis with heavenly qualities, and its faults and conflicts are left behind by the beguiling rhetoric. As a listener/witness, Socrates also experiences a "triumph" over visiting foreigners in the audience who, because they are strangers to Athens, are split off from the solidaristic effervescent ritual (234c).

In the second part of the dialogue, Socrates offers his own speech that serves to underline his critique (or, perhaps, to provide a backhanded compliment to the genre's potency).[33] Socrates's speech, like Pericles's, performs a political history that emphasizes Athenian exceptionalism. Distorting the history of the Persian and Peloponnesian Wars, Socrates claims that the Athenians have stood unbowed and are incapable of being defeated by a foreign power. Despite being "attacked by all mankind," the polis has "gained the reputation of being invincible" (243d). All Athenian "defeats" were merely self-inflicted wounds, meaning that "we were our own conquerors . . . and to this day we are still unconquered . . . by others" (243d). The omnipotent polis can never undergo an external wounding.

Within Socrates's speech, moreover, the Athenians are purified by being split off from "barbaric" others, which allows the citizens to love and hate with one common heart: "The hatred of the foreigner has passed unadulterated into the lifeblood of our city" (245d). Alone among the Greeks, the Athenians are "pure Hellenes . . . uncontaminated by any foreign element" (245d). Athenians' purity stems from their common allegiance to the image of the sanctified polis. The polis mediates between the dead and the living, just as, according to Freud, the superego reaches into the id and, as such, can act as the id's "representative" vis-à-vis the ego.[34] The civic superego redirects the passion and pain of the citizens from lost objects to the still-living (omnipotent and idealized) polis. The citizen-witnesses are reconciled within themselves ("purified") and to the polis through the performance of a coherent and meaningful narrative of political tradition, providing continuity and direction for the fragile life of the individual. Perhaps, as Socrates suggests, the experience of purification only lasts for a few days; if so, he implies, the performance of civic consensus must be frequently renewed if its effects are to be maintained.

The oratorical performances of Pericles and Socrates show the tropes common to the Periclean mode of public mourning: the embellishment or falsification of the past, and the penchant toward omnipotence, idealization, and splitting, whereby the solidaristic bonds of the in-group are renewed at the expense of an identification and exclusion of the stranger. Such speeches have both political and psychological effects. According to well-known theories of social psychology, stigmatization of out-groups alongside the idealization of the in-group activates and reinforces group identification by fulfilling needs for belonging, inclusion, and cognitive clarity.[35] The funeral oration is a political-psychological performance that attempts to divert and manage the circulation of passionate attachment within the polis. Pericles's speech forsakes a more accurate description of Athenian life and history in order to provide an idealized picture that both offers aspirational civic values and virtues for its audience while fulfilling and trading on a psychologically reassuring framework of inside/outside, pure/corrupt.[36] As Nicole Loraux argues, the funeral oration presents the polis not as it is but "as it wishes to be."[37] It is a practice of "civic idealism" and a kind of "political sublimation."[38] Yet this work of civic idealism would not be felicitous if it was not triggering a schema of cognitive-affective processing in which omnipotence, idealization, and scapegoating are appealing defenses against the anxieties inherent to social life. The city might be invented by the funeral oration, but it also has to want to be invented in this way.

If the world of Pericles and Socrates is foreign to our own, a Periclean mourning discourse of political sublimation is still clearly with us. Socrates's experience of elevation, again, seems to be captured by Durkheim's concept of effervescence, and the rhetorical tropes of idealization and omnipotence are still common in modern societies, as Barry Schwartz as shown with regard to the funeral procession of Abraham Lincoln.[39] Simon Stow has also seen elements of Periclean mourning in contemporary American funeral discourse, which he describes in terms of a "romantic" style of public grieving. Romantic rituals incorporate loss into a coherent account of collective identity, heroizing the dead and offering identity-boundary maintenance through a rhetorical enactment of a collective subject. Echoing Socrates, Stow argues that the romantic style of mourning "demands little" of its audience; instead it is "singular in vision, uncritical, [and] purely comforting."[40] Ranging from the annual memorials for the September 11 terrorist attacks, to some of the speeches at the funeral for Coretta Scott King, Stow has charted the ways that a Periclean mode of mourning still operates today.

But why, we might ask, is this problematic? Are not aspirational virtues and values for collective life both important and unavoidable? Stow, in contrast, argues that the fantastical coherence performed by romantic mourning rituals is democratically poisonous because it invokes a consensual politics that obscures the messy and violent struggle for racial justice and social progress in the United States. Romantic rituals of mourning serve to isolate struggles over civil rights to the past, which denies that present inequalities bear any relationship to the past or that the struggle for civil rights might be ongoing and (perhaps) endless.[41] The romantic elevation of the polity and its citizenry promotes an amnesic politics that obscures or ignores historical and enduring injustice. Just as Socrates warned, a Periclean mode of civic mourning can damage our capacity to make effective moral and political judgments. It weakens a skeptical, critical view of the polity that identifies all the gaps between present reality and the "Islands of the Blessed" (or the "Shining City on a Hill") that is depicted in funeral discourse.

Using the work of Melanie Klein, we can see these rituals in a richer light. Klein's work is a sensitive tool for investigating the vagaries of public mourning. As chapters 1 and 2 have described, Klein's theory of mourning is linked to her understanding of the different psychological "positions"—the paranoid-schizoid and the depressive position. The positions, once again, refer to the schematic organization of the ego, which oscillates between different forms of experience depending on a mixture of environmental stresses and internal capacities. It is better to think of the positions less as hard (Freudian) stages of psychic growth than as perceptual-affective filters that are never fully left behind or overcome.[42]

Socrates describes funeral orations as "the games of youth" (236c), and similarly for Klein the paranoid-schizoid defenses are the child's first defense against a bewildering reality. Yet the paranoid-schizoid position persists as a possibility throughout life; it is a perceptual-affective crossroads that we will confront "again and again."[43] Within the paranoid-schizoid position, the lost object assumes an outsized character, and the ego feels compelled to defend it at all costs from internal and external threats. The ego thereby projects the hatred that is mixed up with the object—and, for Klein, every attachment is mediated by both love and hate—into another object, or internalizes it and enters a period of self-loathing. The one-sided, unblemished object requires a corresponding source of frustration and persecution. This stand-in object serves the same purpose as Durkheim's scapegoat; they are a subject *minoris resistentiae* that resolves the "anxiety of disintegration."[44] The harsh, persecutory superego serves to maintain this split reality; it keeps at bay the greater anxiety of disintegration through the perversely consolatory anxiety of punishment and persecution.

By contrast, the depressive position allows for the working through of these intense anxieties by the acceptance of, and interaction with, plural, whole others. The depressive position is characterized by a milder, polyphonous superego. Without the pressing specters of pure objects—whether idealized or demonized—the subject can better engage with the actual conflicts that exist within the self and between self and other. In this respect, we can clearly see how the Periclean mode of mourning and the cognitive-affective schema of the paranoid-schizoid position reinforce one another. The idealization of the polis and the demonization of the subject *minoris resistentiae* provide a temporary resolution to the intense anxieties surrounding separation or trauma. They enthrone a persecutory superego that fantastically purifies the self and distorts self-awareness and political-moral judgment. Periclean mourning forecloses on the space between and within "whole" subjects and mitigates the arrival of the depressive position and the actual mourning, guilt, and reparation therein.

Periclean Mourning and Consensualist Political Theory

At first blush, the placement of the work of John Rawls alongside discourses of funeral orations and mourning rituals might seem strange. Rawls seems closer to Plato, concerned with a philosophical theory of justice, than he does to Pericles, who is charged with the rhetorical performance inherent in his public position. Yet as Stow has argued, there is an intimate connection between a Periclean (what Stow calls "romantic") mode of public mourning and consensualist political theories such as Rawls's. In this section, I show the hermeneutic advances that are possible by placing Rawls's work within the funeral oration framework and reading both through a political-psychoanalytic lens informed by Klein's theories of mourning and the positions. This reading builds on and adds to the critique leveled against Rawls by agonists such as Stow and critical race scholars such as

Charles Mills. By approaching this angle of critique from a psychoanalytically informed perspective, we are able to better appreciate the anxieties (and insights) within Rawlsian liberalism, while pushing Rawls's theory in a more democratic direction.

For Charles Mills, Rawls's troubles begin on the first page of *Theory of Justice*, where Rawls takes up the social contract tradition in order to "generalize" and "carry [it] to a higher level of abstraction."[45] By stepping into and revitalizing the heritage of social contract theory, Rawls inherits that tradition's analytic cachet, its elegant simplicity, and its powerful normative valences. But Rawls also inherits—yet does not reflect on—the historical realities of "group power and domination" that have accompanied the social contract tradition as a shadow. As Mills argues, the social contract has historically been "color-coded": the "free and equal" participants in the contract were axiomatically defined as white, and non-whites were seen as incapable of achieving full human status due to their ignorance of the natural law.[46] The abstract language surrounding the adoption of principles of governance (whether in a pseudohistorical state of nature or a willfully abstract "original position") serves to obfuscate these facts, with the result that the social contract tradition amounts to what Mills calls a "collective self deception" and a "consensual hallucination."[47] As Mills sees it, contemporary liberal theory is typified by a willingness to look past—or not to see in the first place—the historical intertwinement of inclusive moral and political principles and practices of racial domination in European colonies and in the white settler states. By "looking the other way" when it comes to race, modern inheritors of the social contract tradition carry forward what Mills calls the "most pervasive mental phenomena of the past few hundred years," namely, "white misunderstanding, misrepresentation, evasion, and self deceptions on matters of race."[48] These practices of self-deception promote a color-blind reading of Western history and its political traditions, which have been continually shaped by definitions of insider/outsider and rulers/ruled that have themselves been governed by the color line.[49]

Rawls, in his efforts to carry the social contract tradition to a higher level of abstraction, sidesteps the issue of race, articulating the principles of justice as fairness from an abstract original position where participants deliberate beneath a so-called veil of ignorance, which keeps them from knowing their assigned place in the social order. Curiously, given the contentious politics swirling around race in the broader American culture during the composition of *Theory*, racial identity is not one of the things that Rawls explicitly enumerates as being restricted by the veil (although he does include it in later iterations). Rawls does explicitly condemn racial discrimination, writing, "we are confident that religious intolerance and racial discrimination are unjust."[50] Moreover, he maintains that the original position would rule out a racial configuration for a just society's basic structure;

as he puts it, "from the standpoint of persons similarly situated in an initial situation which is fair, the principles of explicit racist doctrines are not only unjust. They are irrational. For this reason we could say that they are not moral conceptions at all, but simply means of suppression."[51] From these remarks, we can discern that Rawls was sensitive to the presence of racial discrimination as a potent force in American history. However, according to Mills, Rawls's thought experiment in ideal theory promotes a pernicious abstraction away from the cruel realities of the American polity.

Of course, Rawls might have responded that abstraction was precisely the point—that we need to get clear of our entrenched biases and prejudices if we are to ever understand what justice requires of us. Mills, however, argues that Rawls has left his readers few "conceptual point(s) of entry to start talking about the fundamental way in which (as all nonwhites know) race structures one's life and affects one's life chances."[52] Furthermore, the abstract quality of Rawls's principles creates its own veil of ignorance that shadows the neutral language in which it is couched. As many scholars of race have argued, the apparent neutrality of principles such as "reasonableness" and "merit" often conceals a racial subtext.[53] Even "justice" has a different meaning depending on one's social position and previous experience with the institutions of justice—Mills quotes the oft-expressed idea among African Americans that "when white people say Justice they mean 'Just Us.' "[54] Echoing Loraux's reading of funeral orations, then, Mills argues that Rawls shows the polity as it wishes to be rather than as it is, absent the racial inequalities that persist in American society.[55]

Rawls courts a Periclean form of amnesia then, by restricting himself to theories of strict (not partial) compliance and to a description of well-ordered (not actually existing) societies.[56] At the least, Rawlsian ideal theory, geared as it is toward social consensus, provides cover for Periclean efforts to whitewash history and obscure enduring injustices.[57] If Mills is correct, and a familiarity with the legacies of actually existing racial domination is an essential part of the struggle for justice, then Rawls's abstract starting point amounts to a politically pernicious form of denial.[58] Rawls maintained that ideal theory was a necessary condition for nonideal or partial-compliance theory, but, as Thomas McCarthy argues, Rawls's work largely neglected to provide anything more than a tacit theoretical mediation between the ideal and the real.[59] Absent a practical mediation, the ideal and the actual are split off from one another in ways that promote exactly the kinds of evasions that Mills diagnoses.[60] Having split off ideal theories of well-ordered societies from descriptive accounts of actually existing injustice, Rawlsians then can decamp—at least temporarily—to the Isles of the Blessed, leaving behind the messy conflicts and complexities of the actual polity as well as weakened faculties of judgment and social critique for those of us left behind.

In his major works and in separate interviews and articles, Rawls fully acknowledged the racial- and class-based inequalities of our actually existing democracy, yet he remained committed to a form of ideal theory that did not give these inequalities a central role. Certainly Rawls's intention was to take up the social contract tradition and to use it as a tool in crafting a conception of justice that could apply to everyone, and not simply to dominant groups ("just us"). Rawls was confident that racial discrimination would be structurally impossible from within the terms of his theory.[61] I argue, then, in distinction from Mills, that the difficulty with Rawls's arguments does not result from the use of ideal theory but more deeply from Rawls's explicit (in *Theory of Justice*) and implicit (in *Political Liberalism*) theories of moral-political psychology. Contra Stow, Rawls is not Periclean (or romantic) because of his emphasis on consensus—Stow himself, as we will see shortly, has not entirely left behind the dangerous game of consensus—but because the same persecutory defenses triggered by the funeral oration also animate Rawls's theory. In both *Theory* and *Liberalism*, Rawls, in Periclean fashion, acknowledges fractious elements within self and society (envy and unreasonable comprehensive doctrines) only to perform a reconciliation of those elements through the advancement of a superordinate univocal principle (the original position and public reason). Although Rawls's explicit moral psychology in his early work is closer to Klein than to Freud, in the end he slips back under the gaze of a Freudian superego: demanding, univocal, and unforgiving. It is this problem that must be addressed in order to move Rawlsian liberalism from an original position of paranoid anxiety toward a depressive position of democratic repair.

A Theory of Justice

In *Theory*, Rawls's theory of justice and his account of moral psychology run on overlapping tracks. According to Rawls, the theory of justice can "generate its own supports" because it is aligned with "the principles of moral psychology."[62] He aimed to indicate the major steps whereby a person could acquire both an understanding of and attachment to the principles of justice. His approach to moral psychology is stylized but, importantly, it is not strictly an exercise in ideal theory; in fact, it is characterized by a strange mixture of ideal and "realistic" psychology. *Theory*'s aim is to indicate an attachment to the principles of justice for a person growing up within an idealized, well-ordered society, yet Rawls states that the psychological account of moral learning had to be "true and in accordance with existing knowledge."[63] The laws of moral psychology cannot be purely the product of an idealized social order because they are also the unavoidable ground for social relations at their most basic level.[64] In other words, without a realistic moral psychology, Rawls implies, the theory of justice cannot get off the ground. Rawls, however, is inconsistent on this point, writing that the principles of moral psychology refer to "an institutional setting as being just" and that these principles reflect deep psychological realities without which "our nature would be very different and fruitful social cooperation fragile if not impossible."[65] This inconsistency, as we will see shortly, allows Rawls an ideal theory escape hatch, when the resources of his realistic moral psychology run out.

Rawls's theory of moral psychology includes three successive stages, which he refers to as the moralities of authority, association, and principles. In developing this account, Rawls leans on two broad paradigms of moral learning. The first, which he associates with Freud, is a deficiency model where learning results from the supplying of missing moral motives. The second tradition, which Rawls associates with Rousseau, Kant, and Piaget, sees moral learning less as a form of imposition than as the free development of innate moral capacities, including the "innate susceptibility to the pleasures of fellow feeling and self-mastery."[66] Although Rawls claims to combine these approaches, he clearly has deeper debts to the latter model. The moralities of authority and association, for instance, are reflective of an innate-capacities approach. During the stage of authority-morality, the child—while driven by excessive and unruly desires—is primarily motivated by a reparative impulse to atone for any transgressions and to "seek reconciliation" with his beloved authority figures.[67] For Rawls, these reparative gestures are at the root of moral sense. They are innate capacities cultivated through repeated experiences of love, trust, and affection; they reflect the "deep psychological fact" of reciprocity, or the desire to give back for what we have received.

Authority-morality flows naturally into the stage of associational morality. As the child begins to associate and identify with a wider range of others, he or she develops a sense for fellowship and the virtues and ideals of being "a good student and classmate . . . a good sport and companion."[68] Social cooperation and competition at the associational level instills—through reliance on the deep psychological fact of reciprocity—a feeling of commitment to a larger group. Identification with the group also creates the possibility of associational guilt, when the individual "fails to do his part."[69] The expansion of commitment to an ever-widening circle of associates sets the stage for the next and highest step in moral development—the morality of principles. Rawls argues that the taking on of a succession of "more demanding roles" leads to a gradual expansion of perspective-taking ability. However, unlike Jürgen Habermas, who bases his dialogic theory of ethics on a similar expansion of perspective-taking ability, Rawls emphasizes the subjective recognition of being the beneficiary "of an established and enduring just institution" as the basis of a passionate attachment to being "a just person."[70] Here the abstract principle of reciprocity returns as the unshakable ground of Rawls's argument. Just as the child received and gave back love and fellowship in the stages of authority- and association-morality, the adult feels tugged at by a love of mankind that is "continuous . . . with the sense of justice."[71] A sense of and passionate commitment to justice must be the result of *experiencing* justice within a well-ordered society.[72]

Before showing how this emphasis creates problems for Rawls's account, I note at this point how Rawls explicitly sets his ontogenetic account of justice against Freud's. For Freud, the sense of justice is a reaction formation rooted in envy. Because envy cannot be fully expressed, lest personal and social relations deteriorate to the point of nothingness, it is transformed into a social feeling that insists on equality.[73] On Rawls's account, the insistence on equality within justice as fairness is the progeny of a marriage between reciprocity and anthrophilia, but for Freud it springs from the sublimation of aggression against others into a feeling of group spirit, guided by a vengeful superego that twists our envy and resentment of others back into a critical voice of self-control. The superego is a harsh and unimpeachable authority because it must hold back the malevolent desire to spoil others' access to the good. If this desire were liberated, all hell would break loose.

Rawls acknowledges Freud's hypothesis about the ontogenesis of justice but sets out to show that envy is not a problem for the theory of justice as fairness. According to Rawls, Freud's account suffers from a serious "defect." Namely, it fails to distinguish between what Rawls refers to as "emulative envy" and "rancor."[74] Emulative envy, which is "benign," arises when we aspire to achieve the good virtues or qualities that others display. It is a "socially beneficial" form of striving and in no way leads us to a twisted desire to deny these goods to others. Rancor, on the other hand, is "what emulative envy may become under certain conditions of defeat and a sense of failure."[75] Rancor is a "collectively disadvantageous" form of misanthropy, and it leads to a willingness to deprive others of their goods even if we have to sacrifice some of our own.[76] Yet because rancor is a product of bad circumstances, in well-ordered societies it would not find hospitable soil. Hence Rawls, sliding into the mode of ideal theory, can set socially destructive envy to the side. The reasoners within the original position can bargain without rancor, and the principles of justice remain untouched by it.

This argument against rancor, however, shows clearly that Rawls's realistic moral psychology and his theory of justice are no longer running together. Our moral sense is a "natural" and "fundamental" attitude and consists of incontrovertible psychological "facts."[77] Yet to dispel the strongest anxieties surrounding the viability of this account, Rawls retreats to the image of idealized, well-ordered societies. Envy is a problem within damaged life, but it is not a problem for ideal theory. And this slippage into ideal theory with regards to the problem of envy betrays further inadequacies in Rawls's account of the ontogenesis of the morality of principles. Namely, unlike the moralities of authority and association, Rawls cannot explain the development of the principled moral stance without recourse to an idealized social order. Reciprocity cannot explain the morality of principles without a vicious form of circularity: If justice is returned for justice received, then where did the "first" justice originate? And while Rawls also claims an innate capacity for anthrophilia, it is hard to see how the principle of love can be extended to the universal human community without some bridging principle. Something essential seems to be missing, something that for Freud was provided by the superego: an agency that turns back our aggressive impulses in ways that make social life possible.[78]

What, then, does Rawls put into the place of this superordinate agency? On my reading, the original position—Rawls's thought experiment by which the principles of justice are laid down—fulfills this function. The original position is a construct of ideal theory, but unlike the sense of justice resulting from an up-bringing in a well-ordered society, the original position is available to reasoners within damaged life. As Rawls puts it, the original position is a "perspective" or gaze that is accessible "at any time."[79] This perspective, moreover, although it is designed as a device for reasoning, cannot be reasoned or bargained with itself. The strict rules that structure the original situation make its edicts unequivocal and final. Regardless of how many times we may enter the position, "the same principles are always chosen."[80] The univocal, final court of appeal provides con-clusive reasons that can then become a means of self- and social-critique.[81] By turn-ing back our penchants for partiality, the original position is the means by which those of us living in unjust circumstances could nevertheless obtain "purity of heart."[82]

Rawls is obviously hostile toward Freud's pessimistic ontogenetic account of justice, but has Rawls really done away with the harsh superego, or has he merely refurbished it? The fact that Rawls ends *Theory* on the note (however hopeful) of "purity" demonstrates clearly that his project is pressurized by paranoid-schizoid anxieties.[83] Fully admitting that the resources within a realistic theory of moral psychology were insufficient to secure the development of social justice, Rawls invokes a kind of Isles of the Blessed from which abstract reasoners could deduce the correct principles of action. Rawls seemed to intuit, in Kleinian fashion, the need for a situation whereby persecutory or disintegrative anxieties could be worked through. This is why, as C. Fred Alford sees it, there are "sound psy-chological reasons" for constructing the original position in the way it is, because it could allow the "self to begin to think about justice in more abstract ... [and] other regarding terms."[84] Yet Rawls's broader social theory does not carry through on these intuitions. He does not look for actual social practices or spaces that might assuage or work through persecutory dread, but instead turns to an always-available superego to overwhelm fantasies of omnipotence rooted in narcissistic partiality. The location of an unimpeachable procedure, however, actually intensifies the very pressures they are meant to alleviate. Because Rawls could only conceptualize the problem of justice "as a problem whose solution is . . . universal, and categorical," his theory remains stuck within the paranoid-schizoid position. As Rawls puts it, the original position must be narrowly construed and geared toward unanimity, lest it "lead to endless wrangling . . . setting the stage for the nastiest individuals getting more than their share."[85] The search for purity drives out the dangerous elements within the self but forestalls the recognition of these dangerous elements and the broader ambivalence of social life. Yet it is this work of recognition that makes possible political judgment and "depressive" forms of agency in which we can share power with others.

This is the secret yet strong source of connection between Rawls and the Periclean mode of mourning. Like the funeral oration, Rawls acknowledges envy and "nastiness" but dissolves them through the production of a superego-like mechanism of surveillance that keeps these fractious forces at bay. In this respect, Rawls's theory of justice, like the Periclean mode of mourning, is motivated by what Loraux calls the fiction of the "unanimous assembly."[86] The dream of purity of heart is the dream of moral blamelessness, of acting consciously in light of universal moral principles to the extent that one would know and feel, with certainty, that one has acted correctly and justly. Yet, as Bernard Williams and others have argued, the very idea of blamelessness denies the fact that human life is lived in a tragic world, in which even morally coherent actions may—and even should—inspire regret, mourning, and reparation.[87] The original position qua unanimous assembly, then, is a reflection of paranoid-schizoid anxieties, in which we require an ideal object to rid us of the persecutory dread that arises when the good and bad elements of life begin to run together. Paranoid-schizoid defenses provide some measure of relief from this anxiety by reinforcing the split within the self and between self and others, but this relief is both shallow and short-lived, and it leaves us ill prepared to negotiate with the complexity or messiness (not to mention the "nastiness") within self, other, and world.

Political Liberalism

Rawls's late work extended and refined his early reflections on liberal conceptions of justice, while overturning key precepts of those original arguments. The basic content of justice as fairness—society as a system of fair cooperation between free and equal citizens, each engaging others in concordance with the principle of reciprocity and the duty of civility—emerges in his later work relatively unscathed. Yet the context of articulation for the theory of justice has been altered by Rawls's recognition of irreducible pluralism in late-modern democracies—specifically, a pluralism of potentially incompatible comprehensive doctrines. These doctrines are comprehensive in that they offer their adherents both a fundamental orientation to the world and a conception of the good. Such worldviews are comparable in their scope to the salvific religious doctrines that clashed violently across Europe in the centuries following the Reformation—competing doctrines whose claims could not be settled or adjudicated on the political bases of compromise or deliberation. These conflicts generally were settled only by "exhaustion and circumstance," or through the development of a modus vivendi social order based on a precarious balance of power between competing doctrines.[88] Rawls begins *Liberalism* by declaring that a plurality of these irreconcilable comprehensive doctrines is not an accident of history but the "normal result of the exercise of human reason."[89] The enduring presence of conflicting doctrines represents the haunting possibility of a slide toward violent conflict, and, therefore, it cannot be lightly passed over. The problem posed by the Reformation is a sobering one: "How is society even possible between those of different faiths?"[90]

Famously, at this stage Rawls no longer believed that the full theory of justice as fairness, as articulated in his early work, could provide the terms for a comprehensive reconciliation of reasonable but incompatible doctrines. The moral "baggage" of *Theory* would have to be bracketed so that the theory of justice can be reconstructed as a "free-standing" and purely political conception.[91] In other words, justice as fairness was to be stripped of its comprehensive philosophical presumptions in order to serve its reconfigured purpose—the securing of a stable and just pluralistic society.

As a central part of this revised project, Rawls crafted a "political" conception of the person, which, he argues, avoids any controversial assumptions about human nature or moral psychology. As he puts it, "Justice as fairness starts from the idea that society is to be conceived as a fair system of cooperation and so it adopts a conception of the person to go with this idea."[92] Rawls cannot make this move without making some claims about human capacities, of course; as he puts it, human nature and psychology "are permissive: they may limit the viable conceptions of persons and ideals of citizenship, and the moral psychologies that may support them, but do not dictate the ones we must adopt."[93] Psychological permissiveness means that there are no structural impediments hindering diverse subjects from "impersonating" the free and equal citizen; abstract citizens can each passionately identify with the principle of reciprocity as fair treatment of (free and equal) others, regardless of their background cultures or "nonpolitical" psychological capacities, needs, or anxieties. Instead of his earlier insistence that our moral psychology gives license to this form of civic attachment, now Rawls only claims that there are no insurmountable obstacles in its path.

The political conception of the person is tied to Rawls's newly adopted "method of avoidance," the result of which is a self split between a "political" or public identity guided by public reason and a "nonpublic" or "background" self in which the passions and partial attachments are given free play.[94] In making these arguments, Rawls fully retreats to an idealized account of the person, crafted to fit "the practical needs of political life and reasoned thought about it."[95] In other words, the theory of moral psychology is developed to fit the model of a stable and just liberal society—the two tracks have been reduced to a single, idealized model. However this model suffers from the same Freudian slip as did Rawls's original moral psychology. As I argue in this section, *Liberalism* in effect replicates, at the social level, Freud's structural model of the psyche (in which the ego is torn between the disruptive forces of the id and the controlling edicts of the superego).[96]

Rawls sets the stage for the work of reasonable justification within *Liberalism* with a reminder about the "extreme violence and increasing destructiveness" of the twentieth century, and his method of avoidance is inspired by the specters of religious warfare and constitutional collapse. In his published lectures on political philosophy, Rawls elaborated on the possibility of disintegration within a society's basic structure.[97] Using the example of Wilhelmine Germany, Rawls argues that the German constitution was ripe for collapse because the country's political parties were a "fragmented" array of "pressure groups . . . [that] held exclusive ideologies which made compromise with other groups difficult."[98] Because they "never aspired to govern," these pressure groups always acted "as outsiders petitioning the chancellor."[99] Like the unreasonable comprehensive doctrines described in *Liberalism*, political pressure groups "cannot support a reasonable balance of political values."[100] They press inexhaustible demands that cannot be met by the liberal order.

The basic structure (call it the Rawlsian ego) cannot bear up under this pressure unaided. Democratic citizens must therefore adopt a normative schema of reasonableness and use it "to express our moral and political thought and action."[101] Passionate identification with the "reasonable," however, seems to represent the return of the (repressed) Freudian superego. Just as the original position—the always-available gaze through which reasoners can develop attachment to the principles of justice—appears when Rawls's moral psychology can no longer support his theory of justice, so does the agency of "public reason" function as a fallback for Rawls's theory of liberalism. Public reason does not claim sovereignty over the entire basic structure, but only "public political forums," such as the spaces of law courts, government affairs, and campaigns for public office. It also applies only to certain questions within these contexts, such as questions of "constitutional essentials and matters of basic justice."[102] Public reason, then, does not eliminate the fractious desires and attachments across the array of comprehensive doctrines, any more than the Freudian superego eliminates the pressing demands of the id. It merely restricts or redirects those demands to the "background culture" of civil society, where they are given free reign.

We can call this, with only slight strain, Rawls's structural model of the polity: the constitution is the container of the basic rights and liberties of the citizen body, the "nonpublic" demands of civil society persist in a free-wheeling "background culture," and deliberation and decisions in constitutional bodies are constrained by the demands of public reason. Public political forums are buffeted on all sides by the demands of parties and pressure groups, but these groups are disciplined and their demands sublimated through the operations of a superordinate guiding voice. Recall that Freud saw the ego in a similar middle position, charged with managing the excessive demands of the id and the superego. For Freud, the ego is a "constitutional monarch"; it is not the actual seat of power but rather the space of an aspirational coherence.[103]

Within *Liberalism*, the structural model of the polity is mirrored by Rawls's political model of the person. The constitutional container is attended to and guarded over by free and equal citizens who are each committed to self-containment as dictated by the "ideal" of public reason. This ideal elevates citizens until they become hypothetical legislators and judges themselves, thereby capable of articulating their political beliefs and desires in the language of public reason guided by the duty of civility and the principle of reciprocity.[104] Because human nature is permissive, Rawlsian discipline encounters no significant obstacles in this work of political subjectification.

On my reading, Rawls's *Liberalism* replicates the paranoid-schizoid defenses that were manifest in his original work; in fact, it seems to intensify them. In *Liberalism* both society and self are split between public and nonpublic sides, the former guided by public reason and thus oriented toward stable agreement and just reconciliation, the latter a supposedly more raucous and contestatory space of competing doctrines and visions full of encumbered and motivated selves posturing, performing, and protesting. This background noise is tolerated until it threatens the constitutional order (and hence the sanctity of the split itself). When it begins to influence the settled constitutional bodies, either as external pressure or internal interference, then all good, reasonable selves must step forward to reestablish the discipline demanded by the ideal of public reason and the conception of justice as fairness. Public reason becomes a civic superego that disciplines the passionate and fractious voices that, without such a superordinate principle, would drag the polity toward disintegration.

The difficulties with this account do not stem from Rawls's supposition concerning the destructiveness of the twentieth century, which is undeniable, or from the specters of religious warfare and constitutional collapse, which only a cursory reading of history would convince us are serious and significant threats. The difficulty stems from the mechanism by which Rawls attempts to disperse these intense anxieties. Namely, Rawls attempts to dissolve the anxieties of loss and trauma through the invocation of a consensualist object of attachment. Public reason serves as a mechanism of self-control that merely (and in passing) mentions, but does nothing to effectively work through, dramatic political conflicts.[105] Rather, it acknowledges these conflicts only to insist that they can be resolved through what Rawls refers to as an "overlapping consensus."[106] The unnerving pluralism within the polity—the ever-present threat of a slide toward violent doctrinal conflict, or toward oppression by unreasonable or mad conceptions of the good—turns out to be an illusion resting on a partial perception of social reality. While each regnant comprehensive doctrine has aspects of belief that fall outside the contours of public reason, there is a happy space of convergence that "when worked up into a political conception of justice" turns out to be sufficient to underwrite a just constitutional regime.[107] Instead of unnerving or dangerous pluralism, we have in front of us ("embedded" in public political culture) the basis of a "reasoned, informed, and willing agreement."[108] Political reconciliation is by this conjuration not only possible but is already implied by the practices and principles built into the political culture. Hence, like Pericles, Rawls acknowledges the presence of discord and fractious desire only to resolve them through the construction of a superordinate, univocal mechanism of self-control.[109] Again, Rawls's (Kleinian) intuition regarding the intensity of anxiety surrounding pluralistic selves and societies is reflected but not mitigated by the elevation of public reason as an ideal of social discipline. As Jonathan Lear has argued with regards to Freud's theory of the superego, its forbidding and unyielding critical voice not only prevents cruelty but also "has its own cruelty in it."[110] While Rawls's political principles aim to be reasonable above all else, the reason on display is the anxious, persecutory reasoning of the paranoid-schizoid position. The challenge remains, then, to develop Rawls's powerful psychological intuitions in ways that effectively modulate rather than exacerbate the anxieties and conflicts inherent to social life in *dis*ordered societies.

Engaging the Transference within Contemporary Racial Politics

How does this interpretation add to or modify the critical race and agonist critiques of Rawls, as represented here by Mills and Stow? Undeniably, Charles Mills is correct that Rawls's work does little to theorize historical and enduring legacies of racial domination in the United States. Yet perhaps this limitation of Rawls's work does not represent an ideological obfuscation so much as an insight into the difficulty of negotiating fair terms of social cooperation in the face of deep and persistent inequalities. Mills and others describe Rawlsian theory as suffering from a pernicious form of amnesia and denial, but perhaps there is a hidden form of denial within this very critique of denial. In short, Mills might neglect the issues of the "transference" circulating within discourses and interactions in our racialized polity. Transference was for Freud and his followers the clearest demonstration that the analyst and the analysand are never the only people in the room during a session. Our relationships with others are mediated by the deep deposits of previous relationships and, *pace* Klein, by the cognitive-affective schemas that reflect different levels of anxieties and our various capacities for working through them. It is true that Freud defined the work of analysis as the removal of amnesias, but the theory of transference complicates such work. Successful interpretive work is uneven and rarely guaranteed of success because of the inexhaustible unconscious and the oft-times unpredictable patterns of interaction within and between selves. The telos of analysis is not a life of purity or blamelessness, but rather, in Freudian terms, liberation from unmitigated misery to "common unhappiness" and, in Kleinian terms, development of an enriched ego in better touch with the "poignant" and ambivalent nature of internal and external realities.[111]

The theory of transference has direct relevance to contemporary racial politics. Scholarship of racial attitudes in the United States has recently undergone a paradigm shift in how it approaches questions of prejudice and bias. Despite persistent levels of racial inequality, overt levels of support for racial equality in the United States have increased dramatically over the past half century since the passage of the Civil Rights Act in 1964. Yet measures of implicit racial bias reveal a stark divergence between the explicit acceptance of racial equality and unconscious levels of racial prejudice across (and within) different racial groups.[112] Racial prejudice in the United States appears to have been sublimated and is now pushed through an ideological filter of values (such as the work ethic) that, in turn, have become racially coded.[113] Because it is increasingly socially unacceptable to express explicit racial bias, "old-fashioned" racism has partly shifted toward symbolic and even unconscious registers.

This shift from explicit to implicit bias has significant implications for Mills's theory and for his critique of Rawlsian abstractions. Namely, the sublimation of racial prejudice both increases the saliency of racial priming and increases the anxieties surrounding racially coded politics and policies. Perversely, the stricter social superego surrounding racial equality, by shaming the expression of racial bias, appears to repress these thoughts in ways that intensify rather than diminish them. Racial priming can then tap into this unconscious affective layer, and, in doing so, actually increase resistance to policies that might address racial disparities.[114] As the literature on affective intelligence has demonstrated, when individuals feel threatened and anxious, their resistance to redistributional politics increases significantly.[115] The symbolic racism literature, moreover, shows that this anxiety is more likely as the gap between implicit bias and explicit norms grows ever wider. Paradoxically, then, the direct thematization of racial disparities and inequalities can interact with this hostile unconscious brew in ways that actually decrease the likelihood of making progress in the areas of racial disparities. A Millsian truth-telling, antiamnesic theory of racial domination and enduring injustice, despite its honorable intentions, risks the provocation of a transference storm in the polity at large. Racial politics then oscillates between manic triumph and the most hostile resentment.

Progressive racial politics, in this light, has to confront and work through the racial transference rather than presuming that clear and obvious truths surrounding racial inequality and injustice will, by themselves, cultivate a cross-racial political coalition capable of addressing these social pathologies. In fact, the recent scholarship on unconscious racism and affective intelligence leads us to assume the opposite—that a righteous insistence on racial justice will actually increase resistance and decrease the likelihood of making progress. Klein's concept of projective identification becomes a valuable explanatory tool in light of contemporary racism's increasingly implicit basis. Projective identification initially results from the paranoid-schizoid defense of splitting, in which the good and bad aspects of experience are isolated from each other and threats are projected out onto an external object. The other becomes the repository for the aspects of the self that could not be tolerated, such as our aggression or our vulnerability. Racial differences create a ripe playing field for these fantasies of splitting and the corollary phenomena of idealization and demonization.[116] Social institutions and cultural norms are deployed to reinforce these defense mechanisms, operating as a screen to obscure intense sub rosa anxieties.[117] As the conflicts and prejudices surrounding racial difference become increasingly subject to social shaming, these anxieties are exacerbated and the need for social institutions to provide this fantastical screening is intensified. Our interactions with others are mediated by these intense, largely unconscious anxieties, promoting, once again, either a politics of manic triumph or of racial resentment (cue liberals and tea partiers after the election of Barack Obama). These outcomes offer temporary satisfaction through release of the pent-up tension, just as Pericles's discourse promotes a temporarily satisfying identification with the idealized polity that simultaneously disavows and expels the dangerous or evil aspects of the in-group onto a safely hated other.

In the late twentieth century, James Baldwin provided eloquent testimony to the idea that race is an illusion born of projective identification, even if Baldwin did not deploy a psychoanalytic framework to do so. Race, for Baldwin, was an "illusion" rooted in basic human needs for security and the fight against anxieties of disintegration. For Klein, similarly, the paranoid-schizoid position is characterized above all by defenses against fears of disintegration—feelings of absolute insecurity and instability that, in turn, call forth defenses such as splitting, idealization, and demonization. Baldwin echoes this idea when he writes that what "drives people" to racist behavior and attitudes is "pure terror."[118] This terror has both psychological and historicopolitical roots. In the American context, the specific terror that drives people is rooted in the (disavowed) knowledge of the historical crimes of white supremacy. As Baldwin puts it, "whites . . . know the crimes they have committed against black people. And they are terrified that these crimes will be committed against them."[119] In other words, Americans' violent racial history locks white citizens into a kind of paranoid-schizoid functioning, in which the terror of their collective inheritance has to be split off or denied. Baldwin sees this nexus of defenses as the strongest source of support for group identity in the racialized polity. As he puts it, "it is . . . comparatively easy to invest a population with false morale by giving them a false sense of superiority," and this sense of superiority is predicated on and held in place by racial inferiors, who serve as a receptacle for the terror that cannot be acknowledged.[120] Identity cannot be imagined outside of these polarized terms, as evidenced by the fact that, as Baldwin puts it, "progress" is imagined only in terms of "how quickly a Black kid can become white."[121] Yet this perverse form of progress implicitly relies on a racial other remainder, who will reinforce the basic boundaries even as those boundaries are surmounted by a fortunate few.

In short, American identity is built on projective identification and paranoid-schizoid defenses, and these defenses are rooted in unarticulated terror: "Americans are terrified . . . they know that they are capable of genocide. History is built on genocide. But they can't face it. And it doesn't make any difference what Americans think they can think—they are terrified."[122]

"Whiteness," then, is a paranoid-schizoid "state of mind."[123] It is rooted in a terror that cannot be expressed because to do so would expose the work of paranoid construction that holds it together. All of this is encapsulated by Baldwin's notion of "innocence." Innocence is both a practiced amnesia over historical violence and an immobility of identity. Innocence is "based on a lie, the lie of Manifest Destiny. [America is] a country immobilized, with a past it cannot explain away."[124] Yet innocence is not simply the refusal to accept historical crimes or to admit fantasies of expansion that accompanied and often justified such crimes; innocence is also an omnipotent refusal of *interconnection*, an insistence on what Baldwin calls the "dream" or illusion of separation.[125] As Baldwin puts it, "people in America have not been able to accept the fact that their reality is entangled and almost defined by the black reality."[126] The very categories of white and black in fact ensure that the entanglements and blood-ties of American history will be denied. Social practices of separation—white flight, gentrification, and racialized drug and prison policies—reinforce these categories and prolong the recognition of entanglement. All of this, however, comes with a significant cost; as Baldwin puts it, "you can't deny your brothers without paying a terrible price for it."[127]

For Baldwin, the innocence of American life is in many ways a product of what Klein called projective identification. For instance, Baldwin repeatedly interpreted race not only as a certain way of seeing but also as the production of certain sights—namely, "the nigger" and the associated stereotypes of black life such as "Uncle Tom, Aunt Jemima, and Little Black Sambo" (now we might say the black "supercriminal," or the "welfare queen").[128] Whiteness as a state of mind is predicated on the projection of intolerable aspects of self and history into the receptacle of "the nigger." Baldwin argues, moreover, that the production of such characters is intertwined with an inability to countenance deep anxieties and terrors of life. As Baldwin puts it, "I am not a nigger . . . [and] if you think I'm a nigger, it means you need it. Why? That's the question you have got to ask yourself."[129] Baldwin focuses as much on the *need* as the defensive production of the image and the social consequences of its production. White people "have a black citizen locked up in their mind . . . and that is why they treat them as they do."[130] The "nigger" in the mind of the white citizen means that "what they do see when they do look at you is what they have invested you with . . . all the agony, and pain, and the danger, and the passion, and the torment—you know, sin, death, and hell—of which everyone in this country is terrified."[131] For Baldwin, then, the historicopolitical practices of white supremacy are inextricably connected to the "heat, horror and pain of human life itself" and to the relatively undeveloped human and civic capacity to face down this horror.[132]

Can paranoid-schizoid projections that reinforce punitive social practices and serve as omnipotent defenses against interconnection be unwound? Stow's depiction of a "tragic" mode of public mourning can be seen as one possible response to this challenge. In distinction from the romantic mode of mourning, which intensifies normalizing pressures within political life and marginalizes disagreement and conflict, tragic styles of mourning, according to Stow, generate an agonistic understanding of democracy "in which conflict and disagreement are recognized as central to democratic politics."[133] Tragic public mourning is "pluralistic, critical, and self-consciously political."[134] It eschews a maudlin sentimentalization of loss in favor of a tragic mode of response that emphasizes paradox, frustration, and conflict. Above all, a tragic style of public mourning "seeks to generate ambivalence in its audience as a productive response" to loss.[135] Ambivalence—or the "prevalence of duality over unity"—casts into doubt both romantic readings of loss and the unity or coherence of a collective subject on which such readings are typically founded.[136]

It is on the basis of the distinction between romantic and tragic mourning that Stow describes an African American mourning tradition that is both "tragic and self-consciously political."[137] This tradition grew out of the experiences of oppression under slavery and coalesced into a political force that galvanized struggles against de facto and de jure segregation and discrimination. By offering its audience the doubled consciousness of violent oppression alongside a hopeful expectancy of justice, African American mourning practices embodied a democratic pedagogy, which generated solidarity among the oppressed and galvanized countless acts of courageous resistance to legal and social discrimination. They also engendered a mode of "critical remembrance" that challenged dominant interpretations of American history and identity.[138]

For Stow, the historical and contemporary exemplars of this African American funeral tradition—from Frederick Douglass to Joseph Lowery—have been insistent critical voices, continuously calling citizens to respond to the tragic side of American life. Frederick Douglass's multiple funeral orations for Abraham Lincoln, for instance, were agonistic reminders that fought against both "historical amnesia" and the tropes of romantic eulogy. In the years following the Civil War, Douglass repeatedly refused a hagiographic frame for Lincoln's life and death. For instance, in a speech before Congress in 1876, Douglass excoriated Lincoln as "the white man's president."[139] In so doing, Douglass "performed . . . [a] productive disorientation" that forced his audience "to reconsider their own position."[140] Douglass's funeral orations provoked dissonance and revealed ambivalence—the combination of stirring promises and pernicious realities.

Stow's disaggregation of public mourning into competing traditions, his development of a twofold typology that links these traditions to distinct conceptions of democratic politics and identity, and his subtle treatment of African American mourning practices as an instantiation of the tragic mode of mourning are an invaluable contribution to debates about the link between mourning and politics. Moreover, Stow's description of a democratic pedagogy drawn from an acceptance of ambivalence and conflict has great potential for engaging the transferential battlefield surrounding racial politics in the contemporary United States. Anti-Periclean, dissonant mourning practices can act as a counterweight to idealized accounts of national histories and civic norms that feed cycles of manic denial or omnipotent triumph. Because these countermemorial discourses are rooted in a tragic awareness of fundamental ambivalence, they are also less likely to enflame persecutory anxieties that actively work against cross-racial sympathies and coalitions.

Yet there remain some difficulties within Stow's account. For instance, Stow acknowledges that there is "something of a paradox" with regard to his claims about Frederick Douglass, whose "unequivocal commitment" to a definite view of the Civil War seems to conflict with the emphasis on tragic ambivalence and the essential partiality of any particular viewpoint.[141] It is clear that Douglass's discursive register—as much as it emphasizes a critical uprooting of convention—also had moments of closure and a drive toward a (reconfigured) social consensus. This paradox creates an internal conflict that causes Stow's essay to rove across the typology of public mourning he has described—alternately tragic and romantic, agonistic and consensualist. For instance, he describes Douglass's eulogies as demanding "that those who had hitherto considered their position natural, given and unassailable, defend it against his more compelling arguments. By inviting his white audience to engage him in reasoned argument, moreover, Douglass enmeshed them in a performative contradiction: undermining white supremacist claims by forcing them to recognize him as a person worthy of reasoned engagement."[142]

Stow's emphasis on "reasoned" and "compelling" arguments, the work of "performative contradiction," and the telos of "reasoned engagement" reveals a tacit consensualism within his agonistic approach. Agonists cannot fully quit the dangerous game of consensus without their own performative contradiction. Somewhere there lurks a good object, which licenses the critical uprooting of rooted biases. The good object, for Klein, is a dynamic psychic entity that has a characteristic influence on the individual's way of experiencing life and relating to others.[143] In the depressive position, the heretofore-idealized "good breast" is restored to wholeness and morphs into the good object, which still carries a measure of idealization but whose ideal features are now filtered through an awareness of the object's overall imperfection and complexity. The good object is what allows us to appreciate the "trauma of a flawed world" without that experience tilting us toward endless cycles of despair, fear, or defeat.[144]

Klein's idea of the good object has relevance beyond the intimate world of analyst/analysand in which she was enmeshed. The basic insight contained within the concept of the good object is that the experience of tragic dissolution cannot be borne without a corresponding source of reassurance. In order for us to mourn and accept the imperfections of self, other, and world, there has to be a reliable, whole object that gives us hope for the continuity of life and the possibility of understanding or mutual recognition. We can only be disappointed in an object that we also need; we can only experience disappointment (instead of living it) if at some very deep level we also experience security, comfort, understanding, and hope. All of these experiences are very fragile, and that itself is a tragic recognition that requires a certainty that they are possible, perhaps even unavoidable.

Therefore, instead of thinking about the praxis of mourning from the perspective of separate ideal types, I suggest that we see consensualist and agonist modes of public mourning as ultimately inseparable and complexly intertwined. The work of agonist or tragic disruption cannot function purely on its own power. Tragic and moral narratives must necessarily shadow one another because each makes the other possible. For Klein, the acknowledgment of the tragic (our conflicted and fractious self) stands on and educates the moral or normative core within her theory, represented by the depressive position and the hope for reparation undertaken through the work of acknowledging and accepting the imperfections of self, other, and world.[145]

The danger, then, resides not within the game of consensus or the agonistic clash of wills in themselves, but where either of these narratives manically denies the other. As Meira Likierman argues, morality for Klein "must assume the possibility of irrevocable loss all the time" if it is to retain its sense and its connection with lived experience.[146] Morality must be disciplined by tragedy if it is to avoid the rigid moralism of the paranoid-schizoid position, which serves as a protection of the fantasized sanctity of the self and precludes open interaction and engagement between selves. If we build from Klein's insights, the challenge for democratic theory and practice is to locate good objects and potential spaces that license the acknowledgment of tragedy—to search, in essence, for means of mourning that do not eliminate either agonistic struggles for recognition or the consensualist search for background norms but holds these moments together in tense coexistence. In short, the challenge is to *combine* the tragic and the moral in ways that mitigate one-sided agonism or consensualism.

Let us go back to Rawls, then, and to what I have described as the Kleinian intuition behind his ideas of the original position and public reason. Instead of asking, *pace* Mills and Stow, whether or not a theory such as Rawls's promotes denial, perhaps we ought to ask if the denial at work is pernicious or democratically adaptive. In other words, do the abstractions of Rawls's approach help us to negotiate the transferential field surrounding racial discrimination, prejudice, and inequality? I want to argue that this is (potentially) the case. With the increasingly symbolic and implicit nature of racial bias, a direct rhetoric of aggressive and unvarnished truth telling may, perversely, have a backfire effect on support for policies that could ameliorate racial injustices. Because racial prejudices are both intense and partly unconscious, Rawls's intuition to base public reasoning on deracialized stick figures has some merit. The original position and public reason, in this light, might provide some measure of relief from the intense anxieties surrounding race in the contemporary polity, leading to the development of terms of negotiation and engagement that could form the basis for political coalitions forged in the teeth of the racialized transference.[147]

However, as previously discussed, Rawls's theory cannot fulfill this function because of the narrow way in which the original position and public reason—as civic superegos—are theorized. I argued that the reason was Rawls's Freudian slip toward a severe, univocal superego within his explicit and implicit theories of moral psychology. In Rawls's lectures on Joseph Butler, for instance, he describes the work of conscience as a "supreme principle" that specifies "conclusive or decisive reasons for what we are to do."[148] Conscience, like the original position, is always available and accessible; we come to it within what Butler called a "cool hour" of reflection.[149] From this space of solitary consideration, we can come to understand how we should act, and from these judgments "there is no further appeal."[150] Here again, we detect the specter of Loraux's unanimous assembly and the search for moral blamelessness or purity of heart. Yet, according to Klein, the univocal and severe superego is precisely that which intensifies paranoid-schizoid defenses such as splitting, idealization, and demonization. The search for blamelessness is a symptom of desperate omnipotence, and purity of heart is a pernicious fantasy that cuts the ambivalent self off from its aggression and hatred. The alternative to the unanimous assembly fantasy is an understanding of conscience as a polyphonous assembly of diverse voices and ambivalent objects.[151] This involves the activation of the depressive position as a cognitive-affective schema by which we can acknowledge the "poignant psychic reality" of whole, ambivalent others and by which we can face up to the conflicts that persist within the self and between self and other—preparing all the while for inevitable regrets and the work of reparation.[152] What makes this possible is the interminable work of mourning where we work through, again and again, the differences and distances between and within selves across the battlefield of transference and amid the uneven, unequal, and contested terrain of the social. Abstract others and univocal principles cannot accomplish this work. Only by engaging concrete, whole others can we effectively modulate the anxieties and pathologies plaguing both intersubjective and social life.

Yet all of these possibilities are denied to the representatives in the original position, which is intended only as a "guide to intuition" or a Butlerian "cool hour" of reflection—a process of introspection that all rational agents can take up and practice. Hence it has limited value. In the absence of concrete others and actual social practices whereby paranoid-schizoid defenses can be countered, anxious fantasies of persecution will continue to plague us. The original position cannot, by itself, effect a transition from paranoid anxiety to depressive anxiety; this happens only when our internal objects and fantasies come to more closely match our external experiences. Klein did not extend her theory to social-political practices, but by helping us to see and accept the ambivalence and conflicts within the self while mitigating persecutory fantasies of dissolution or idealized dreams of perfect union, she, in the words of Isaac Balbus, has "taught us something new and important about the emotional demands of democracy."[153] As Hanna Segal puts it, Klein's description of the transition from the paranoid-schizoid position to the depressive position is the "evolution from an insane world determined by misperceptions into a saner world . . . in which conflict and ambivalence can be faced."[154] This transition requires the repeated presence of concrete others who can hold and effectively dispel characteristic defenses against anxiety such as splitting and demonization. Yet Rawls neglected to theorize the political practices and experiences that could replicate—and make real—the psychological and cognitive development that he seemed to hope would take place in the original position. Rawls's sound psychological presumptions (that we need distance from persecutory anxiety in order to sympathetically engage with others in the difficult work of sharing and re-creating a common world) seem to be compromised by the most "liberal" of fears: the fear of politics.[155] But it is perhaps only through such concerted political engagement with whole, ambivalent others that we can achieve integration.[156] It is to this possibility that I now turn.

Conclusion: Viable Others and the Democratic Superego

In her study of the Athenian funeral oration tradition, Nicole Loraux asks, "Is there a democratic way of speaking about democracy?"[157] This project asks a similar question: Is there a democratic way to mourn in a democracy? The Periclean mode of mourning, whose tropes persist, seems problematic on this score. By transforming the democratic polity into an idealized, harmonious whole, Periclean-styled civic discourses and rituals surrounding public traumas seem to obscure ongoing conflicts and injustices, which impoverishes public discourse and impairs political judgment. Guided by Melanie Klein's theories of the paranoid-schizoid and depressive positions, I have argued that these mourning rituals are politically felicitous and effective because they trigger psychological defense mechanisms such as splitting, idealization, and denial. Yet these defenses have pernicious consequences. Consensualist political theories feed this same cycle of denial and persecutory anxiety. What Periclean mourning and consensualist approaches to public life have in common is the reliance on a superordinate, univocal principle of self-control and social order. Far from providing the means of moral-psychological maturity, however, the univocal superego reflects and feeds the anxieties of the paranoid-schizoid position, which isolates subjects from each other and from the less-tolerable aspects of their selves—their hatred, envy, vulnerability, and fear. When social life is mediated by a severe, unequivocal superego, the intense anxieties that circulate around public trauma and enduring injustices are exacerbated rather than being effectively worked through. The result is an autistic politics characterized by episodes of manic triumph and hostile resentment.

The approach to mourning proposed here, however, provides room for an alternative. With her idea of the depressive position, Klein describes a schema by which the conflicts within and between selves could be acknowledged and the capacities for tolerance, guilt, and reparation could be cultivated and practiced. Klein's simultaneous tragic and moral narratives license both an agonistic struggle for recognition and a consensualist search for defensible social norms—but more importantly, they warn against the excesses or pathologies attendant on each of these struggles in isolation from the other. The challenge, then, is to develop Klein's insights by anticipating and describing the political institutions and social practices that could provide space for what I am calling the democratic work of mourning.

In part we can do this by developing Klein's concept of the superego as a fractious assembly. Unlike the Periclean civic superego, which emphasizes and enforces social consensus and coherence, Klein's concept of "depressive" conscience takes into account the differences and distances between and within selves.[158] For Klein, the acceptance of ambivalence—the expression of hatred and disappointment toward loved objects, for instance—is the key component of moral-psychological maturity. By accepting ambivalence, we mitigate the temptations toward the temporarily satisfying defenses of idealization or demonization. By facing up to the *otherness* within the self, we can increase our tolerance toward actual, whole others. This is the integrative work of mourning in the crucible of the depressive position. It does not eliminate conflicts within and between selves, nor does it make injustice, violence, or terror impossible, it merely and temporarily (and this is still quite a bit) helps us to clarify the sources of conflict and to mediate this conflict through a depressive or mournful awareness of complexity and ambivalence.

What makes this work of mourning possible? Thomas Ogden argues, following Winnicott, that the "containing" function of external others is crucial.[159] What we might call "viable others" unsettle the perceptual-affective habits within the paranoid-schizoid position. They simultaneously hold and disrupt the fantastical projections emitted by the defenses of splitting, idealization, and demonization. Viable others, as Klein described them, are *whole* others; they reflect ambivalence and fractiousness in ways that objects within the paranoid-schizoid position cannot. In reflecting ambivalence they help to inaugurate the depressive position, which disalienates the anxiety, frustration, and fear that had been heretofore split off and disavowed. From within the terrain opened up by viable others, reparative impulses can be liberated and tolerance of self and others can be strengthened.

Moving beyond an anxious emphasis on consensual theories (or rituals) of democracy, then, we need to identify viable others and spaces in which interaction with such others can cultivate a more polyphonous, democratic superego. Once again, on this front we have much to learn from analytic approaches. Freud, for instance, defined the work of analysis by invoking Oedipus's gradual recognition of his tragic origins. The work of analysis proceeds in like fashion: engaging the transference in ways that allow the analysand to recognize herself, to *re*-cognize her thoughts, actions, history, and future by a new light. Klein, however, moves us beyond recognition toward productive or generative *reversal*. Reversal occurs when the projected or disavowed aspects of experience are returned to the self. Reversal happens when the internalized objects talk back, when they object to the flattening and obscuring discourses that embellish them (either as angels or demons). Reversals can themselves be disavowed, of course, which starts the paranoid-schizoid cycle afresh. Yet reversals can also inspire what James Baldwin referred to as a "good-natured reconciliation" to the complexity and ambivalence of self and other.

How are these viable others made to appear? In part, viable others appear from the rubble of a destroyed or overturned projection. Take, for instance, the work of perceptual-affective reversals in Michelle Alexander's *The New Jim Crow*, which powerfully details the affects imbuing racialized policing and prison policies in the United States, ranging from the easy scapegoating of black and brown criminals to the cognitive dissonance-inspiring efforts to exclude white, middle-class, or suburban drug users from the stigma of criminality.[160] Racial discrimination finds a ready outlet in the officially color-blind but intensely racialized war on drugs. Alexander provides a thorough genealogy of these policies, revealing them to be related to and in some respects an outgrowth of historical patterns of racial stigmatization. Although Alexander does not mention Klein or projective identification, what she describes as the collective American "permission to hate" criminals can clearly be read as an accessible outlet for paranoid-schizoid defenses such as denial, splitting, and demonization.[161] Alexander also models viable otherness with several reversals that hold and disrupt penchants for racialized disavowal. For instance, she argues that—if justice were really color-blind—the drug war could have been waged in a very different manner:

> From the outset, the drug war could have been waged primarily in overwhelmingly white suburbs or on college campuses. SWAT teams could have rappelled from helicopters in gated suburban communities and raided the homes of high school lacrosse players known for hosting coke

and ecstasy parties after their games. The police could have seized televisions, furniture, and cash from fraternity houses based on an anonymous tip that a few joints or a stash of cocaine could be found hidden in someone's dresser drawer . . . all of this could have happened as a matter of routine in white communities, but it did not.[162]

Alexander's racial transposition reverses the easy projections and disavowals that stand behind prison and drug policies in the United States. Because Americans have permission to hate criminals, and because those criminals are so persistently coded as racial others, the cognitive dissonance that occurs when the frame is switched can challenge or dislodge the nexus of anxious projections that maintain a rigid split between innocence and guilt. In this example, the white, suburban, middle-class drug users are viable others insofar as they disrupt easy stereotypes and complicate the perceptual-affective schemas on which those stereotypes rest. Viable others become the basis for a more honest dialogue about the enduring traumas and intense anxieties surrounding racial politics in the United States. Even more importantly, honest dialogue or cross-sectional deliberation can reveal those viable others.[163]

Rawls, it turns out, had it right the first time around: the struggle for justice not only relies on psychological capacities but calls for a kind of soul-craft. James Baldwin never shied away from this claim, or from the idea that there is a connection between a political struggle for racial justice and a human struggle against the terrifying aspects of our interconnected, ambivalent lives and the desperate strategies we deploy to deny our terror. The struggle against racial injustice is more than a battle against unjust laws, exclusive institutions, or even "racism." As Baldwin puts it, "The battle is elsewhere. It proceeds far from us in the heat and horror and pain of life itself where all men are betrayed by greed and guilt and blood-lust and where no one's hands are clean."[164]

For Baldwin, viable others that clarify the "heat . . . horror and pain of life itself" were what he often referred to as "poets." The poet, according to Baldwin, does not simply reflect his or her own experience but gives witness to the pathologies and disasters of the world in ways that bring a semblance of order and understanding to those disasters. As Baldwin puts it, in describing Billie Holiday: "Billie Holiday was a poet. She gave you back your experience. She refined it, and you recognized it for the first time because she was in and out of it and she made it possible for you to bear it. And if you could bear it, then you could begin to change it. That's what a poet does."[165]

Poets "hold us together," that is, they make experience bearable in part by offering new ways in which individuals can understand themselves, new forms for experience that make this experience, and the experiencing self, more coherent, whole, enriched—*assembled*. Viable others, however, are necessary but insufficient for the ongoing praxis of the democratic work of mourning. The limitation of the poet is that while they may indicate blockages in particular vocabularies, they cannot create a new vocabulary by themselves. Only groups in assembled spaces can create—and contest, and re-create—a vocabulary.[166] Therefore, in chapters 4 and 5, I look beyond both Antigone and Pericles toward spaces of acknowledgment and assembly through which citizens might mourn democratically in the name of democracy.

"THERE IS TROUBLE HERE. THERE IS MORE TO COME"

Greek Tragedy and the Work of Mourning

> **The Furies: What shall I do? Afflicted, I am mocked by these people. I have borne what cannot be borne. Great the sorrow and the dishonor upon the sad daughters of the night.**
> **Athena: No, not dishonored. You are goddesses. Do not in too much anger make this place of mortal men uninhabitable. . . . Put to sleep the bitter strength in the black wave and live with me. . . .**
> **In the terror upon the faces of these**
> **I see great good for our citizens.**
>
> —Aeschylus, *Oresteia*

> **The only way to get through life is to know the worst things about it.**
>
> —James Baldwin

In this chapter, I begin to sketch out in more detail the constitutive aspects of what I am calling the democratic work of mourning. The democratic work of mourning involves the public spaces and practices by which the traumas of collective life are publicly worked through in ways that enliven social struggles for recognition while mitigating denial, disavowal, and distrust. In articulating this concept, I lean heavily on the work of object relations psychoanalysis and, in particular, the approach to mourning found in Melanie Klein and D. W. Winnicott. Klein's concepts of the depressive position and the good object, supplemented by Winnicott's idea of potential space, provide the kernel for a sociopsychological theory of mourning that constructively responds to the paradoxes and pathologies that shadow dominant modes of public mourning. With the depressive position, Klein articulated a developmental possibility whereby individuals are sensitized to the ambivalences and tensions of intersubjective life, a process with incipient political content. Winnicott's concept of potential space supplements Klein's theory by showing how cultural symbols, public discourses, and civic practices can create the conditions for successful efforts to acknowledge living legacies of misrecognition and undertake concrete steps toward social repair.

The work of mourning responds to the pressing needs of late-modern democracies, such as the challenge of findings ways for loss, vulnerability, and suffering to become opportunities for constructive social action rather than occasions for reaction, resentment, and misrecognition.[1] Public acts of mourning can be called democratic insofar as they cultivate inclusiveness while falling short of (fantastical) social consensus and insofar as they promote interaction and social cooperation across lines of division. Inclusive practices honor and exemplify the equal respect and treatment that are due to members of the democratic polity.[2] Yet, as Rosemary Nagy argues, reconciliatory efforts that demand social consensus are "too thick" insofar as they come "at the cost of private difference."[3] Efforts to address historical and enduring traumas of misrecognition and to work through a violent past should not sacrifice heterogeneity and difference for the sake of an impossible ideal of social unity.[4]

Alongside this emphasis on ineliminable social differences, however, democratic processes of mourning must aim to facilitate what chapter 2 described as the "agency" of the depressive position. Depressive agency treats power as fluid, relational, and many-sided, and this form of agency is best cultivated through interaction and collaboration across lines of social division. Working through traumas by the actual work of public organizing, association, and problem solving promotes the recognition and acceptance of difference through cross-group contact, dialogue, and interactive problem solving.[5] In the democratic work of mourning, then, the stress should be placed on the work by which citizens acknowledge and address traumas of misrecognition. We have good reasons to believe that such work is indeed possible, even in the face of significant historical traumas. We have even better reasons to hope that this work can be expanded and intensified, to cope with the violence and pain that is daily on display in our world.

In this chapter, I begin to develop the idea of a democratic work of mourning by first displacing it from the immediate context of contemporary dramas of reconciliation and social repair. In particular, I turn back to the city-state of Athens in the fifth century BCE and specifically to its annual festival the Great Dionysia (where the tragedies of Aeschylus, Sophocles, and Euripides were originally performed). The Athenian tragic festival offers an intensely rich practice of representing and honoring trauma and violence. Through a reading of the dramatic festival and of Aeschylus's *Oresteia*, I lay the conceptual groundwork for a theory of democratic mourning. Using Klein's essay on the trilogy, I argue that Aeschylus and the Athenian experience can help us to think about an "Oresteian" politics of mourning that is irreducible to either a Periclean or an Antigonean approach.[6]

Greek tragedy and Athenian democracy are conceptual and practical spaces that—once surveyed—will give us a richer vocabulary and store of practices for working through the traumas of our own time.[7]

The Athenian experience of tragedy, like contemporary dramas of reconciliation, was paradoxical by its nature. I will argue that this ambivalence was part of its democratic function in the polis, contributing to what Christian Meier has called the "mental infrastructure" of Athenian citizenship.[8] I will also argue that tragedy also provided a "psychological infrastructure" that made Athenian democracy possible—a psychological infrastructure understood as an acceptance of ambivalence, conflict, and trauma within intra- and intersubjective life. Tragedy nurtured the civic identity of the Athenian citizens, but it also nurtured what Josiah Ober has called the "democratic soul."[9] This understanding of tragedy is reinforced by Klein's reading of the *Oresteia*, which, I argue, captures some of the democratic importance of the trilogy even if Klein's theory itself focuses on the "micro" reconciliations inherent in interpersonal life. Klein's conceptual innovations, however, can be used to go much further than Klein herself was willing to go; they contain incipient political content that the space and practice of Greek tragedy helps us to unpack and develop.

If Klein gives us some purchase on the sociopsychological meaning of tragedy, then the Greek polis and its practices in turn give us a means of sounding out Klein's undeveloped areas from the perspective of political or social theory. For instance, Klein's theory of mourning/integration misses (or at least downplays) the foundational role that power plays in the politics of mourning. An appreciation of the Great Dionysia as a cultural and political institution at Athens, then, will correct an absence in Klein—an absence, as it were, of the polis itself, with its native fractiousness and radical disparities. In making the argument that tragedy was an "analytic" space, then, it is also worth emphasizing how the analytic space is also a "political" space—in short, how the individual and the democratic work of mourning are intertwined and mutually implicated in each other. By recognizing the connection between these two spaces, we are already some distance beyond Klein. As argued in chapter 1, Winnicott's idea of potential space builds on Klein's insights while turning them outward toward cultural and institutional spaces that both embody and cultivate the developmental possibilities she envisioned. Yet, more importantly, an analysis of the Athenian dramatic festival can usefully "politicize" Klein and object relations psychoanalysis. I argue that Greek tragedy gave space for the articulation and interpretation of the micro- and macrodramas of reconciliation within the life of the polis. In my terms, then, the Greek tragic festival represented an ongoing democratic work of mourning, from which contemporary efforts to face down and work through a violent past and conflicted present have much to learn.

In the penultimate section of this chapter, I take on two challenges to my reading of Greek tragedy in the wake of Klein—namely, tragedy's imitative and distancing character (tragedy by and large assiduously avoids the representation of actual traumas in the polity's history in favor of distant places and mythical heroes), and the supposed "cathartic" effect of tragedy. Catharsis is a term that haunts both tragedy and psychoanalysis, and I argue that to understand it in terms of purgation or healing keeps us from appreciating the full relevance of tragedy as a piece of the democratic work of mourning. Instead, we should understand catharsis as the act of making pity/fear (and the trauma and terror that elicit these emotions) public—giving them a public account in the interests of working through or mourning them. Doing so provides a means of engaging—rather than displacing—the paradoxes of mourning and reconciliation.

In the final section, I reconnect the strands of this argument to the contemporary politics of mourning by returning to the context of postapartheid South Africa. The South African Truth and Reconciliation Commission (SATRC) can be usefully seen as a good object that licenses social critique and depressive forms of agency. In this light, I give an interpretation of South African playwright Yael Farber's *Molora*. In *Molora*, Farber repurposes Aeschylus's *Oresteia* within the context of South Africa after the fall of apartheid and the experience of the SATRC. Read in a Kleinian light, the play offers a glimpse at a simultaneously tragic/moral practice of mourning that leaves the audience with both reasons for doubt and for hope. It stages an apparently ritualistic reconciliation through the performance of communal norms, but certain ambiguities within the text and its performance cut against the ritualistic movement toward closure. I argue that the play shows the SATRC as a Kleinian internalized good object that—while not without its faults—has become a reflective means of accounting for the enduring conflicts within South African society. Farber's play is a powerful representation of the challenges inherent in the democratic work of mourning, and it helps us to think about other objects, practices, and spaces that might carry forward this work in South Africa and elsewhere.

The Great Dionysia and Athenian Democracy

The extant Greek tragedies—all composed during the fifth century BCE—display a frankness about violence, cruelty, hatred and injustice that continues to grip the contemporary imagination.[10] Tragedy's representation of transgression and trauma show "a world ripped apart," a world with "civic foundations shattered and the noble values of citizenship turned against themselves in violence, confusion, despair, and horror."[11] In tragedy, mothers murder sons, sons kill mothers and fathers, husbands are slain by wives, queens become slaves, cities are leveled, and legendary families are brought to utter and complete ruin. The strong are laid low, the pure are polluted, the peaceful turn violent, and the certain become confused. Yet tragedy is not simply the waking dream of a violent society; it reveals a keen sensitivity to the dilemmas of collective life and the often-disastrous consequences of our actions. Tragedy shows the unforeseen costs of our necessarily blind choices and provides room for the regret and lamentation that follows from the realization of disaster.[12]

What makes the tragic spectacles even more compelling is that the audience members could not maintain a detached posture of aesthetic appreciation. The theatergoers (*theates*) at the Great Dionysia were also the citizens (*polites*) at Athens: just as they sat in the theater of Dionysus and witnessed the potential consequences of action, so too would they sit in the assembly in order to debate and decide on the polis's best course of action. The same citizens who watched representations of Trojans, Persians, and Thebans bemoan the disastrous effects of warfare would later sit in the assembly and vote to support (and to fight) wars of their own. The same citizens who beheld Athena's delicate negotiations with the Furies would sit in the law courts and adjudicate between competing claims of guilt and innocence. Participation in the theater, then, was but one aspect of a comprehensive political experience for Athenian citizens.

Over the past thirty years, a scholarly consensus has developed that the Great Dionysia—the Athenian festival held annually in the spring at which the tragedies and comedies were performed—had an important civic function, and therefore that our understanding of the plays is enhanced by an attentiveness to their location within the larger context of political life in Athens.[13] The Great Dionysia is now itself seen as a constitutive part of the Athenian democratic experience—a "vigorous civic practice" as relevant to the democracy as the institutions of the assembly, the council, and the law courts.[14] Accordingly, Josh Beer reads the extant tragedies in the light of the "conflicts and policy decisions" faced by the enfranchised demos; as he sees them, "the plays raised serious ethical, social, religious, and political problems that provided a major part of all Athenians' education."[15] Peter Euben notes that funding of a chorus was "a liturgy equal to the maintenance of a trireme . . . as if to suggest that the cultural survival of the Athenians depended on the courage of its people in confronting the risks of tragedy in the same way as its physical survival depended on its sailors' courageously meeting the risks of battle."[16] Helene Foley identifies the reciprocal connection between democratic debate and tragic narrative, arguing that drama required its audience to "negotiate among points of view as it would in a court of law or an assembly."[17] The festival itself is said to have had a "democratic ambience"—

ordinary citizens danced in the choruses and acted on the stage,[18] and judges were selected by sortition.[19] The procession—or *komos*—on the first day of the festival mixed rich and poor citizens together in a celebratory atmosphere that emphasized the commonalities binding Athenians together over and against the class and factional lines that cut across the polis at all other times.[20]

The tragedies were performed, then, in a "political forum" that "allowed the Athenians to consider the nature of their own society."[21] The Great Dionysia was a "democratic institution" and tragedy was "a form of public discourse."[22] Because ordinary Athenian citizens had to exercise agency—to "engage in politics on a grand scale"—they needed to "have answers ready for all the conscious and unconscious questions and doubts that arose."[23] Tragedy (perhaps) provided some of these answers, but, more importantly, it provided a space for the examination and exploration of questions, doubts, and anxieties. The Great Dionysia was one of the crucial components of the democratic imaginary at Athens; it responded to the Athenians' need to "think themselves into being democratic citizens."[24] Tragedy by its very nature as a periodic but extraordinary liturgy could "introduce perspectives which might otherwise have been overlooked" in a polis concerned with day-to-day survival.[25] Freed from immediate pressures of decision, Athenians could reflect on the values and practices of their polis, explore alternative imaginaries, sound out new and even uncomfortable ideas, and then return to the challenges of self-government, their skills of discernment and judgment (ideally) sharpened by the experience. Ultimately, tragedy "helped the Athenians to work through difficulties, threats, and uncertainties which would otherwise have hampered them in their thinking, feeling, and acting."[26] Tragedy was not only a democratic space, then; it was, as Euben argues, "a theoretical institution" insofar as the "form, content, and context" of tragedy provided "a critical consideration of public life."[27]

Sara Monoson argues that three primary elements of Athenian democratic culture emerged in part from the experience with tragedy: unity, reciprocity, and what she calls "strong-mindedness," or the ability of the common Athenian citizen to judge important matters skillfully and prudently.[28] Unity emerges from the admixtures of the processional *komos* and the visual "mapping" of the polis in the theater of Dionysus. Yet importantly, according to Monoson, this mapping of the unified polis did not erase social and factional differences but, rather, brought attention to them. Prominent citizens were marked by where they were seated for the performances, and wealthy elites at Athens were made visible through their liturgical duties as chorus sponsors. The festival emphasized commonality, but not at the expense of particularities and differences. Instead, these differences were negotiated through reciprocal acts of participation and service—particular citizens filled different roles, but the entire polis shared in the burdens and the rewards of the festival. Reciprocity was also exemplified through the public benefaction of citizens in the ceremony that initiated the festival. The bestowing of honors for citizens whose service had benefited the polis during the preceding year sent a message that such actions would not go unacknowledged. Lastly, there is the value of "strong-mindedness." The difficult and trying subject matter of the performances reflected the assumption that the ordinary Athenian citizen was capable of making careful and thoughtful judgments. For Monoson, even the physical rigors of spectatorship (the audience sat through a tragic trilogy, a satyr play, and a comedy performance each day of the festival), lent credence to the Athenian citizenry's claims of intellectual and physiological fortitude.

Athenian unity as represented (or performed) by the tragic festival, scholars argue, did not come at the expense of social heterogeneity and conflict. As Mark Griffith reads them, the surviving tragedies provided an occasion for Athenians to think through the clashes and inconsistencies between aristocratic and democratic norms. However, rather than glorying in aristocratic family failures and frailties, the tragic poets "reinforce[d] a notion of mutual inter-dependency between elite families and their communities."[29] Tragedy helped to foster a sense of social solidarity, but for Griffith it was "solidarity without consensus . . . among the different social groups and ideologies that comprised the theater audience."[30] Following Nagy's treatment of discourses of reconciliation, Athenian tragedy could be seen as cultivating a "thinner" form of social solidarity, which did not paper over social differences or deny ongoing conflicts.

In fact, it was the Athenians' ability to practice solidarity without consensus that may have provided the groundwork for the polis's success in areas of social innovation and interpolis competition. As the work of Josiah Ober has demonstrated, Athenian society was consistently responsive to self-critique and capable of significant cultural and political innovations in the wake of this critique. According to Ober, tragedy was one of the crucial venues through which such critique filtered into and influenced the Athenian imaginary.[31] The tragic performances, then, demonstrated a keen awareness of (if not an obsession with) the fraught tension between norm and transgression in a fluid society. As a result, Athenians could remain highly conscious of the vertigiousness and contingency of democratic action. Athenians of the fifth century could rewrite the structure of the polis at every assembly meeting. In this way, they were attuned to the tension between continuity and change—a sensitivity that shows forth in tragedy. By participating in an ambiguous and contradiction-rich discourse—where social roles were upended, and boundaries between man and woman, nature and polis, pure and polluted were constantly troubled or blurred—Athenians learned both to "think alike" (to share common values or norms) and to "think differently" (to question those very same norms when challenged by unexpected events or ideas).[32] In this way, they were able to maintain a dialogue between the desire for constancy and the need for innovation.

Moreover, the broader culture of participation (in which even a staged performance would elicit active engagement and critique) promoted "an enlarged understanding of common predicaments"[33] that prepared the Athenian citizenry for the demands of self-government. As Bruce Heiden puts it, "tragedy . . . [gave] the Athenians the flexibility to play a variety of roles as situations might require, especially the role of friend to a former enemy."[34] Role-playing and sensitivity to role *reversal* perhaps explains the Athenian capacity for high levels of social cooperation despite a heterogeneity of social interests and often deep social divisions.[35] On these terms, we can see how the Athenians might have used tragedy to understand and practice solidarity without consensus and social cooperation without homogeneity.[36] In other words, tragedy facilitated a depressive form of civic agency in which power was seen as fluid and relational, not as something located in a central place but available to a variety of actors and circulating through a variety of spaces.

Although it was not its only purpose, tragedy provided a venue for the Athenian citizenry to practice and hone the skills necessary for democratic life. Moreover, as I will argue shortly, by witnessing and working through the traumas represented on stage, the Athenians also nurtured a psychologically resilient and integrated identity. This nested sociopsychological challenge is captured by Ober's idea of the "democratic soul," which includes the "moral psychology, ethical judgment and conception of justice and law that is appropriate to the democratic citizen."[37] The Great Dionysia was not only a democratic and a theoretical institution but an analytic space, and it not only provided an occasion for intellectual reflection and social cooperation; it was also a scene of mourning that honed an integrated psyche.

The Internal Assembly and the Democratic Soul: Melanie Klein at the Great Dionysia

The developmental goal of Kleinian analysis is the "integration" of the ego, a process that takes place through repeated moments of recognition or understanding by which the individual accepts and comes to terms with the painful losses attendant to their relationships with imperfect others, who, by necessity, both fail and fall away from them. These moments of recognition facilitate a process of mourning whereby losses of purity and innocence are acknowledged and worked through. The work of mourning within the depressive position mitigates pathological states of mind such as omnipotence, denial, and splitting. The depressive position and its labor of mourning, however, are precarious achievements. Klein's understanding of the positional nature of these cognitive and psychological states means that integration names a perpetual aspiration more than a reachable endpoint. The archaic defenses of the paranoid-schizoid position remain a live possibility throughout life. These defenses persist as a powerful hedge against intense anxiety and feelings of powerlessness, and they provide a fantastical consolatory extension for desires of omnipotent control or sovereign agency because it is through these defenses that we create a space of frictionless belonging populated by one-sided part objects that exist only for the gratification of our needs (for a scapegoat; for an enemy; or for something hideous, twisted, and corrupted so that we might feel beautiful and pure).

Although Klein did not extend her analysis into group life, others have noted the ways in which social pressures exacerbate paranoid-schizoid tendencies or entrench persecutory interpretive frameworks.[38] The effectiveness of symbolic politics—demonization of "the immigrant," for instance—rests in part on the deep grammar of psychological functioning that Klein locates in the paranoid-schizoid position.[39] Inchoate, painful experiences and the anxiety and frustration therein are often displaced through what Wilfred Bion calls a "psychotic" form of group identification. For Bion, in fact, one of the primary functions of groups is to contain the destabilizing and psychotic anxieties that we cannot cope with ourselves by giving them expression through the idealizing empowerment of insiders or the demonization of abject outsiders.[40] The group is able to act out individual pathologies, such as omnipotence and denial, in ways that the individual cannot; as Fred Alford puts it, "only a madman would say, 'I am the most wonderful and strongest person in the world. Yet, groups say things like that all the time about themselves."[41]

The mitigation of denial and splitting inherent in many forms of symbolic politics requires the integration of the psyche, which involves practice with ambivalence and acceptance of conflict within the self and between self and other. Mourning is the hinge of this practice. The psychological weaning from the idealized objects of the paranoid-schizoid position requires, once again, the internalization of the good object, a process that begins with the depressive recognition that this object's purity was a fantastical construct. The good object shifts the superego from a univocal, harsh voice into an internal, polyvocal "assembly" of whole objects.[42] The internal assembly in turn enables more reciprocal connections or encounters between self and other. Idealized internal objects, by contrast, *pre-interpret* the world. The (melodramatic) story of absolute love and pure hatred is already written in the paranoid-schizoid position, whereas the depressive position marks a shift toward the risky or "treacherous field of communication through language."[43] In essence, our ability to mourn for a lost pure other is tied to our ability to engage with complex, whole others within the inherently risky terrain of the political, and vice versa.

At this point, we might begin to see the relevance of tragic drama for Klein's theory of integration. Greek tragedy portrays the dilemmas and ambivalences attendant to intersubjective and intrasubjective life with delicate precision. Tragedy is replete with viable or ambivalent others, who unsettle the emotions, judgments, and habits fed by paranoid-schizoid fantasies and anxieties. For instance, in tragic drama conventional judgments and norms are called into question and often undergo dramatic reversal. Heroic characters and those in positions of authority are often indecent and hubristic, and those who are of lower status often gain the sympathy of the chorus. Antigone is a case in point. Antigone shocks her sister Ismene and the chorus of elders at Thebes by refusing to obey Creon's edicts surrounding the exposure of her brother's body. Yet this shock seemingly yields to a growing acceptance of Antigone's choice, and then even to sympathy with the ill-fated daughter of Oedipus (the chorus joins the lament with Antigone as the latter is led away by the henchmen of Creon). As Helene Foley interprets this sympathetic shift, "it appears that it is possible to be both subversive and at least partially right on the tragic stage—that the notorious and dangerous 'female intruders' who often stalk the tragic stage have a point."[44] Antigone is an unacceptable danger, a threat to the social order, violently transgressive, *and* justified in her actions. Accepting this mixed picture is part of the chorus's (and ultimately Creon's) growing awareness of the fragility and ambiguity of the situation.

That the hero is often mistaken and the denigrated other often "at least partially right" is what Simon Goldhill has described as the "unsettling force" of tragic drama.[45] Perhaps it is impossible to recapture the difficulty of experiencing such cognitive and emotional dissonance. But with Klein, we can ask a slightly different question: What precisely is unsettled by this incessant practice of unsettlement? It is not simply the idealized picture of the hero (or the god, or the polis) that is disrupted or put askew—it is the psychological mode of functioning in which such idealized images are necessary. The great heroes are upended and exposed as partial and failing beings. In the wake of the unsettling of this (fantastic, imaginary) world, the audience can achieve a clearer understanding of the often-fraught relationship between self and other. This is the recognition, at its root, of how our fantasies and fears can keep us from appreciating the full range of the other's character—recognition of our *mis*recognitions.[46] According to Klein, "It is an essential part of psychoanalytic therapy . . . that the patient should be enabled by the analyst's interpretations to integrate the split-off and contrasting aspects of his self; this implies also the synthesis of the split-off aspects of other people and of situations."[47] Greek tragedy was, then, a social analytic practice whereby the Athenians could integrate the split-off and denigrated parts of their collective identity. This view mirrors the work of mourning as depicted by Klein, and it has similar effects. By making the world difficult on stage, we might say, tragedy was a fantasy or waking dream that could mitigate the more destructive fantasies of escape and omnipotence to which we are often prone. Tragedy made more likely what Sedgwick calls the "agency" of the depressive position, in which collaboration across divisions and differences requires power that is fluid, shared, and relational.

Famously, Aristotle thought that the effect of tragedy was to elicit pity and fear among the witness-participants.[48] The elicitation of tragic pity and fear is an aesthetic achievement on the part of the poet, but it is also ethically and politically relevant. Pity establishes a connection between the suffering hero and the audience members, expanding and educating the latter's sympathetic imagination. However, pity does not obliterate the distance between the self and the other. Identification does not imply incorporation, where the suffering is taken into the witness-participant as their pain. We do not take the character's place on stage; instead, Aristotle implies, we project ourselves into a similar situation as the protagonist. We imagine the enacted suffering as potentially our own, but we do not collapse the difference between self and other. Rather we come to better appreciate that distance in the light of common bonds of sympathetic identification. As Martha Nussbaum interprets Aristotle, the appropriate amount of pity and fear nurtures the ethical/political virtue of *suggnōmosunē*—fellow feeling and/or "thinking-along-with."[49] This leads to a new understanding of shared vulnerability and interconnectivity that allows us to see the other outside the frozen dichotomy of friend/enemy.[50]

Yet why exactly, we might ask, does the experience of mimetic terror or trauma serve to make us more sensitive to the plight of others—why does it not lead to quietism or resignation, cold indifference, or hostility toward others born of overwhelming fear? Again, Klein helps us to see the mechanism at work—primarily because it is the same mechanism behind her notion of analytic interpretations:

> Very painful interpretations—and I am particularly thinking of the interpretations referring to death and to dead internalized objects . . . have the effect of reviving hope and making the patient feel more alive. My explanation for this would be that bringing a very deep anxiety nearer to consciousness, in itself produces relief. But I also believe that the very fact that the analysis gets into contact with deep-lying unconscious anxieties gives the patient the feeling of being understood and therefore revives hope.[51]

Confronting and giving some form of articulation to deep-seated anxieties tied to trauma, suffering, and death can elicit a shared experience of pity and *suggnōmosunē*, akin to the attainment of the depressive position. Yet this only takes place, we might say, if the act of working through does not reinforce paranoid-schizoid fantasies. Enter Aristotle's famous emphasis on reversal and recognition.[52] Reversal—change "by which the action veers round to its opposite"—and recognition—the "change from ignorance to knowledge"—are, according to Aristotle, the "most powerful elements of emotional interest" in tragedy.[53] We can see obvious parallels between Aristotle's description of the emotional/cognitive transformations inherent in tragic pity and fear and Klein's view of a successful analysis. Take the example of the analysis of "Richard," presented in her *Narrative of a Child Analysis*. Richard suffered from persecutory fantasies and a rigid internal split between idealized and denigrated objects. Yet in the course of his analysis, Richard's internal world began to morph—the idealized mother image was implicated in the menacing persecutory figures (reversal), and the ambiguity of the situation was fully acknowledged (recognition). By bringing together the isolated and split images of the internalized objects, Richard's persecutory fantasies decreased and his hopefulness surged. This did not signify a removal of psychological discomfort or difficulty; in fact, Richard reflected that it was "difficult" to operate with "so many kinds of parents" in his internal world.[54] The analytic space did not erase life's difficulties; rather, it helped to remove certain obstacles that blocked the acknowledgment of the manifold complications inherent in existence. As Richard said to Klein, in a remarkable insight for a ten-year-old, "I have discovered that there is no happiness without tragedy."[55] Richard's internal and external conflicts were not fully resolved by his ascension to the depressive position; they were instead faced fully for the first time:

> Richard, before leaving, inspected his jacket, which was stained with soot. He did not seem perturbed and said that though there would be a row with Mummy over this, it would not be too bad. He parted in a friendly way, neither particularly excited or elated, nor persecuted or depressed. . . . Richard's insight into the need to dirty himself, if he wanted to clean something, seems to me of some significance. His whole development at this stage showed a diminution of idealization, progress in integration, and therefore a greater capacity to acknowledge that a person can be good without being perfect . . . dirty yet useful, helpful, valuable.

Richard's internal and external worlds were dirtied yet valuable, and even all the more precious and secure for their imperfections. The life instinct—enhanced and inflected by positive object relations—had gained predominance as Richard's envy, greed, and persecutory anxiety had dimmed and as his ego was increasingly able to integrate the tensions within and between internal and external worlds.

In the analytic environment, Richard's conflicts with his actual parents began to emerge, become conscious, and find expression. By successfully leaving behind idealized part objects, Richard was able to gain a measure of security and independence that he had heretofore lacked. By internalizing the clashing objects into a fractious but coherent multitude or assembly, Richard was able to look forward to and accept new relationships. This narrative is Klein's clearest portrayal of a healthy work of mourning, through which the analysand develops an identity that is capable of reflecting on loss and damage without succumbing to the defensive temptations of idealization or denial.

I argued earlier that integration marked Klein's understanding of the goals of analysis. Yet again we must understand "goal" here less as a telos toward which we are progressively moving than as a fraught achievement from which we perpetually fall away. Well-integrated selves have nurtured habits of interaction and reflection to mitigate pathological compromises that uphold a false sense of stability through the repression of conflict and tension. By remaining committed to engaging or facing the small-scale traumas of intersubjectivity (our disappointments and frustrations; our imperfect relations with others whom we both hate and love), integrated selves better appreciate the complexity and ambivalence of life. Following Klein, I have taken to calling the mechanism by which this takes place the work of mourning. Mourning is endless—we have to do it, in Klein's words, "again and again"—because our dependency on and relationships with others put us under constant pressure of a sudden oscillation between persecution and respect, fear and empathy, hate and love.[56] The drama of the self is a drama of loss, mourning, and recovery, repeated ad infinitum.

In the figure of Orestes, Klein discovers a character that models the promise and the difficulties of life in the depressive position. Orestes is cognizant of the ambiguity of his objects of affection, sympathetic to even those he must defeat, and able to face down his mortality, partiality, and guilt through reparative acts of love. Unlike (Freud's favorite) Oedipus, who flees from his fate only to fall into it, Orestes is able to act in full awareness of the terrifying consequences, and, with a little help from Athena/Athens, he is able to bear the suffering and guilt that follows from his actions. Unlike Oedipus, who is an object of sheer horror and pity,[57] Orestes is a "good object" of identification because he overcomes paranoid-schizoid functioning and restores the plurality to his superego. Orestes models the difficulties inherent in achieving integration between internal phantasy and external reality—or between unconscious needs and desires and conscious aptitudes and actions.

Orestes first appears to the audience in the grips of an idealized fantasy of his father, Agamemnon. Because of his absence from Argos, Orestes had failed to prevent his father's murder; as a result, Orestes is persecuted by feelings of guilt, which could not be expressed or properly contained ("I was not by, my father, to mourn for your death" [8]) and which has turned round into a desire for vengeance ("Zeus, grant me vengeance for my father's murder" [16]).[58] Grief unexpressed and unworked is projected out only to be reabsorbed as persecution, which feeds a murderous passion. The idealized Agamemnon exists alongside the persecutory Clytemnestra, the "cruel, cruel all daring mother" (429–30). But there are costs to Orestes' blocked grief over Agamemnon. The idealization of his father leads him to dismiss Agamemnon's ambivalence. For instance, the memory of Orestes' sister Iphigenia, sacrificed at Aulis by her father, is seemingly repressed. As a corollary, Clytemnestra is demonized; she becomes a "deadly viper" who is "all unworthy" of her deceased husband.

Orestes, according to Klein, is suffering from a delusional state of mind characteristic of the paranoid-schizoid position. He is unable to tolerate his grief and his guilt, and he is haunted by persecutory fantasies of heralded punishment should he fail to avenge his father's death: "Apollo's oracle . . . told me to cut them down in their own fashion, turn to the bull's fury . . . He said that else I must myself pay penalty . . . and suffer much sad punishment; spoke of the angers that come out of the ground. . . . The wrath of the father comes unseen on them to drive them back from altars. None can take them in nor shelter them. Dishonored and unloved by all the man must die at last, shrunken and wasted away in painful death" (270–96).

The weight of these persecutions leads Orestes to put faith in a *passage a l'acte* that will absolve him of his guilt.[59] Yet when he has murdered Aegisthus and has turned to confront Clytemnestra the watertight distinctions he has drawn between purity and corruption, justice and evil, begin to be troubled. Clytemnestra begs for her life—"Hold, my son. Oh take pity, child, before this breast where many a time . . . you would feed" (897)—and suddenly Orestes is at a loss: "What shall I do, Pylades? Be shamed to kill my mother?" (898). This moment of doubt and deliberation may seem incidental because it only takes a brief reminder ("of the oracles . . . and sworn oaths") by Pylades to convince Orestes to proceed: "I judge that you win. Your advice is good" (903). But the meaning of the pause becomes clear through its distinction from what has come before and what will follow. Until this point in the trilogy, all violent acts have been justified by an appeal to the gods, and the agents behind the violence use such a pretext to claim blamelessness and innocence. Agamemnon, fresh from genocide at Troy, avoids guilt through his faith that the gods "in one firm cast" had given to him ("the beast of Argos," a "wild and bloody lion") the joy of conquest. Clytemnestra, astride her husband's corpse, was "made glad" by the "sacrament" of Agamemnon's blood that "spattered" her as she, "in thanks and reverence to Zeus" struck him "with this right hand that struck in the strength of righteousness" (1394–

1406). In Klein's terms, Agamemnon and Clytemnestra each suffer from a persecutory superego, which has grown increasingly malignant through repeated acts of denial.[60] Moreover, once their deeds are committed, they succumb to manic triumph that serves to seal off the possibilities of culpability and guilt. As Clytemnestra says, "You can praise or blame me as you wish; it is all one to me" (1404). Neither praise nor blame affects a manic self who is incapable of showing regret for her actions and who refuses to acknowledge their implication in the lives of others or to treat those others as anything but one-sided part objects.

Orestes breaks this cycle of denial, even if he carries forward the cycle of violence. Orestes's moment of doubt—"Hold, my son"—is where unthinking repetition yields to deliberation and public judgment. It marks the repopulation of Orestes's superego, which had been flattened under persecutory pressures and unbearable guilt.[61] The fantasized "viper" of Clytemnestra is rejoined with the image of the nurturing mother, which had been repressed in order to feed a murderous passion. We can think here of Klein's analysis of Richard, and the latter's admission that it is "difficult" with "so many kinds of parents" in his mind.[62] Orestes, unlike both Clytemnestra and Agamemnon, is able to acknowledge the competing pressures of his multiple identifications. He acts, but it is a self-conscious action in that he understands its costs and consequences. After the deed has been committed, far from absolving himself from punishment and blame, Orestes acknowledges that this "victory is soiled, and has no pride" (1017).[63] Orestes does not succumb to manic triumph, à la Agamemnon and Clytemnestra, who presume that their acts of violence will set things right once and for all. By contrast Orestes "grieve(s) for the thing done, the death, and all our race" (1017), and the chorus joins the lament: "There is no mortal man who shall turn unhurt his life's course to an end not marred. There is trouble here. There is more to come" (1018–20).

The heralded trouble, of course, soon arrives in the form of the Furies—"the mind of the past"—who appear and become the main protagonists in *The Eumenides*. Their presence reminds us that the *Oresteia* is not only the story of Orestes. In fact, most readings of the trilogy within political theory neglect the narrative arc of Orestes's microdrama and instead focus on the final scene between the Furies and Athena, which takes place only after Orestes has left the stage. As Klein would have it, however, the final agon between the Furies and Athena is a replaying of Orestes's struggle for integration. Athena/Athens joined by the Furies represents the mature superego that Orestes has already obtained by acknowledging his guilt and publicly mourning (in concert with the chorus) his loss and the brute fact of loss.

I read the ending somewhat differently than Klein. To me, the negotiation between the Furies and Athena—on the behalf of Athens—shows that Orestes's individual work of mourning is nested within Athens' democratic work of mourning. The larger social challenge of recognizing and understanding the presence of terror and trauma is both reflective and partially constitutive of the intersubjective task of integrating the self. The success of the conclusion to the trilogy is not that the Furies/Eumenides have been transformed—after all, they are still terrifying, even if they are given a less terrifying title—but that Athens has, following the example of Orestes, committed itself to seeing the "great good" that can come from the practice of working through terror and trauma.

How does Klein's interpretation of the *Oresteia* (and my modifications to it) compare with other readings of the trilogy? Richard Seaford is a strong representative for one prominent line of interpretation, as he reads the conclusion of *The Eumenides* as an origin myth of the Aeropagus court. The dangerous disorder represented by the Furies has been restrained, and their "eye for an eye" brand of *dike* has been subordinated to an open process of public adjudication. Athena's tie-breaking vote and her mollification of the Furies are, for Seaford, reminiscent of the "controlled ambiguity" inherent to ritual, a process whereby "ambiguous power is canalized . . . the negative elements separated from the positive."[64] Emphasizing the transformation of the Furies into "the kindly ones," Seaford sees the ritualistic procession at the close of the play as signifying that the trilogy's troubling dilemmas have been successfully remedied: "The questions are indeed answered and the conflicts resolved."[65] The audience would leave the festival reassured that the polis could incorporate older practices (and gods) into its new rituals and institutions.

However, it seems that Seaford overstates both the transformation of the Furies and the implications of this transformation. The Furies have been integrated into the polis, but this integration involves not merely their mutation but also that of Athens—the "terror" in their faces has been modified, but only insofar as Athens has accepted this terror and committed to honoring it. Indeed, we see that it is only after Athena has shifted her tactics from force to persuasion that her dispute with the Furies begins to soften. Instead of asking the Furies to "put away" their hatred and anger, she says, "I will bear your angers" (847). Athens has morphed into a holding environment; instead of asking the Furies to give up their claims, Athena offers to integrate them into the structure of the polis: "Do good, receive good, and be honored as the good are honored. Share our country. . . ." (165). The Furies do not seem reconciled with Athens so much as Athens has reconciled with the Furies. Moreover, the mutual reconciliation is a momentary achievement that must be repeated again and again. Even in the guise of the "Kindly Ones," should the polis ever return them to a condition of wandering and exile or neglect to honor them properly the Furies retain a right of disturbance. Lastly, the ritualistic resolution at the end of *The Eumenides* does not appear to subsume or cancel out the tragic denouement that closes the *Libation Bearers*, where the chorus and Orestes share a scene of public mourning and acknowledge that "there is trouble here . . . there is more to come." In light of Orestes's (and Athens') attainment of the depressive position, the *Eumenides*'s claim that "life will give you no regrets" seems dissonant. For that reason, the processional that follows is all the more unsettling.

If Seaford overstates the case for a ritualistic resolution of the dilemmas and conflicts of the drama, Christopher Rocco makes the opposite mistake by overstating the case for irresolvability.[66] Rocco rightly rejects a "rationalist" reading of the trilogy, one that would see in the conclusion a salutary progression "from chaos to order, darkness to light, perversion to normalcy, miscommunication to mutual understanding and reconciliation."[67] For Rocco, the ambiguities in the *Oresteia* reassert themselves throughout and upset or overturn this progressive narrative. None of the negative forces have been defeated or cancelled out; instead, they've been held momentarily to bring about (temporary) relief. For Rocco, then, instead of ritualistic closure, the trilogy models a "democratic politics of disturbance" that "problematizes the sedimentations and accretions of cultural practices and norms that constitute the self and other."[68] Aeschylus becomes the first genealogist, and his trilogy "elaborates the contours of a . . . politics of disturbance that resists the sedimented norms of a consensually achieved self and order even as it provides democratic norms against which to struggle."[69]

Rocco's account of the *Oresteia* is persuasive in its details, but it is compromised by a larger interpretive framework that sees norm and disturbance as necessarily opposed forces. Norms for Rocco exist "to struggle against," and disturbance is seemingly always a salutary process of undoing oppressive sedimentations of identity. However, a Kleinian view of precarious identity through repeated acts of mourning could not accept such a simple and rigid dichotomy between norm and disturbance. Disturbance is not something that we take *to* norms in a heroic act of theorizing; disturbance is *in* the self/polis, and the work of integrating split-off and dangerous elements through a public work of mourning requires norms of speech and action in order to exist and persist.[70] Instead of focusing on a struggle between norm and disruption, we might instead pursue and practice norms whereby we can recognize and honor the disruptions that are already there. Tragedy, like Kleinian analysis, partially fulfills this function;[71] it was the annually refreshed commitment to breaking through denial and triumph and reestablishing communication with the dangerous, the terrifying, and the unbearable.[72]

Perhaps Simon Goldhill is correct that any interpretation of the *Oresteia* that reduces its meaning to a simple message distorts the trilogy's "democratic *paideusis*" (culture or education) which emerges from the trilogy's presentation of contradictions and tensions without the possibility of a finalistic redemption.[73]

In such a nonreductionist interpretation, Orestes's microdrama of mourning would gain in importance relative to the ritualistic resolution of *The Eumenides*, and the Eumenides's claim that "life will give you no regrets" would be leavened by a depressive awareness of impurity and a commitment to the inevitable regrets accompanying our actions and inactions in the world. Klein's reading agrees with Goldhill's insofar as she emphasizes the precariousness of depressive integration heralded by Orestes's (and Athens') recognition of the Furies. The appearance of Athena/Athens, joined by the heretofore split-off Furies, as the mature superego for the city is a momentary pause—*Hold, my polis*—but the opposing votes of the Aeropagus "show that the self is not easily united, that destructive impulses drive one way, love and the capacity for reparation and compassion in other ways. Internal peace is not easily established."[74]

But can Klein speak not only to the microdramas of reconciliation inherent in interpersonal life but to the contemporary dramas of public mourning such as those described in the chapter 1? In part, Klein sheds light onto these processes because of her insight into the causes and consequences of sociopsychological defenses such as denial, splitting, idealization, and demonization, which inevitably surround scenes of transitional justice and a multitude of other political conflicts.[75] These defenses not only maintain social divisions or support acts of violence, but, as Robert Meister and others have argued, they also exist within public efforts for reconciliation and forgiveness. Klein gives us a grammar of psychological functioning that can help us to identify when the messy work of mourning is being spurned or avoided. Beyond this diagnostic contribution, however, Klein's depressive position forms the kernel of a democratic theory of public mourning that emphasizes ambivalence and discord while pursuing a fractious coherence or solidarity. Klein's theory is both tragic and moral; it provides a sober means of acknowledging the native discord and distance within the self and between self and others, and yet it also sketches out a developmental possibility with both interpersonal and broad social relevance.[76] Still, Klein herself did not develop the social implications of her theories, leaving it to others to chart this course.

The Great Dionysia as Potential Space

D. W. Winnicott wrote, "Cultural experience starts as play, and leads on to the whole area of man's inheritance. Where do we place this third life of cultural experience? I think it cannot be placed in the inner or personal psychical reality, because it is not a dream—it is a part of shared reality. But it cannot be said to be part of external reality, because it is dominated by dream."[77] At this point, it is worthwhile to step back from Klein's portrayal of the inner world and to return to the broader questions about the politics of mourning that inaugurated this project. As noted earlier, Klein misses a crucial scene of identification in her reading of the *Oresteia*—namely, the tragic audience itself—which keeps her theory from applying without modification or translation to the ongoing dramas of mourning within late-modern democracies. Surrounding the tragic performances, and both joined together and separated *by* those performances, was the democratic polis in its fractious and multiplicitous array. Contemporary dramas of reconciliation, unlike Klein's picture of the work of mourning, involve much more than the individual psyche's struggle for integration. Klein reads the drama of the *Oresteia* in terms of the subject's struggle for the depressive position, but if we are going to discuss a sociosubjective work of mourning, we will need to take this larger scene into account, lest we risk reducing the meaning of Orestes's struggle to the intimate struggles between mother and son, brother and sister. The *Oresteia* is a microdrama of family politics, but it is also a story about Athens' integration of the mind of the past. As we have seen, the Athenian willingness to "collectivize suffering" and share each other's pain—represented in and by the tragic festival—was part of a larger project of collectively sharing the burdens and responsibilities of self-governance.[78] In Athens the work of mourning was a democratic project, and democracy involved public labors of mourning.

Moving out to this broader scene of mourning requires a supplement to Klein's ideas of the depressive position, the good object, and her tragic/moral approach to psychological development. D. W. Winnicott's idea of "potential space" provides one such supplement insofar as it calls attention to the social spaces and practices that can unsettle frozen dichotomies held in place by paranoid-schizoid functioning. As discussed in chapter 1, potential spaces provide social breathing room; they are, according to Winnicott, "the space in which we are alive as human beings, as opposed to being simply reflexively reactive beings."[79] They represent occasions when the melodramatic story of good and evil can yield to a more subtle appreciation of viable others, or when the individual can discover new or repressed things about themselves and the world around them. Winnicott describes interactions within potential spaces in terms of "play," but these forms of play are a serious matter insofar as they make it possible for individuals to recognize the wholeness and complexity of self and others.[80]

Potential spaces may weaken the defenses inherent in the paranoid-schizoid position. Yet it should be emphasized that this weakening does not presume the overcoming of social conflicts. Nothing in Klein or Winnicott suggests that the macrodramas of reconciliation are reducible to the microdramas of self and other, or that "integrated" selves will not find reason to disagree or even violently clash with each other. Psychological developmental possibilities aside, collective life will still be marked by tensions and conflicts that may often tilt into pathology—which is why a training in pity, fear, and *suggnōmosunē* is an ongoing and ever-refreshed task dependent on a receptive environment. The work of public mourning supports the conditions for solidarity without consensus by effecting not only a cognitive appreciation of the difficulties and dilemmas of collective life but also by providing space for the play of an assembly of viable others that reveal and upend strategies of omnipotence, denial, and splitting. By integrating the split-off features of our subjective and social inheritance, by confronting the traumas that form the crucible of collective identity, and by accepting the imperfections of ourselves and others, we are better able to participate in political life without reducing or collapsing it into a zero-sum struggle for power. In short, the Athenians, by identifying with the nightmares of tragedy—forcing and integrating them into a shared public account—were better positioned, politically and psychologically, to turn these conflicts into occasions for constructive social action.

Oddone Longo has offered a deceptively similar interpretation of the mechanism of identification at work in tragic drama. For Longo, there are "two levels" of identification in the tragic theater. The spectator identifies simultaneously "with the dramatic characters *and* with the theatrical space."[81] The experience of witnessing/participating in the downfall of the tragic protagonist leads to an individual identification that offers "resignation" or "consolation" regarding one's own fate. Our own failings receive compensation because they resemble the protagonists'; in feeling sorry for the tragic protagonist, therefore, we are better able to feel sorry for ourselves. In addition, by identifying with the theatrical space, the audience member also comes to a "heightened consciousness" of their "determinate membership in a group." The larger identification operates as a more compelling form of compensation for suffering, as we come to see ourselves in a larger organism that absorbs our idiosyncratic sufferings and lives on. This latter identification, on Longo's reading, is an "imposition" of a fantastical communal intimacy and consensus that serves to obscure the "inevitable conflicts and cleavages" of the polis.[82] For Longo, identification is an act of displacement—the building of a false account of the collective body in order to cover the emptiness of the subject.

Longo is right to focus on the process of identification, but he does not give voice to the full range of mechanisms at work. For Klein, mourning is the means of identifying with or "integrating" the terrifying, split-off parts of the self—forces that have been excommunicated through fantasies of purity and innocence and by practices of denial. The work of mourning animates a repopulation of the superego by reopening these blocked lines of communication and emphasizing the fluidity of identifications through which we locate ourselves. When read through the experience of tragedy and the challenges of life in the democratic polis, this repopulation implies the clarification of social conflicts, such that fantastical projections are withdrawn as others evolve from persecutory or helpful part objects into whole others with whom collaborative action might be possible. Tragedy supports this process by honoring a commitment to speaking the unspeakable, which empowers a public process of working through the ambivalences within collective life. According to Goldhill, this commitment was itself reflective of a democratic norm of openness born from identifications with imperfect and failing heroes:

> Tragedy again and again takes the ideology of the city and exposes its flaws and contradictions . . . tragedy depicts the hero not as a shining example for men to follow, but as a difficult, self-obsessed and dangerous figure for whom transcendence is bought only at the cost of transgression. The Greeks, as ever, had a word for it: *es meson*, which means put "into the public domain to be contested." Democracy prides itself on its openness to questioning. Tragedy is the institution which stages this openness in its most startling fashion.[83]

Jonathan Lear has spoken of the goals of analysis in terms similar to Goldhill's reading of tragedy—as putting the analysand and his or her plight *es meson*—into a more public, open space. This publicizing process is chancy because its work is mocked and threatened by the psychological tendency toward *es anonymia*—toward namelessness. Lear attributes this process to transference, which bespeaks the "psyche's characteristic activity of creating a meaningful world in which to live . . . a world endowed with its own peculiar meanings and structures," or what Lear calls the "idiopolis."[84] Following Freud, Lear sees transference as a "battlefield" where the analyst and analysand gradually confront and unpack concentrated and isolated worlds circulating with fantasies, fears, and internal objects (partial and whole). Psychoanalytic therapy is a scene of recognition that gradually lends reality to our idiopolis by "allowing us to migrate and share the larger polis."[85] Integration by means of a shared process of working through becomes the precarious and time-consuming collision and readjustment of idiopoleis until they mutually connect and reconnect with the broader public world.

Integration implies that the fractious spheres of the idiopolis and the broader polis will remain unruly, but that this unruliness will be better and more openly acknowledged—not denied and disavowed. Moreover, these spheres will remain distinct. *Pace* Winnicott, the broader polis and the idiopolis of the psyche are intertwined but never entirely overlapping spheres. However, these spheres interact most fruitfully in a third space that Winnicott refers to as "potential space." Potential space is neither purely internal nor purely external. As Winnicott puts it, "it is not a dream," yet "it is dominated by dream."[86] Potential space has to be understood, then, as a medium in which internal and external objects shift in and out of position, as a way of testing out new possibilities in response to felt needs, anxieties, hopes, or frustrations. Potential spaces enable the creative deployment of available objects—internal and external—because these objects are loosened from the codes of dominant symbolic and political orders and susceptible to radical rearrangement.

The democratic work of mourning requires the creation and activation of potential spaces in which inclusive, dialogic encounters across entrenched lines of difference might take place. The inclusiveness of these processes not only fulfills democratic norms of equal respect but is a psychological necessity insofar as it might repopulate idiopoleis with a fractious assembly of voices and experiences. Interaction and cooperation across lines of discord, once again, are less occasions for social unity or political consensus and more opportunities for individuals and groups to mirror viable otherness and solicit a rearrangement of spaces that have caused and continue to perpetuate patterns of misrecognition.

Turning Klein's account of the intimate drama of reconciliation out into the broader sociopolitical world requires an appreciation of how aspects of social life prey on and exacerbate deep-seated anxieties and entrench sociopsychological habits of abjection, idealization, and demonization. Klein's depiction of the anxieties and defenses inherent to the paranoid-schizoid position provide crucial insight into the intersection between psychological and social life. Moreover, Klein's concept of the depressive position and the developmental account of ego integration through an endless process of mourning provide the kernel for a novel approach to the ongoing dramas of social reconciliation.[87] Klein's theory, then, explains more than she thought that it could. It not only provides a powerful interpretation of the *Oresteia* but also helps us to appreciate the full democratic meaning and importance of the tragic festival itself.

With this approach in mind, we can now return to Longo's reading of identification at the tragic festival and better see his missteps. First, the identification with the tragic hero—in this case, Orestes—does not necessarily serve to console the audience members about their own particular sufferings. Rather, the identification with Orestes puts the audience in touch with that suffering, insofar as they, like him, overcome the pathologies of denial and splitting and achieve an integration of the split-off and terrifying parts of their selves. Second, on this reading, the more crucial identification is not with the idea of the unified polis in which idiosyncratic sufferings are absorbed. Instead, following Klein, we might say that the audience identifies with the "good object" of the tragic drama itself, which in turn heralds the appearance of a broader assembly of whole objects that enrich and deepen the ego. The festival becomes an object of identification that reenfranchises the excommunicated or split-off parts of the self/polis. As Fred Alford argues, tragedy reflects the "anxieties of the audience rather than its confident truths," and the poet provides a holding environment in which those anxieties can be engaged and worked through.[88] Tragedy provides a pluralistic assembly of voices and a more realistic portrayal of the paradoxes and conflicts attendant on collective life. Democratic mourning fails or becomes maladaptive when the helpful internalized objects that mitigate pathological compromises go silent, and the external world becomes a flat space of part objects through paranoid-schizoid fantasies and fears. Tragedy facilitates democratic mourning because it provides a potential space of critique, rupture, and rearrangement, a space that makes critique possible because it also provides reassurance about the polis's strength and continuity—the paradox of the good object.[89]

Transference and Catharsis

At least two potent objections could be raised against the arguments developed earlier about tragedy's role as a good object and about the potential of reflective identification that made possible a democratic work of mourning whereby the Athenian citizens were able to confront and work through conflicts and violence by integrating the experience of trauma into their public lives. The first is that the traumas presented on stage were never directly Athenian traumas: Sophocles never brought forward a "Plague in Athens," nor did Euripides ever stage a "Sicily Expedition" or "Alcibiades." Rather, the characters were drawn from the great store of Greek legends and myth—Heracles, Philoctetes, Oedipus, and Pentheus; and the dramas were set in places that were distant from Athens geographically and culturally—Persia, Argos, or (most commonly) Thebes. On the face of it, this selection of characters and setting looks more like the avoidance of trauma (or its displacement into a safely distant other) than it is a wrestling with trauma. It is important to address this apparent limitation of the tragic genre.

The second objection that could be raised at this point is that the effect of tragic drama on its audience was not a depressive acknowledgment and acceptance of loss but the "purgation" of pity and fear (i.e., "catharsis"). The audience participated in this festival not in order to integrate these experiences of trauma into their subjective and political identities, but to ritualistically remove from their minds the polluting forces of fear and pity. Athenians went to the theater of Dionysus for the same reason that (some) people today go to horror movies: for a giddy peek at acts of transgression that provide a fleeting thrill. This objection is even more important to address than the first, because catharsis is a term that haunts psychoanalysis as surely as it does tragedy. A clearer understanding of its meaning for the Athenians will help us to give it a richer meaning in our own time.

Herodotus did record one instance of tragic performance at Athens that dealt with a trauma in the polis's immediate history. In 494 the poet Phrynichos presented a drama entitled "The Capture of Miletos" at the annual Dionysia. Miletos was a polis on the coast of Asia Minor that had been encouraged by Athens to rebel against creeping Persian influence. This encouragement had emboldened the citizens of Miletos, who had assumed that Athens might provide support should the Persians retaliate. When the retaliation came, however, Athens stood by as Miletos was razed to the ground and its population enslaved or killed. According to Herodotus, when Phrynichos staged his dramatic recreation of the events, the "whole theater burst into tears."[90] The poet was in turn fined 1,000 drachmas for "recalling to them [the Athenians] their misfortune."[91] As P. J. Wilson reads it, this story "illustrates the sensitivity of the Athenians to the boundary between tragedy and the immediate affairs of the city."[92] The genre had been chastened and disciplined: from this time forward, tragic drama avoided direct contact with the immediate traumas of the polis.[93]

As I read it, the Phrynichos incident testifies both to the incredibly powerful affects tied to grief and the inescapable relevance of transference for the work of mourning. As Freud reminds us, mourning can involve a "grave departure from the normal attitude towards life"—a "loss of interest in the outside world," an "inhibition of all activity," and a "loss of capacity to love."[94] For Freud, the work of mourning (Trauerarbeit) gradually overcomes this painful state of mind, by weaning the subject from its unrequited libidinal attachments. For Klein, the pain of grief is doubled by the fact that the loss of a loved object touches off the original traumas of painful recognition whereby our first objects came to be established in the psyche. Analysis—for both Freud and Klein—helps to reestablish the broken circuits of identification that can be shattered by grief. Yet both Freud and Klein appreciate that the success of the analytic relationship is dependent on working with/against the myriad of defenses that potentially poison this relationship and forestall the work of mourning. Above all, the analyst and analysand have to respect the "battlefield" of transference on which our psyches are perpetually encamped. Interpretations that are too direct—that do not respect or work within and against this battlefield—will provoke a "transference storm" that short-circuits the precarious tendrils of communicative action between analyst and analysand.[95]

Phrynichos—like another famous Athenian[96]—perhaps took the felicitousness of frank speech too much for granted. He did not respect the peculiar mix of immediacy and distance that makes for a communicative act—the necessary slack between self and other that allows for identification rather than incorporation. As both Freud and Klein would remind us, interpretations without affect are meaningless, but overwhelming affect can keep the interpretation from reaching across the gap that separates us on the battlefield of transference. Klein maintained the value of "very painful interpretations," but the impact of these interpretations is dependent on the relationship that precedes them—on the establishment of a potential space where the analyst can "appear alternately in the role of good and bad objects, is alternately loved and hated, admired and dreaded."[97] Such oscillations engage the transference and enable the analysand to "work through, and therefore to modify, early anxiety situations; the splitting between the good and bad figures decreases; they become more synthesized, that is to say, aggression becomes mitigated by libido."[98] Painful interpretations can become too much to bear—especially if the analyst does not offer to bear these sufferings with the analysand. In these cases, the work of mourning will slide back into the pain of grief, and the world will lose all interest for us. Only in "good-enough" circumstances will the experiences of fear and trauma become an occasion for identification and growth.[99] I argue that the tragic festival evolved into this good-enough space, which supported the civic and psychological infrastructure for democratic life at Athens. But Phrynichos did not respect the precariousness of this communicative field.

Yet what about catharsis—that most enigmatic and infamous of Aristotelian ideas? Catharsis is a term that haunts interpretations of both tragedy and psychoanalysis. For centuries, it was understood to mean purgation or ritual cleansing (Aristotle's most frequent usage of the term is in reference to bodily discharge).[100] Freud himself seems to have understood catharsis in this light when he used the term to describe his early assumptions about psychological pathologies.[101] And yet the purgation interpretation has come under increased scrutiny and is now rejected by almost all interpreters of Aristotle and Greek tragedy.[102] In its place are a variety of competing (and often overlapping) theses. Catharsis is an "intellectual clarification"[103] of fear and pity, an emotional "refinement" of dangerous affect,[104] an education in civic relations,[105] or a cognitive pleasure drawn from an aesthetic appreciation of a well-crafted plot structure.[106] Yet all of these interpretations agree that the image of catharsis as purgation is ill-fitted to the Athenian experience of tragedy. As Amelie Rorty memorably puts it, "Aristotle does not have a hydraulic or drainage ditch model of catharsis . . . a room that has been cleaned has not been emptied. . . ."[107]

Catharsis in its purgative usage is too crude for psychoanalysis as well. Freud dropped the term as he moved to the topographical and ultimately to the structural view of the psyche. Klein never used it. Yet this does not mean that a more generative understanding of catharsis cannot shed light on psychoanalytic categories (or vice versa). In fact, if, as Steven Salkever has argued, catharsis can be seen as part of tragedy's larger purpose as a treatment for "the dream of pleonexia" or avarice, then we can appreciate catharsis in terms of Kleinian mourning—marked, as the latter is, by a transition from persecutory fear to depressive anxiety, which allows for sympathetic engagement and identification with plural, whole others.[108] Salkever even interprets Aristotelian catharsis in terms similar to what I have been calling the democratic work of mourning: "Tragic catharsis . . . is part of the process of transforming a potentially good democracy . . . into one that is actually such."[109] Catharsis is an integral part of the education or cultivation of the democratic polis/soul.

Perhaps the best (or at least the most Kleinian) definition of catharsis has been provided by Simon Goldhill:

> In 1990 a production of Sophocles' *Electra*, starring Fiona Shaw, opened in Derry, Northern Ireland, during a week when eight people had been killed in sectarian violence. The production was brilliantly acted and directed, but when the performance finished something wholly out of the ordinary happened. The audience refused to leave the theatre without a discussion of what they had watched. The play is a brutal exposure of the distorting psychological traumas which a passion for revenge creates, and drama's shocking dissection of self-inflicted anguish spoke so powerfully to an Irish audience that to leave without the *catharsis of debate* proved too disturbing.[110]

In this instance, we see catharsis less as ritual than as discourse—not as the elimination or purgation of dangerous affects, but as the bringing of split-off and dangerous forces into the public realm as objects for contestation, deliberation, and rearrangement. Such acts of public making and public meaning making bespeak a commitment to communicative fluidity whereby split-off and terrifying aspects of the self/polis are not denied, repressed, or pushed out of consciousness, but actively engaged and worked through.

Ashes to Ashes: Yael Farber's *Molora*

In this chapter, I have argued that political dramas of reconciliation are intertwined and never fully separable from psychological dramas of integration and that the object relations approach of Klein and Winnicott provides a grammar for understanding the conflicts and constructive possibilities within these nested processes. Through a reading of Aeschylus's *Oresteia* and the Athenian civic festival at which it was performed, I have articulated a concept of the democratic work of mourning that promotes inclusive dialogic encounters and cooperative public action, which forms the basis for a politics of depressive agency that could clarify social conflicts surrounding traumas of misrecognition and work toward their concrete improvement. The democratic work of mourning cultivates a comfort with ambivalence through repeated encounters with viable others that challenge the omnipotent and fantastical frames of mind through which public life is often perceived. Klein's idea of the depressive position represents a kernel around which such practices might grow, even if Klein's tragic/moral account of psychological development shows their precariousness. Winnicott's idea of potential space in turn compels us to search for practices and spaces that provide social breathing room in order to mitigate the suffocating pressures of the paranoid-schizoid position. The paradoxical experience of the tragic festival, I have argued, provided this breathing room for the Athenian citizenry and can be seen as a Kleinian good object that facilitated the simultaneously difficult yet essential democratic work of mourning. The *Oresteia* embodies this paradoxical charge by refusing to resolve the tensions inherent in the life in the polis; instead, it makes these tensions and conflicts "lucid" through a "prodigious integration of life."[111]

Returning to the context of postapartheid South Africa, however, we can think more concretely about the spaces and practices that might re-create the risky or treacherous terrain represented by the Greek dramatic festival in our own (very different) age. To anticipate the arguments of chapter 5, I argue that truth and reconciliation commissions, like the tragic good object and potential space of the Athenian polis, can unsettle rigid social identities and patterns of misrecognition, by opening up spaces for social critique and depressive agency. The South African Truth and Reconciliation Commission, for instance, has often been described in terms that resonate with my depiction of the democratic work of mourning. According to James Gibson, for instance, the public truth process of the TRC was able to partially unsettle rigid habits of mind that reinforced in-group and out-group distinctions within South African society. The TRC's inclusive and participatory approach made possible measurable changes in social perspective.[112] The TRC has become an internalized object that serves to make reconciliation a "persistent" question in South Africa.[113] In the language of object relations approaches, it makes possible a civic superego qua assembly, repopulating idiopoleis in South Africa devastated by centuries of segregation and misrecognition. Moreover, and more importantly, the TRC has ramified other potential spaces in a society still torn by deep conflicts and inequalities.

The TRC has also surfaced as an object of reflection in contemporary works of South African literature and drama, allowing the questions and perplexities surrounding South African history and identity to reappear, again and again, in and beyond South Africa. One of the most compelling appearances of the TRC in contemporary South African literature is within Yael Farber's *Molora*. With *Molora*, Farber retells the story of Aeschylus's *Oresteia* within the context of postapartheid

South Africa, focusing on the tortuous relationship between the (white) Klytaemnestra and the (black) Elektra, who mourns endlessly for her murdered father and pines for the return of her brother, Orestes. Farber sticks closely to Aeschylus's trilogy, repeatedly lifting entire lines from the original text. Yet the struggle between the characters is displaced from the ancient context and filtered through the spatial imagery of South Africa's recent history. Klytaemnestra, for instance, performs the "wet-bag" method of torture on Elektra in an attempt to extract information about Orestes's whereabouts. The wet-bag technique was an infamous form of torture used by South African police against antiapartheid activists. At his amnesty hearing, security policeman Jeffrey Benzien demonstrated the procedure, and the images and video from this testimony proliferated and have come to be strongly associated with the brutality of the apartheid regime. The TRC derived much of its evocative power from such scenes, which captivated the attention of a wide swath of South African society. Farber powerfully invokes this brutal form of torture at an early point of the play, in a scene that includes the unsettling stage direction, "Suffocation should be performed longer than the audience would be comfortable with."[114]

The wet-bag scene, however, is only one of the ways in which the SATRC makes an appearance in Farber's play. Klytaemnestra and Elektra re-create the spatial framework of the TRC hearings when they initially confront each other from across two plain wooden tables beneath fluorescent lights, and the testimony tables are reused and repurposed throughout the performance. Farber also recontextualizes Aeschylus's drama by using members of the Ngqoko Cultural Group as a substitute for the Greek chorus. The Ngqoko group members perform a dissonant style of "split-tone" singing and speak exclusively in the Xhosa language throughout the performance (without translation). They provide an inharmonious presence that contrasts with Klytaemnestra (who speaks exclusively in English) and also with Elektra and Orestes (who alternately speak Xhosa and English, often repeating the same lines in each language). Farber selected the Ngqoko group to represent what she called the "weight and conscience of the community," yet even this claim carries a dissonance given the radical separation between the play's characters. Klytaemnestra, for instance, does not interact with the chorus or respond to its presence.[115]

Farber's most significant transformation of Aeschylus, however, occurs at the play's climax. At the tense moment when the revealed Orestes confronts Klytaemnestra, his hand is stayed as the chorus raises a "haunting" song that fills the performance space.[116] Claiming that he is "tired of hating," Orestes breaks down and cries that he "cannot shed more blood." He drops the axe that was held above Klytaemnestra and asks Elektra to help "rewrite this ancient end."[117] Enraged at the betrayal, Elektra picks up the axe and lunges toward Klytaemnestra. Yet before the blow can be struck the members of the chorus envelop and restrain her. Held and cradled by the chorus members, Elektra weeps uncontrollably until the slow beat of a drum begins to calm the scene. She is released, and she and Orestes stand with Klytaemnestra before the latter backs away and retakes her place at the testimony table. At that moment, the chorus members break into song and encircle Orestes and Elektra, who embrace in silent sorrow.

From amid the split-tone singing of the other chorus members, the Diviner of the chorus then steps forward and offers a ritualistic prayer that is redolent of the closing of Aeschylus's *Eumenides*. The prayer invokes the wisdom of ancestors and offers hope for "unity" between "black and white."[118] In some respects, then, the play's conclusion gives the appearance of a manic form of reconciliation, in which Ubuntu transcends fear and hatred and the fractured community restores itself through forgiveness and hope for the future. Does *Molora*, then, displace the necessity of ongoing political struggle through the performance of consensus and an image of beloved community? As with Aeschylus's *Oresteia*, there is plenty of evidence for a ritualistic reading of Farber's conclusion. Yet certain dissonant elements in the play work against this conclusion. For instance, the community/chorus embrace of Elektra and Orestes pointedly excludes Klytaemnestra. Klytaemnestra is not incorporated by the communal ritual, but neither is she shunned or expelled by the force of community reconciliation. She remains outside the circle of Ubuntu as performed by the chorus, but she is not displaced from the performance space, persisting instead at the testimony table. In this respect, her twisted pain and anguish remains—not just as a reminder of the past but as a demonstration of the ways in which the past still lingers in the present.

Klytaemnestra is also given the last words of the play, which are adapted from the lines that the chorus in *The Libation Bearers* speaks immediately before Orestes presents to them the bodies of Aegisthus and Klytaemnestra. These lines precede another dissonant moment that works against a closed or consensualist reading of the play:

> Look now—dawn is coming
> Great chains on the house are falling off.
> This house rises up,
> For too long it has lain in ash on the
> ground.[119]

By themselves, these lines seem to promise a redemptive transformation or rebirth, but this possibility is then instantly unsettled. As Klytaemnestra finishes her testimony, a fine powdery substance resembling ash begins to fall gently onto the stage. The falling ash (*Molora* is the Sesotho word for ash) directly challenges the redemptive hope that dawn will bring a rebirth of a South Africa that has "lain in ash" for "too long." The heralded dawn only brings more ash. Moreover, as Glenn Odom notes, the idea of ash in South African culture has an inescapable ambivalence. In the Xhosa language, children who are neither of the royal line nor diviners are described as *abantwana bo thuthu*, or "children of the ash heap."[120] Ashes, then, are associated not only with ancestors or the past but also with the future of the community. The house that "rises up" from the ash can be an expression of hope for a new dawn, a manic wish to reject the past, or a melancholic plaint that we are buried not only by the past but also underneath the burden of an unknown future. *Molora's* ambivalent ending matches the ambivalence of postapartheid South Africa, a country of both stark divides in social well-being and interesting democratic experiments, a society of intense violence but one that has been (for the moment) rescued from the disintegrative chaos of an all-out civil war. Democracy in South Africa, Farber implies, depends on how the mixed legacy of ash is taken up.

Instead of offering ritualistic closure, then, the end of *Molora*—like the end of Aeschylus's *Oresteia*—is a discordant rather than a harmonious one that acknowledges social difference, distance, and conflict. The play itself—like the TRC testimony tables—does not unambiguously join ex-combatants into a new, reconciled community. Instead, it both joins and separates the characters, the chorus, and the members of the audience.[121] The play shows how the TRC functions as a social good object that, if internalized, licenses both a critical examination of its own shortcomings and a broader process of mourning in which the ambivalent legacies of social trauma can be acknowledged and democratically worked through. The TRC opens up a potential space that can gather together an assembly of dissonant voices that, by the act of assembly itself, implies the possibility of a more democratic future of recognition and repair.

A SPLINTERING AND SHATTERING ACTIVITY

Truth, Reconciliation, Mourning

> **The experience of searching for truth around November 3rd has been a toxic one. To talk about race, class, police, capital and labor all at the same time is not just divisive, but is a splintering and shattering activity that can leave you standing on a lonesome precipice for a long time.**
>
> —GTRC Commissioner Muktha Jost

> **We were shattered by what we heard.**
>
> —Archbishop Desmond Tutu

> **Let's open my bulging files of tales of ordinary murder. You choose your weapons and I'll choose mine, and we'll annihilate the certainties in one another's brains.**
>
> —Rian Malan, *My Traitor's Heart*

In chapter 4, I argued that the Greek tragic festival marked a psychopolitical innovation in Athens of the fifth century BCE. The Great Dionysia provided a space within which the members of the polis could work through public traumas and intense anxieties by facing down the ambivalence of self and other and by advancing simultaneous moral and tragic narratives about the political project in which they were engaged—including an awareness of this project's fragility, contingency, contestability, and susceptibility to radical rupture. The Great Dionysia was a Kleinian good object, shaped by psychosocial defenses such as idealization and omnipotence that offered reassurance in an uncertain world, but mitigating these same defenses by containing a space for social critique and shared experiences of vulnerability and disappointment. The tragic festival was also a potential space that both joined and separated the audience members and promoted practices of communication to span the revealed distances and fissures. In this respect, the festival cultivated a form of civic agency in which power could be seen as fluid and multisourced, making the Great Dionysia as much a democratic an institution as the assembly and the law courts. The Athenian experience, I argued, can help us to think about similar practices and spaces of democratic mourning, in our time and for our own traumas.

However, the Greek festival—and the Athenian experience as a whole—can also be a site of projective identification, in which we invest our frustrated democratic desires back into a distant past in ways that distort our perception of the present. Suffering from a kind of "polis-envy," we can neglect the imperfections of the pristine object of admiration (for instance, the exclusion of women or the use of slave labor in Athens) and create outsized expectations for what we might accomplish in our own time. Therefore, this project would remain incomplete if it did not return to the place where we started in the first chapter: Greensboro, North Carolina, in the early twenty-first century and its practices and spaces of public mourning.

While the proper names used in this project—Antigone, Pericles, and Orestes—have drawn attention to the fact that political communities have long struggled with the question of public mourning, contemporary practices of mourning operate within a political context that has been shaped by recent events and by the development of novel political institutions and international norms. In particular, thinking about mourning today requires an examination of the rapid proliferation of "truth and reconciliation" processes across the world, which inspired and made possible the Greensboro Truth and Reconciliation Commission. Critical discourses of mourning and sociopolitical projects of reconciliation have developed hand in hand over the past several decades. Whether described in terms of a "justice cascade" in which human rights norms have eroded cultures of impunity surrounding state violence or seen through the lens of transitional justice or the "age of apology," the last decades of the twentieth century and the first years of the twenty-first have seen a remarkable expansion of mechanisms or procedures by which societies, in Martha Minow's words, express some level of "rejoinder to the unspeakable destruction and degradation of human beings."[1] Efforts to create a truth and reconciliation commission in Greensboro were explicitly motivated by this context of rejoinder or reconciliation and by its most prominent example—the South African TRC. Therefore, before describing in more detail the politics of mourning exemplified by the GTRC and its ripple effects in Greensboro and elsewhere, it is essential to examine the proliferating politics of reconciliation and the institutional forms that they have taken. The politics of reconciliation display all of the pathologies of the Antigonean and Periclean politics of mourning, yet they point to a space and practice amid these pathologies that represent what I am calling the democratic work of mourning.

In this chapter, I examine the nettlesome politics of reconciliation from within the framework of public mourning developed over the preceding chapters. Like many interpreters of the politics of reconciliation, I will focus primarily on the South African experience. Not only has the South African TRC been the most widely surveyed and scrutinized reconciliation process, it has also become exemplary for communities seeking an extrajudicial "rejoinder" to traumatic events in their past, such as Greensboro. South Africa's transition from apartheid rule in the 1990s is commonly seen as the paradigmatic case of how societies torn by deep and seemingly intractable conflicts can account for or in some respect come to terms with a violent past and all the ways in which the present has been shaped by that past.[2] The postamble to the South African interim constitution set the terms for this project when it declared, "For the sake of reconciliation we must forgive, but for the sake of reconstruction we dare not forget."[3] To embody the charge of reconciliation, the parties established a truth and reconciliation commission to hear victim testimony about gross human-rights violations, to undertake amnesty hearings for perpetrators who stepped forward to acknowledge their deeds, and to recommend reparative measures to be undertaken by the new government.[4]

Despite its immediate tasks of taking testimony and preparing a final report, at the heart of the TRC process was the ambivalent term "reconciliation."[5] For Desmond Tutu, the chairman of the SATRC, reconciliation implied "forgiveness," understood as both a moral and political practice of relinquishing hatred and bitterness in order that new social arrangements might grow up in a space that had previously been coded by violent resistance and struggle. This understanding of the term is best expressed in Tutu's pithy formulation, "without forgiveness, without reconciliation, we have no future."[6] The implicit framework for social reconciliation, then, was a consensualist process by which perpetrators, victims, and bystanders could mutually acknowledge an evil past as a means of entering into a more equitable and just future. Critics of the SATRC, however, find the language of reconciliation—and especially its accent on forgiveness—problematic for what it leaves behind in the rush toward this supposedly brighter future. Robert Meister, for instance, sees reconciliation as the foundation stone of a "sentimental humanitarianism," which has supplanted revolutionary, political struggles for social justice with bromides about common humanity. For Meister, the idea of reconciliation is the strongest root of the transnational human-rights discourse (and industry) that has developed in the post-1989 world, but this discourse offers little more than "mock" or manic forms of reparation that delegitimize agonistic struggles against the prevailing social order.[7]

Truth and reconciliation processes, then, seem to acutely express the pathologies attendant on the politics of mourning as described in chapters 1 through 4. Insofar as they replicate the Periclean politics of amnesic consensualism—displacing political contestation and social differences and offering nondivisive norms and social visions—they feed psychosocial defenses of denial and splitting whereby historical and enduring injustices are marginalized. Those who benefited from engrained patterns of misrecognition continue to enjoy their ill-got advantages, though they now may be joined within their gated communities by some new faces from previously disadvantaged groups.

Reconciliatory processes, then, provoke—while simultaneously delegitimizing—a resistant, Antigonean response. The (now-forsaken) project of revolutionary social justice is crossed out by the new norms of human rights and reconciliation. As Meister argues, the underlying project of truth and reconciliation is "to deconstruct revolutionary victimhood," but this leaves agonistic voices little social or political space to make claims about how the past still ramifies in present inequalities and injustices. The discourse of forgiveness marginalizes those who insist on remembering injustice, in effect replicating Creon's banishment of Antigone to her living tomb.[8] The delegitimization of revolutionary resistance in turn feeds a melancholic attachment to the lost (but unmourned) object of a struggle aimed at structural social transformation.[9] The surface consensualism of the reconciled community, then, is little more than a thin covering over a roiling subterranean conflict.

Reconciliation seems to provoke a hypomanic response, one either of over-admiration or contempt. It is either a salvific force enabling peaceful social reconstruction or an elaborate ruse designed to mollify and marginalize more critical voices. Yet as Meister acknowledges, there is ambivalence within the idea of reconciliation that makes it possible for its practice to exceed (without transcending completely) both the amnesic politics of manic consensualism and the melancholic politics of endless agonistic struggle. This inherent ambivalence of truth and reconciliation processes—their precarious perch between pathology and democratic possibility—leads to problems in how scholars and activists conceptualize the practice and discourse of reconciliation and understand its potential effects. Political theorists such as Aletta Norval emphasize the exemplarity of the TRC as a means of triggering a broadscale "aspect change" toward a democratic subjectivity.[10] Critics such as Heidi Grunebaum, however, see truth and reconciliation discourses as a neoliberal ruse that overlooks the need for state intervention into durable patterns of injustice.[11] The discourse of reconciliation, like the discourse of mourning, is a political tool (concealed in moral garb) to soothe grief rather than to change the conditions of grief's production. On Grunebaum's reading, the TRC moralized and psychologized an inherently political struggle. Once again, we seem strung between Pericles and Antigone, consensualism and agonism, with the advocates of each talking past each other while using the same words.

In this chapter, I advance a reading of truth and reconciliation processes in the terms of the democratic work of mourning as previously developed. On this reading, TRCs do not necessarily herald the appearance of a new democratic subjectivity, nor do they inevitably displace political struggles for recognition through ethical discourses of forgiveness, reconciliation, or reparation. TRCs should be better seen as a Kleinian good object—as both desirable and disappointing, and desirable in part because they disappoint manic wishes for frictionless belonging only possible among part objects. Critics of TRCs often resist the idealized picture of reconciliation implicit in voices such as Tutu's, but I argue that some measure of idealization is necessary in order for truth and reconciliation processes to cultivate or inspire potential spaces in which citizens can erode habits of denial and come to new terms of social cooperation, which is precisely the work that many of these critics, including Grunebaum, are calling on citizens to do. The inability to acknowledge the tensions at the heart of TRCs has led to problems in how reconciliation and its effects are conceptualized. In response, I argue that we should approach truth and reconciliation processes as neither salvation nor sham, but as messy, conflicted, yet novel and vital parts of the ongoing democratic work of mourning.

To make these claims, I focus in part on how truth and reconciliation processes have been repeatedly described as "shattering" or "unsettling" events. As Tutu, reflecting on his service on the SATRC, put it, "we were shattered by what we heard."[12] Halfway across the world, Muktha Jost, a commissioner on the Greensboro Truth and Reconciliation Commission, echoed Tutu when she reflected on how "the experience of searching for truth around November 3rd has been a toxic one. To talk about race, class, police, capital and labor all at the same time is not just divisive, but is a splintering and shattering activity that can leave you standing on a lonesome precipice for a long time."[13]

Klein also described loss—defined broadly as feelings of anxiety and pain resulting from frustration, suffering, or misrecognition—as a "shattering" experience.[14] For Klein, what is shattered by loss is in part the assembly of internal objects and the reassuring presence of the good object.[15] Survival in these moments requires a struggle against the "chaos inside"—the misplaced, out-of-place, or wandering objects dislodged by loss—a struggle carried out within the depressive position.[16] The external world either provides a stabilizing space for this struggle or it compounds the chaos by withholding recognition. Without a holding space that mimics—and gradually restores—the reassuring good object, loss cannot be experienced but instead is split off or manically denied. For Klein, mourning is the process by which we repair the multitude or assembly of our internal world, and this in turn enables us to acknowledge the wholeness and ambivalence of self and other in ways that mitigate persecutory forms of interaction. The ability to mourn, however, clearly hinges on the presence of reassuring objects and relationships beyond the (permeable) boundaries of the idiopolis.

In chapters 1 through 4, I have argued that Klein's theory of mourning can form the kernel of a psychopolitical theory of mourning motivated by the struggle for mutual recognition and carried out through the cultivation of potential spaces where historical and ongoing traumas of misrecognition can be acknowledged. Potential spaces make possible "depressive" forms of civic agency, in which power is relational and fluid, because they can weaken the hold of the symbolically loaded subject positions of friend/enemy. Depressive forms of agency can thereby mitigate persecutory forms of politics and the affective-cognitive defenses that feed them. There are no guarantees—mourning can always fail, and so can depressive forms of agency—and Klein's tragic theory of psychic life sensitizes us to the conflicts that will remain within and between selves. Communities marked by traumas of misrecognition, however, have much to gain from a theory and practice of the democratic work of mourning. It provides a suitably capacious framework for understanding the ambivalent promise of the discourse and practice of reconciliation, giving citizens reason for hope and space for action in places as different as Cape Town, South Africa, and Greensboro, NC.

In this chapter, I explore the work of the South African TRC in light of Klein's ideas of the good object and the work of mourning as well as Winnicott's notion of potential space. I argue that defenders and critics of the SATRC often both understate or misunderstand the democratic relevance of the event. Meister—in part because he turns to the work of Klein—has pinpointed the paradoxical nature of the discourse and practice of reconciliation, yet Meister does not go far enough with Klein or object relations psychoanalysis. Meister acknowledges that reconciliation implies not just new political relationships or institutions but also a changed psychological relationship to self and other, but he misses the opportunity to conceptualize this shift in terms of Klein's depressive position and its attendant work of mourning. This causes Meister, like so many other interpreters of the TRC, to miss the democratic ripple effects that, while still marginal and fragile, represent the most promising legacy of the event. I describe a few such effects in South Africa before returning to North Carolina in order to more fully examine the experience of the GTRC and its still-unfolding aftermath in Greensboro and beyond.

TRCs and the Work of Mourning

The steady expansion of the discourse and practice of "truth and reconciliation" over the past three decades has been nothing short of remarkable. The International Center for Transitional Justice reports that, as of 2011, over forty official truth commissions have operated on six different continents since Argentina convened the National Commission on the Disappearance of Persons in 1983.[17] Commissions, though they vary in scope and purpose (not every truth commission is a truth and *reconciliation* commission, for instance), are broadly motivated to uncover and publicize episodes of state violence, traumatic social injuries, or patterns of abuse, neglect, and marginalization. TRCs reflect the idea that it is incumbent on democratic societies (or societies that aspire to democracy) to provide an account for human rights violations and, in some instances, to make reparations or alter state policies. For many advocates, TRCs are the outgrowth of a developing transnational ethical norm or "duty to remember."[18] As Martha Minow argues, the "failure to remember" mass violations of human rights or everyday patterns of misrecognition constitutes an "ethical breach."[19]

Beyond ethical imperatives, the work of TRCs is seen as a way of reestablishing political space in the aftermath of civil conflicts or episodes of mass violence. By including narratives of exclusion or violence in public histories of communities, such processes can restore (or acknowledge for the first time) political standing for marginalized or persecuted groups. The inclusion of shameful events in public commemorations and histories, as Thomas McCarthy argues, has a "public-pedagogical significance" insofar as it allows for a more accurate view of political traditions and of the connection between historical patterns of domination and present realities.[20] The pedagogy of TRCs, however, often meets with stiff resistance. Political leadership rarely embraces a truth and reconciliation process for its own sake, which is partly why TRCs most often take place during moments of political transition. Resistance to TRCs is not restricted to official spaces, however, but often extends far into civil society. For Jürgen Habermas, this resistance stems in part from a social tendency to focus on simple stories of culpability while downplaying the broader context within which traumatic events take place. Such events therefore appear as exceptions or interruptions, even as they are inevitably shaped by a particular "historical milieu" involving the "mesh of family, local, political and intellectual traditions" that makes "us what we are and who we are today."[21] As Habermas puts it, "no one among us can escape unnoticed from this milieu"; we are all touched in a myriad of unseen ways by the habitual aspects of social and cultural life. Truth and reconciliation processes offer one means of providing this honest historical accounting. By reckoning with all the "subtle capillary ramifications" of our social milieu, we potentially mitigate the pathologies of denial and disavowal. For Habermas, this process reflects an imperative political responsibility; in his words, we "have to stand by our traditions"—including their difficult or unspeakable moments—"if we do not want to disavow ourselves."[22] Reckoning resists a "narcissistic" relationship to history that serves to split off traumas of misrecognition in the interests of a sanitized version of the past with which we can identify without guilt or cognitive dissonance. Narcissistic histories, however, elide the importance of a "suspicious gaze made wise by . . . moral catastrophe."[23]

TRCs seem well positioned to cultivate a suspicion of the historical milieu and the mesh of relationships, habits, and etiquettes that inevitably surround social traumas, in part because they can focus on broader patterns of abuse and bring heretofore-marginalized accounts into public space. As Tutu argued, one of the most significant achievements of the SATRC was "to bring events known until now only to the immediately affected communities . . . into the center of national life."[24] By virtue of their difference from trials, mechanisms of lustration, or other punitive or retributive measures, TRCs cultivate "new vocabularies of truth and justice," and "a new institutional repertoire for pursuing them."[25] In this respect, TRCs seem to embody a shift away from what Iris Marion Young called a "liability" framework of justice, in which the identification and punishment of perpetrators takes precedence over tracing the subtle ramifications of traumatic events.[26] In the context of structural injustices or patterns of misrecognition, Young argues that a "social connection" framework of justice is normatively and politically preferable because it enjoins a forward-looking process of responsibility that can only be discharged through collective action, instead of focusing on the identification of culprits or scapegoats. For all of these reasons—the public-pedagogical significance of a more difficult, painful collective history; the possibility of cultivating suspicious gazes toward identity-producing traditions and milieus; and the development of a new practice of justice in which social actors connected to traumatic events have an obligation to act—TRCs represent a significant institutional innovation in contemporary societies.

Nevertheless, there are elements within the discourse and practice of TRCs that seem to undercut the possibilities just outlined. For instance, there is a seductive tendency within truth commissions, with the South African TRC being the most notable example, toward a strong notion of reconciliation that insists on holistic ideas of social healing or resolution. The language of healing presupposes a lost level of communal oneness in need of restoration. Yet this language can obscure ongoing conflicts through false narratives of consensus or unity.[27] The emphasis on sundered unity betrays fantasies of a prelapsarian state of peace, or it projects citizens into a future in which hatred and misrecognition will merely be a bad memory—as Tutu did when he told the South African commissioners that they "were part of the cosmic movement towards unity, towards reconciliation, that has existed from the beginning of time."[28] Myths of unity—past, present, or future—however, can demonize resistance and license social amnesia. Moreover, the use of moral or spiritual categories such as evil, redemption, and reconciliation can overwhelm the importance of an in-depth understanding of social conditions that formed the context in which the violence occurred.[29] At their worst, insistent demands for forgiveness and healing can serve as a silencing tool against those who remain incapable or unwilling to forgive and forget.[30] The discourse of reconciliation, then, seems to contain an inner moral pressure that stigmatizes continued disagreements and grievances.[31] In this vein, Mahmoud Mamdani has asked whether reconciliation in South Africa involved "an embrace of evil," because "truth . . . replaced justice."[32] Placed alongside the persistent inequalities within contemporary South African society, some commentators see the "truth" of the TRC to have been, ultimately, of "little value."[33] If anything, these critics aver, the experience of the truth commission has applied a thin veneer of moral self-congratulation over a society still torn by radical disparities of wealth and health.

When TRC proponents such as Tutu insist that "revealing is healing," they betray a certain cathartic understanding of trauma and its resolution. TRCs are seen as therapeutic tools whereby victims and perpetrators can unburden or purge themselves of traumatic memories, and the witnessing nation can simultaneously undergo a collective abreaction from the pathogenic forces of social trauma.[34] This view appears to be nothing so much as an omnipotent wish to leap out of history. Even if we can see claims for healing and closure as symptoms of a defensible struggle for recognition, this struggle has to countenance the ambivalence of selves and societies that are not only interested in, or motivated by, this struggle.[35] The moral psychology on offer within truth and reconciliation processes, then, seems to trade on what Klein would see as the defenses of the paranoid-schizoid position. The past is manically separated from the present in an effort to supersede historical cruelties and traumas, and irredentist voices and claims are split off by nondivisive relational norms and expectations.[36]

Reconciliation, then, becomes not just an aspiration but also a manic wish and even a normalizing injunction. For instance, Tutu often implored those who gave testimony before the SATRC to speak the language of forgiveness, asking whether victims could forgive their persecutors or whether those who committed acts of violence could ask for forgiveness. For Sonali Chakravarti, this dynamic "hampered opportunities to cultivate trust and a greater responsiveness to the needs of citizens" because instead of "listening to anger" the members of the commission repeatedly attempted to turn anger and bitterness into forgiveness and reconciliation.[37] For Chakravarti, the privileging of forgiveness turned anger into an "individual psychological problem" instead of seeing it as a form of "political commentary."[38] Even if participants such as Tutu explicitly acknowledged that reconciliation should not be understood in terms of undoing or healing the past, or erasing social conflicts, his performance on the commission and the language of forgiveness both seemed to marginalize and delegitimize anger, conflict, difference, and disagreement.

Yet the normalizing impulses of one archbishop should not distract us from the broader significance of the TRC. For Aletta Norval, TRCs have become exemplary of a norm of civic accountability, the "idea that citizens may be called upon to account for themselves in the presence of fellow citizens."[39] By giving equal treatment to victims, the TRC staged a scene of recognition that had been impossible under the conditions of apartheid. The SATRC, then, forged "a space in which hitherto unheard voices could express themselves and articulate . . . their experiences."[40] For Norval, this space was not overcoded with forgiveness, healing, or a postpolitical erasure of conflict. Rather, the "whole process, including the debates around it, inaugurated, embodied and inspired a . . . democratic openness to contestation."[41] In other words, the TRC should not be reduced to the terms of any of its particular contributors—even the most prominent voices, such as Tutu's—because the process as a whole was inherently polyvocal and, as such, "constitutively incomplete."[42] According to Norval, the incomplete, polyvocal process of civic accountability is what provokes a democratic "aspect change"— the felt sense of distance from a former, less democratic subject position and an inspiration to be more responsive to the work of building and rebuilding a democratic tradition.[43]

However, does the aspect change on offer in truth and reconciliation change democratic subjectivities or simply change the subject? Norval argues that the inherent openness and contingency within democratic traditions requires that citizens take up agency and responsibility, but this requirement is broadly consistent with the rise of neoliberal discourse and practices. Under neoliberalism, the state necessarily retreats from its historical responsibilities to address social injustices or economic dislocations, leaving citizens to pick up the pieces themselves.[44] In this vein, Heidi Grunebaum argues that truth and reconciliation is little more than a neoliberal ruse. The "civic language of remembrance and reconciliation" has replaced the "social debt of responsibility," which facilitates neoliberal practices of responsibilization in which victims of structural forces are compelled to craft a response to their victimization.[45] Just as workers have become, under the framework of neoliberalism, "entrepreneurs"—eroding the discursive distinction but not the lived difference between bosses and employees— victims of historical injustice are rebranded as democratic agents, charged not only with fitting into the new democratic order but actively shaping that order, despite the heavy burden represented by histories of marginalization, discrimination, and violent misrecognition.

Perhaps, then, Norval's democratic openness is just an updated, subtler version of Periclean consensus, in which community norms discipline discord and police the boundaries of a certain community. Perhaps then it would be better to reject altogether the discourse and practice of reconciliation as the sources of pernicious myths of social consensus and to affirm instead the importance of contestation or "dissensus" against the chords of democratic harmony.[46] Agonist critics of the discourse and practice of reconciliation have argued that the search for common ground and the moral psychology of reconciliation (which delegitimizes continued contestation and instead elevates norms such as mutual respect) amount to an amnesia over "irresolvable" conflicts that marginalizes victims of abuse.[47] The discourse of reconciliation only seems to offer symbolic forms of reparation, and it depoliticizes ongoing struggles over the past and in the present.[48]

In turning away from the supposedly hegemonic regimes of meaning and reference offered by the TRC, however, where exactly do agonist critics turn? Grunebaum's alternative to the neoliberal "regimes of meaning and reference" on offer in the SATRC is what she refers to as "counter-memory initiatives" of "non-forgiveness."[49] As an example, Grunebaum cites the efforts of the Western Cape Action Tour Project (WECAT), organized in the late 1990s by former members of Umkhonto we Sizwe, the military wing of the African National Congress (ANC). WECAT sponsored tours of townships in which guides would point out how the landscape and layout of the area were shaped by racially motivated policies and state-enforced displacements. Instead of focusing on democratic subjectivities inaugurated by the end of apartheid, these countermemorial practices show how the legacy of apartheid continues to impact the life chances and everyday landscapes of millions of South Africans. These tours do not focus on a post-apartheid horizon but show in painstaking detail how the past has not passed.

For Grunebaum, the reclamation memory work of WECAT and other such projects insists that "collective and individual processes of mourning" must "include . . . the marking of outrage, identifying and working through internalized forms of degradation, reclaiming . . . stolen property and unrestituted land."[50] Yet this position shows clearly that Grunebaum's favored form of mourning work—indignant, resistant, and nonforgiving—is not attempting to play a different game from Norval's (or, for that matter, Tutu's). Countermemorials are trying to play the game of social consensus and democratic openness differently or better. WECAT, in fact, seems to embody Norval's notion of democratic innovation, and it trades on the same ideas of aspect change and exemplarity. Townships and slums replace the Robben Island prison and other official memorials of apartheid, but the lesson remains the same: this injustice cannot stand; *du mußt dein Leben ändern.*

Grunebaum is self-consciously *uncritical* of countermemory initiatives such as WECAT. As she puts it, "Because these practices represent new and creative interventions . . . I do not hold the counter-initiatives which I describe for the same critique" as the "TRC process."[51] Yet the TRC was itself a new and relatively creative intervention, and not just in South Africa since it has established a precedent and a model that has reached into a variety of unexpected places. Grunebaum, perhaps anxious that the subtle capillary ramifications of apartheid will fail to be traced in a rush toward Ubuntu and social harmony, has seemingly split off the "bad breast" of the TRC from the "good breast" of WECAT. The idealized object in turn cannot be criticized, and any pathologies attendant to its practice must be denied or passed over in silence.

Agonists and consensualists, then, seem to be locked in a kind of Sufi whirl, spinning between positions that are individually untenable and that mirror each other's inadequacies. Consensualism offers a normative vision of reconciliation, intending to motivate personal and political acts of forgiveness that might clear space for new relationships predicated on mutual recognition. Yet this vision risks an idealizing abstraction whereby the living ramifications of the past are split off and denied because they cannot fit into the narrative of social transformation. On the other hand, agonists such as Grunebaum challenge selective discourses of commemoration and recognition while failing to criticize their own, similarly idealized, practices of countermemory. They also neglect the ways in which such alternatives implicitly rely on a desire for recognition that has been denied by hegemonic "regimes of meaning and reference" but might be made possible by different "collective and individual processes of mourning."[52]

The South African TRC, in short, traces the edge of the various pathologies of public mourning identified in the preceding chapters. However, TRCs seem to avoid falling fully into a manic form of idealization that would effectively marginalize agonistic voices of resistance. In fact, countermemorial projects such as WECAT are actually more likely to appear in the wake of official processes such as the TRC. Because of its inherent openness traceable to its inclusive, polyvocal performance, the TRC is both a settled, organized space and a social setting that provokes experiences of unsettlement or contestation.[53] Polyvocality—if it is listened to—can mitigate romantic hope for reconciliation understood as frictionless belonging, simple unity, or easy forgiveness. Those who expect more than what Leigh Payne calls "contentious coexistence" are set up for disappointment. As Payne puts it, "those anticipating reconciliation, consensus, and an end to human rights violations will find the limited outcomes [of confessional truth processes] . . . less than satisfactory."[54]

The "unsettling" experience of contentious coexistence, however, requires a somewhat settled space supported by a commitment to coexistence. In this respect, we come back to the paradoxical idea of the good object—the exemplary entity that, because it gathers an assembly of contentious voices around itself, provides a hedge against the internal excesses of exemplarity. Seen by the light of a Kleinian theory of mourning, truth commissions can be seen as an object, a space, and a practice that, while idealized, also licenses a process of deidealization by which the ongoing conflicts and fissures of democratic societies can be clarified and made subject to social action. From this light, the discourse and practice of reconciliation is irreducible to either an amnesic consensualism or a melancholic and self-contradictory defense of dissensus. As Eric Doxtader and Fanie du Toit argue, the TRC has allowed South African citizens to "neither forsake the project of reconciliation" nor "succumb to unrealistic expectations about its power."[55] Doxtader and Du Toit, moreover, conceptualize the "question" of reconciliation as a social good object; it exists "between us" as a precedent, goad, and guide for action.[56] Viewing TRCs from the perspective of the good object helps us to see how reconciliation processes can "open up a space of contestation" even if their "telos" lies in the dangerous game of consensus.[57] The good object is desired and disappointing, necessary and problematic, moral and tragic.

Ambivalence is not an eradicable feature of TRCs. The very idea of a truth and reconciliation commission has been described as a concept "at war with itself," caught between the seemingly exclusive demands of those seeking truth and those counseling reconciliation.[58] Truth and reconciliation are not obviously mutually reinforcing concepts, either logically or politically. To the contrary, opposition to a TRC process is often linked with an anxiety that acknowledging the truth of past atrocities will make collective life impossible.[59] The public search for truth involving victim testimony can have an aggressive—if not traumatizing—aspect.[60] On the other hand, reconciliation, even understood as negative peace, is often achieved only through official declarations of amnesty whereby the agents of violence are given immunity from prosecution for crimes committed during the preceding period.[61] If reconciliation involves amnesty (from the Greek *amnestia*, meaning "oblivion"), then it is, at best, in tension with any pursuit of truth; in fact, the Greek word for truth, *aletheia*, could be literally translated as "unforgetting."

The ambivalence at the heart of TRCs, however, might constitute their greatest promise. Commissions can offer a public gathering place where marginalized or suppressed accounts of the past are recognized and integrated into accounts of collective history.[62] Truth commissions have a perhaps unique ability to not only describe particular events but to investigate and reveal broader social patterns and contexts that made traumatic events possible in the first place. Insofar as TRCs promote public reflection on violent or traumatic events in a polity's past and present, they simultaneously promote the idea that such reflection is a necessary component of democratic politics and identity. Although no report will eliminate all competing interpretations of history, they can serve, in Michael Ignatieff's phrasing, to "reduce the number of lies."[63] By countering current and often heavily distorted frames of the events, TRCs can articulate a public "universe of comprehensibility" that can serve as the basis for the mutual adjustment of competing versions of the past.[64] In weaving together different narratives of the same event, TRCs contest idealized versions of the past and present while disappointing desires for easy consensus or coexistence.

Among critics of the SATRC, Robert Meister seems the most sensitive to its inherent ambivalence. Meister echoes other TRC critics such as Grunebaum and Mamdani when he argues that the discourse of reconciliation amounts to little more than sentimental humanitarianism, which has supplanted revolutionary struggles and aspirations with moralistic bromides about forgiveness and coexistence. According to Meister, sentimental humanitarianism reflects a broader, transnational movement in the post-1989 world through which universalistic claims surrounding human rights have displaced social justice struggles. Human rights culture, as Meister reads it, is "no longer addressed to victims who would become revolutionaries but to beneficiaries who do not identify with perpetrators."[65] The SATRC embodies this shift by recasting "the central dyads of revolutionary political thought . . . as . . . ethical relations among surviving witnesses to human cruelty."[66] Yet in doing so the TRC has forsaken claims for structural reform that were at the root of decades of ANC resistance. The discourse of reconciliation substitutes ethical categories of forgiveness for political categories of injustice and therefore displaces the need for continued political struggle—for the rejection, rather than the acceptance, of the neoliberal postpolitical order.[67]

The newly developing social consensus around the idea that the apartheid past was evil, Meister argues, was purchased through a discourse of reconciliation that sees *evil as past*. The price of reconciliation is a manic amnesia/amnesty that draws a line between past and present and therefore disavows the capillary ramifications that reach across this divide. For Meister, claims that evil is past rest on practices of "mock reparation," in which the collection of victim testimony and meager reparative efforts are undertaken while efforts to make structural changes to the South African economy and society are postponed—perhaps indefinitely. Mock reparative efforts speak the language of justice but in so doing they isolate contemporary social configurations from historical patterns of misrecognition. Mock reparation also draws a line between "reconciled" and "unreconciled" victims. Unreconciled victims—who refuse to grant legitimacy to the new system—are marginalized by a discourse that looks forward, not backward; they are seen as melancholic holdouts or relics who cannot countenance the new social arrangement. Beneficiaries and "reconciled" victims, on the other hand, can step into the space of a new social order, united by their common rejection of the historical violence of apartheid. However, these fantasies of splitting only serve to deny ongoing social problems and their root in structures of misrecognition and to stigmatize ongoing critical resistance.

Once again, however, Meister is sensitive to the ambivalent or paradoxical nature of reconciliation in ways that the TRC's most vociferous critics often are not. The paradox, as Meister presents it, is that the discourse of human rights represents both a political ideology that can displace real grievances and postpone a search for social justice, *and* a plausible ethicopolitical standpoint because it acknowledges "the pathological guilt of victimhood, which stands in the way of recovery."[68] Agonistic doubts about the limits of reconciliation can ossify into a reactive pessimism that denies any actual social progress and rejects on principle the search for mechanisms of such improvement. The revolutionary project of social justice in turn becomes incorporated as a pristine object of attachment, feeding a kind of leftist melancholia.[69] For Meister, the salient question, then, is not how one can carry forward the revolutionary struggle at all costs, but how one can reconcile the legitimacy of the fight for justice with the "moral attitudes that make it possible (and legitimate) to *stop*" the fight; that is, how to create new social practices and spaces in such a way that struggles for justice can relinquish the idealized object of revolution without falling into the traps of a fantastical consensualism that agrees on past evil only by manically asserting that all evil *is past*?[70]

Meister's question sharply expresses the paradox of public mourning that has motivated this project. How can the struggle for social justice and recognition avoid the dead ends of wounded identity or melancholia, and how can social practices of responding to traumas of misrecognition avoid manic forms of denial? As previous chapters have argued, the challenge in confronting this paradox is to conceptualize mourning in ways that resist a befogged sentimentalism that obscures ongoing conflict or disagreements, but that also acknowledges the potential spaces and practices by which communities and citizens can bend social norms and narratives in a more inclusive, democratic direction. The discourse and practice of truth and reconciliation—from South Africa to Greensboro—helps to concretize these ideas.

Meister uses the work of Klein to argue that regnant discourses of human rights offer "mock" forms of reparation and that discourses of reconciliation often split victims into idealized and demonized (or "unreconciled") categories. Mock reparation and discourses of splitting serve to marginalize political struggles for justice in the name of an ethical coming-together of reconciled victims and former regretful beneficiaries. For Meister, Klein helps to unpack the cognitive-affective defenses that are intertwined with these discourses and practices of reconciliation. Yet Meister does not go far enough with Klein; according to him, Klein's account of integration cannot "provide a viable alternative to the pursuit of social justice."[71] Although this claim might be reasonable on its face, Meister does not entertain the possibility that Klein's work could form the kernel of an alternative conceptualization of the *means* and *mode* of this pursuit. Klein's ideas of the good object, the depressive position, and the ongoing work of mourning—along with Winnicott's notion of potential space—help us to make sense of the ambivalence of the discourse and practice of reconciliation in South Africa and elsewhere. Klein was not a political thinker, but we can and must, I argue, use Klein to think politically. Klein and Winnicott help us to see the promise of truth and reconciliation practices in light of the democratic work of mourning, by which their consensualist and agonistic moments are seen as simultaneous narratives that must draw on and learn from each other if the dead ends of wounded identity and amnesia are to be avoided.

Because TRCs are organized by democratic norms of facing up to violent events in a polity's history, they allow for marginalized voices and experiences to challenge dominant understandings of the past and to complicate the identities and attachments based on that history. Truth and reconciliation commissions carry many of the dangers associated with consensualist mourning rituals—the temptation to embellish the lost object, to split off its discomforting features (often in the interests of scapegoating and demonization), to aestheticize the loss and the community of the bereft, and to replace conflict in the past with a depoliticizing discourse of consensus or unity in the present. Yet because TRCs necessarily involve multiple speakers and motives and because they consist of opposed memories and accounts of the past, they are essentially ambivalent objects that provide a measure of resistance to consensualist fantasies. Like the tragic festival at Athens, TRCs can "represent the polis to itself" by displaying the fissures and conflicts within the polity's past and present. They do more than this, however, because they carve out and offer up a public space for working through these fissures.

We can see how this might work by reflecting on how a process like the SATRC—organized by ambivalent ideas such as justice, truth, and reconciliation—has provoked a searching, critical, public conversation about these terms both in South Africa and beyond. Contestation takes place not only over "justice"—coded alternately as punishment, retribution, reparation, restitution, forgiveness, cohabitation, tolerance, restoration, healing, or recognition—but over "truth" and "reconciliation" as well.[72] These terms become problematized within the process of a TRC—their various meanings are put on display as participants identify points of conflict and disagreement. Such processes seem to be inherently frustrating, yet frustration has a political value; it can help to mitigate cognitive dogmatism and create the basis for dialogue and mutual acceptance.[73] In other words, truth and reconciliation processes do not represent an inevitable script so much as a Winnicottian potential space, which can be created and re-created by its direct participants. As Pablo de Grieff argues, transitional justice processes such as TRCs enable "spaces where identities can be tried out, including the

identity of a rights claimant."[74] Just as transitional objects stretch between familiar and unfamiliar worlds, TRCs can provide liminal experiences in which individuals can take up new roles, achieve new levels of standing, and try out new
forms of agency.

Because of their inherent tensions and frustrations, truth commissions have
the potential to pry open public space for broadscale discursive contestation over
the meaning of the past and its continued presence within collective memory and
identity.[75] Episodes of contestation, in turn, can have significant ripple effects as
part of the work of cultivating depressive forms of agency and building democratic culture. These ripple effects following from the commission should be seen
as just as important as its original performance.[76] For instance, Priscilla Hayner
recalls the story of a sugar-producing concern in South Africa that was asked
to participate in the TRC's sectoral hearings on the business community. The
company undertook an internal review of its record under the apartheid regime,
which resulted in its own unexpected—and unexpectedly political—modes of
conversation: "The first meeting was very intense: we spent an hour and a half
just on what to call each other; we weren't supposed to say 'black,' which is what
the whites thought, but rather 'African.' We wanted to call those of Indian descent
'Asiatic,' but they said 'No, call us Indian.' Thus we came to understand, 'black'
included African, Indian, and coloured. We'd never talked about this before, nor
talked about the past."[77]

Such microlevel conversations and engagements are an essential part of building a democratic culture of contentious coexistence, and their potential significance should not be understated. Take, as a more impactful example, the story of
the Solms-Delta winery in the Cape region of South Africa. Mark Solms, a sixth-
generation landholder in the area, decided in the early 2000s to turn his family's
landholdings into a wine estate. The Cape region is the heart of South Africa's
$3 billion wine industry, an industry that was historically built through centuries
of slavery, indentured servitude, legal discrimination, and exploitation. In a social
climate charged by the public work of the SATRC, however, Solms decided that
his venture into winemaking should also be a venture into the history and living
present of the reverberating traumas of slavery and apartheid. Among the first
new employees on the wine estate were archaeologists, who began to excavate the
area. They quickly uncovered evidence of precolonial communities whose ways
of life had been buried by centuries of expropriation and exploitation. Joining
the archaeologists were teams of historians, who helped compile evidence of what
life had been like in the area for the generations of the slave and indentured la-
borers who had for centuries toiled the rich countryside but had reaped none of
its riches themselves.

The result of these excavations was the Van de Caab Museum at the Solms-Delta estate. The museum shows the interconnected history of the wine industry and practices of slavery and legal discrimination. The goal, as Solms put it, was to "counteract the picture-postcard view" of the Cape region and its prized industry.[78] As Solms notes, "slavery was absolutely fundamental to the working and building of all these farms, and we're still living with the consequences today . . . the owners are always rich and white, and the workers are poor and brown, and that stems from slavery."[79] Everyday objects in the area are stained by the history of enslavement—antique bell towers that compose the backdrop of so many tourist photographs, for example, rang for decades to call slaves to their daily labors—and current patterns of wealth and social well-being are the living legacies of these historical inequalities. Because of the Van de Caab Museum, however, current workers on the estate can discover and relive the history of their predecessors and ancestors. In and of itself, this is a powerful means of documenting abuses of the past and creating a space for critique about these abuses. For instance, while exploring an excavated site of the estate, a farmworker lifted a stone tool and addressed Solms for the first time: "You see, professor, my people were here before yours. How come I work for you?"[80]

In part because of the difficult questions made possible by the potential space of the Van de Caab Museum (itself licensed, at least in part, by the good object of the SATRC), the work of historical excavation and critique proved to be only the first step in an unfolding process of social rearrangement at Solms-Delta. In partnership with a neighbor, Solms secured a loan that allowed the farmworkers to purchase a one-third share in the estate. The creation of a worker-owned cooperative is itself remarkable in an industry that has just 1 percent black ownership (in a country where blacks make up 80 percent of the population) and in which workers continue to suffer from meager wages, poor housing, and low safety standards.[81] The cooperative in turn led to the establishment of the Wijn de Caab Trust, which provides estate workers with upgraded housing, health and dental benefits, a full-time social worker, and afterschool tutors. The single biggest allocation from the trust has gone toward improved educational opportunities for both adult farmworkers and their children, but other successful ventures include a vibrant music program called Music van de Caab. The music program was inaugurated through interviews with local musicians and academic research into the history of traditional Cape music styles. There are now four bands on the farm, including an eighty-person marching band. Since 2008, there has also been an annual harvest festival at which the variety of local musical styles blend together as people gather to celebrate the cultural heritage of the Cape—a heritage involving love and murder, cooperation and exploitation, stunning beauty and the ugliest forms of violence. What makes the example of the Solms-Delta estate so compelling is that the good and bad aspects of this history are expressly held together in an honest and open manner.

Each of the concrete actions undertaken by the Solms family and the estate workers is an acknowledgement of interconnectivity and an example of depressive agency. Workers are involved at all levels of production on the estate (including cultural production) and build equity from their labors. As Solms put it, the principles of shared agency stem from the awareness that "our fates are inextricably linked to each other . . . we must recognize our mutual needs and find a way they can be met."[82] What the experience of Solms-Delta shows is that the democratic work of mourning begins with, but soon must exceed, the work of memorialization. The labor of democratic mourning shows up in concrete efforts to create the conditions for mutual recognition, and the ramifying changes in the Cape region show that such efforts can gain traction in the most difficult of contexts. Obstacles to this work—external and internal—are of course legion. Most of the neighboring farms and estates in the area have shifted from an attitude of bemusement toward one of hostility. As Solms put it, "many farmers find my point of view treasonous," and Solms and his partners have received death threats.[83] Yet there was also internal resistance to collaboration and shared agency. When Solms first broached the idea of a cooperative model to the estate's workers, he was met with stiff opposition and incredulity. As he put it, "I felt the impossibility of communicating. I didn't understand it."[84] The creation of communication across stark divides reinforced by centuries of expropriation and mistrust required repeated listening sessions in which Solms and the workers slowly began to erode old patterns of interaction and create a new vocabulary of collaboration. From those sessions, Solms learned that his initial approach had been rejected as the vainglory of another white "messiah" who would "save" the poor, benighted workers.[85] The listening sessions created, then, in Winnicott's terms, a potential space in which the "messiah" owner and the "grateful" workers could slip out of their symbolically loaded subject positions and develop new forms of communication about their intertwined lives. The difficult work of building a more democratic community required that Solms acknowledge not only his family's complicity in the living legacies of slavery and apartheid, but also acknowledge his personal complicity in a subject position of the white messiah, which further entrenched distrust and made communication impossible. Playing within this space, however, enabled new relationships and forms of agency. Perhaps it is no coincidence or small matter, then, that Solms is also a psychoanalyst.

It could be argued that the Solms-Delta estate is an exceptional and marginal experience in a country still characterized by significant differences between haves and have-nots. Some might argue that it is actually less of an exemplar than a distraction from the kinds of large-scale, revolutionary projects that would be necessary to make South Africa a more equal, just, and democratic society. Yet I would argue that it is precisely because they started "small" that the worker-owners on the Solms estate have been able to build something of democratic value in their community. The efforts have focused on the "human-scale" work of building relationships and democratic culture—traditions of education, music, food, and culture that do not exclude a painful history but operate in tandem with a work of memorialization regarding that history. The South African TRC, while not often explicitly invoked by workers or Solms, is a persistent, haunting presence behind these efforts—a good object that licensed an examination of a painful history and helped to create the conditions for a series of concrete rejoinders.

As the example of the Solms-Delta winery shows, then, TRCs have the capacity to catalyze practices of social learning and civic action aimed at preventing future episodes of mass violence or interrupting entrenched patterns of misrecognition.[86] As James Gibson has shown in his studies of the SATRC, the creation of a broad, public means of accounting for the past has led to some significant shifts in social perspectives.[87] The inclusive, public, and participatory nature of the TRC was an essential aspect of this work. By including a multitude of voices and experiences, TRCs promote an inclusive form of public participation through which more citizens can imagine themselves into the process and feel "ownership" over it.[88] The decision to eschew strictly legal proceedings had the consequence of allowing ordinary South Africans to engage with the process.[89] Empirical studies have demonstrated that the public and participatory nature of the South African TRC—because it "captured the attention of ordinary people"—was what made possible large-scale perspective change within South African society.[90]

Yet it is important not to overstate or to read in purely consensualist terms the aspect changes in South Africa inaugurated by the TRC. The reconciliation heralded by such processes is less a collective form of healing or forgiveness than the possibility of ongoing interactions across social divides through which democratic norms and practices might extend and deepen their reach. As Doxtader puts it, "far less than redemption, reconciliation interrupts the historical justifications for endless conflict in the name of fostering argumentation that affords enemies an occasion to begin the task of debating how to best make history."[91] Reducible to neither an Antigonean politics of agonism nor a Periclean politics of mourning, the work of reconciliation is best approached in terms of the ongoing—and ultimately endless—democratic work of mourning.

In the next section, I return to the place where this book started—Greensboro, North Carolina, and its complex recent history of trauma and mourning—in order to continue to think concretely about what this work of mourning could look like and what it might offer to communities and citizens in their pursuit of an imperfectly perfectible democracy. Once again, the work of TRCs during their official existence is perhaps less important than the work that citizens do with the ideas of truth and reconciliation. The ripple effects of such commissions involve (unpredictable) moments of depressive agency in which social actors take up the living legacies of a traumatic past and engage in collaborative exercises of social repair. As the example of Greensboro demonstrates, these ripple effects are not limited to a wine estate in the Cape region of South Africa.

Greensboro's Truth and Reconciliation Commission: Mourning in America

Truth and reconciliation commissions have, by and large, been exceptional events in a nation's history, usually occurring during moments of political transition or at the end of periods of civil strife. But there is nothing inherent in the form that limits it to these exceptional or liminal moments. Perhaps, then, the work of these commissions should be seen less in terms of a discrete, bounded process and more in terms of a society's ongoing struggle for democratic recognition. Hence the value of Greensboro and the GTRC. As the first such commission in the United States, it has challenged the assumption that these processes are exceptional by their nature. The very appearance of a truth and reconciliation process in Greensboro usefully overturned several established myths and assumptions about such practices. It demonstrated, for instance, that the process is not restricted to transitional societies emerging from periods of intense civil conflict or war. The citizens of Greensboro moreover demonstrated—in the words of a South African TRC commissioner—that "many so-called stable democracies have a number of skeletons in their closets . . . [that] there are several historical acts of national shame [in these countries] that will not go away until the wounds are cut open and addressed."[92] Finally, as a grassroots campaign organized, financed, and operated through nonstate agencies, the GTRC demonstrated that everyday citizens and civil society groups could authorize a respected and serious examination of traumatic events in a community's past without the official sanction or support of the state.

The GTRC looked to other experiments with truth and reconciliation and relied on resources within the growing sphere of nonprofit transitional justice organizations, yet this should not detract from the unique and innovative nature of this rooted, local process. As an "unofficial truth project," the GTRC had limited powers to compel participation and no direct means of changing official policies in response to its findings.[93] Yet despite—or perhaps because of—these origins, the commission was able to heighten social awareness of racial disagreements and distrust and to contest elite-driven accounts of civil rights progress.[94] As a local-level, community-organized process, the GTRC provoked a broader reaction in the community that an official process would likely have failed to generate—especially because one of the main topics of the commission's work was the historical distrust between certain largely African American neighborhoods and public institutions in Greensboro.

Unexpectedly, the process of creating a TRC in Greensboro met with stiff resistance. Even the proposal of a commission revealed points of tensions and conflict. For example, advocacy for and resistance to the GTRC tracked largely along racial lines. This is not altogether unsurprising, given both the immediate and more-distant history of racial disparities and distrust in the South. The labor activist Si Kahn, in his testimony to the GTRC, noted that if you "scratch the surface of any issue in the South . . . you will find race."[95] As discussed in chapter 1, Greensboro has a prominent place in the history of the mid-twentieth-century struggle for civil rights because it was the site of the first widely publicized lunch-counter sit-in in February 1960. White progressives in the South often saw the city as a model for moderate race relations, as the "city of civil rights."[96] Yet while it is true, for instance, that Greensboro was the first city to announce that it would comply with the Supreme Court's desegregation order in *Brown v. Board of Education*, it was also one of the last cities in the South to actually act in accordance with federal desegregation orders.[97] Comforting illusions surrounding norms of "civility" and moderation cultivated what William Chafe has called a "progressive mystique," which obscured a violent social reality not all that different from other cities throughout the former states of the Confederacy. Moreover, the emphasis on "civil" speech often enforced silence over uncivil or traumatic realities, and the events of November 3, 1979, were no exception. As Allen Johnson, an editor of Greensboro's most widely circulated newspaper, put it, "Greensboro has trouble talking about things; Greensboro likes to talk about good stuff . . . Greensboro does not like to talk about bad stuff."[98]

The GTRC put pressure on these consensualist norms and narratives, which led to some intense moments of cognitive dissonance. The city council, for instance, voted along racial lines against official involvement. One white council member explained her vote by arguing that racial divisions no longer existed in Greensboro—apparently oblivious to the fact that the vote in which she had just participated had revealed a stark racial division among the city's official representatives.[99] The impact of this vote was profound. The racial split served to validate commission advocates' insistence that the traumas of the Greensboro

Massacre had a vibrant afterlife in the city (coated by a thick layer of denial), and it gave the process a deeper legitimacy among those community members who distrusted official institutions.[100]

As the process developed, additional fractures and fissures came into view, even within the group of TRC advocates and participants. It became apparent, for instance, that white participants often emphasized "reconciliation," whereas black supporters maintained that the purpose of the TRC was "truth."[101] The commission itself was internally divided by these competing priorities, but the GTRC's capacious mandate helped to facilitate repeated discussions about these issues both within and beyond its circle of supporters. The process of creating and operating a TRC in Greensboro, then, like the tragic festival of Athens, represented the polis to itself, complete with its most significant fractures and lines of division. Yet it also made possible painful conversations about those fractures. The fundamental ambivalence of the polity was reflected back into public space, creating a dissonance that could not be quickly or without remainder subsumed under a principle of unity. Although these divisions were certainly known by many of Greensboro's citizens, they did not typically break into broader public consciousness because they were policed by norms of civility and broadly held assumptions of slow-yet-steady progress (and because Greensboro—like many cities and communities—lacks public space and precedent for these kinds of conversations).

Norms such as civility serve a psychopolitical function. They betray an anxious fear of loss (and subsequent duty of mourning) that would arise should the idealized object prove to be implicated in a history of violent persecution or misrecognition. As Lisa Magarrell and Joya Wesley put it, opposition to the GTRC stemmed in part from the sense that "something held dear to individual and community self-image might have to be given up if a new narrative was to be told."[102] The melancholic defense of an idealized "civil" or "moderate" Greensboro, which could never be implicated in the ugly violence of the Klan or the radical agitation of the CWP, formed a subterranean layer of resistance to the work of the commission. But the life and the afterlife of the commission have shown that while something (the ideal object) had to be lost, something by that very process could also be gained (the *good* object, which is neither manically idealized nor requires a corollary process of denial and demonization). For Klein, once again, mourning only takes place insofar as part objects are relinquished and the whole object is internalized. The internalized, ambivalent object forms the kernel of an internal assembly that pushes aside the consolatory company of one-sided objects of pure hatred or unblemished love.

Democratic mourning is performed by describing not only the actual traumatic event, but also by revealing the broader cultural and political contexts that made such an event possible in the first place. By acknowledging these broader social patterns—living legacies of racial discrimination and durable patterns of poverty, police abuse, and social distrust—the GTRC problematized bystander innocence and identified sins of omission as well as commission. Once again, this process is consistent with Iris Marion Young's recommendation to shift from a liability to a social connection model of justice when dealing with complicated structural situations of injustice or misrecognition. Acknowledging a broader context for the event challenged the dominant account in Greensboro that had alienated the source of the trauma from the "real" community. This process of alienation resembles a paranoid-schizoid defense of splitting, whereby violence is attributed only to outsiders. In Greensboro, this strategy took the form of othering not only the Klan members—seen as "relics" of an earlier time—but demonizing the CWP and GAPP as "outside agitators" who had invaded the sleepy mill town only to stir up trouble.[103] Within the official civic cover story, the events of November 3 were framed as a "shootout" between two equally repugnant groups that had "nothing to do with Greensboro."[104] Mark Sills, one of the GTRC commissioners, reflected on the persistence of this myth:

> The city managed through the press to completely distance itself from the event and pretend it never happened, which is why we needed this Commission in the first place . . . I gave a talk to a church recently about our work and I had people raising their hands and saying, "we thought these were all outsiders and you're telling us that these folks had been living in this community and working in this community and were a part of this community. We've been here all of our lives and no one's ever told us this before. We thought they were all outsiders."[105]

An institution such as the GTRC goes some distance toward showing the indigenous quality of traumatic events—to show, despite their appearance as exogenous shocks, a connection to the mundane habits and patterns of behavior that surround and penetrate the life of the community.[106] The *GTRC Final Report* contained a particularly powerful example of spatial implication with an imaginative transposition of the events via racial reversal:

> Imagine for a moment that these elements [of the event] would have been racially reversed, viewed as a photographic negative. Imagine a group of demonstrators is holding a demonstration against black terrorism in the affluent white community of Irving Park. A caravan of armed black terrorists is allowed to drive unobstructed to the parade starting point, and photos are taken by the police as demonstrators are shot dead. Most of the cars are then allowed to flee the scene, unpursued,

even as they threaten neighborhood pedestrians by pointing shotguns through the windows. The defendants are tried and acquitted by an all-black jury. The first shots—fired by the blacks screaming "Shoot the Crackers!" and "Show me a Cracker with guts and I'll show you a black man with a gun!"—are described by black defense attorneys and accepted by jurors as "calming shots." Meanwhile, the city government takes steps to block citizen protest of black terrorist violence including a curfew in the white neighborhood."[107]

By staging these moments of reversal and recognition, the GTRC offered a tragic perspective on the events, making for a "difficult" history that could not be reduced to slogans about the city of civil rights.[108] In Greensboro, public testimonies during the operation of the commission, public hearings and dialogues surrounding the release of the final report, and subsequent scattered events have opened up a dialogic space within the community that did not exist before the commission began its work. By implicating citizens in a violent past, TRCs like the GTRC make it harder to appropriate this past for a flat or dogmatic version of collective identity in the present. A public process like the GTRC can break down not only a simplified account of history but also simplified accounts of group (and individual) identity based on this history, preparing the ground for dialogue across lines of conflict and tension.[109] The commission was a public object of reflection that carved out social space for conversation and contestation over the past and present of the city.

The GTRC, in Klein's terms, can be seen as a good object of identification that mitigated persecutory defenses of splitting, denial, and demonization, and challenged circuits of collective identification based on a romanticized version of history. The good object, first integrated under paranoid-schizoid pressures, later becomes the center or "focal point" of the integrated ego.[110] The integrated ego is able to bear the poignant conflict of the circulating assembly of objects within its internal and external worlds. On this basis, the integrated ego is increasingly tolerant of the complexities and unevenness of its internal and external objects and experiences.[111] The good object conjoins a search for integration and understanding with a tragic awareness of the native fractiousness and ambivalence within and between selves. The tragic and the moral coexist under the reign of the good. In similar fashion, I have been arguing that the agonistic insistence on political contestation and the dangerous game of social consensus can be brought together within an ongoing democratic work of mourning as exemplified by the GTRC. Just as some citizens in Greensboro had to give up "something dearly held," agonism and consensualism both have to relinquish the idealized objects at their core—the agonist insistence on fundamental antagonism and bottomless resistance, and the consensualist fiction of a unanimous assembly. The democratic learning represented by the GTRC shows that agonism and consensualism can and must coexist if pernicious forms of denial are to be effectively challenged and overcome. Ed Whitfield, a local activist associated with broad-based organizing in North Carolina, personally embodied this possibility of social learning and change. Although initially skeptical of the process, Whitfield came to see it as an important means of what he called "chipping away at a lie":

> I think it's all connected with a deeper story that is in the minds of most people—the kind of common narrative about what this country is about, in both its opportunities and its responsibilities. There's a narrative that I think leaves much to be desired . . . that's why truth processes strike me as being useful movements from the standpoint of what I'm concerned with, which is social justice. It's not just about telling the truth . . . it's about chipping away at a lie that I think prevents people from reaching their full potential in terms of their relationships with each other and even in terms of their growth individually as we're all out here engaged in a process of creating meaning in our lives.[112]

Truth and reconciliation commissions can reflect the ambivalence of the polity's past and present—the deeply unsettling or tragic aspects existing within any political tradition—yet they can do so in part because they are organized by aspirational norms of social coherence and democratic recognition.[113] TRCs create a holding environment in which crisscrossing interpretations of a community's values can interact and collide; they are a potential space because these interactions can lead to unpredictable outcomes and perhaps even the development of new vocabularies. In this respect, they are a different type of political space than either a protest march or a city council meeting. Instead they are more like a crossroads. A crossroads does not imply difference or unity so much as interconnection, uncertainty, and choice (or agency).

TRCs best fulfill this public-making function when they promote broad citizen engagement, facilitating the creation of an ambivalent and polyvocal narrative and allowing more citizens to imagine themselves into the process, which promotes ownership of the difficult past across a broad spectrum of the population. This does not replace agonism but places agonistic voices *es meson*—in the public for contestation. For instance, in one of the GTRC's public hearings a representative from the American Federation of Labor–Congress of Industrial Organizations, Richard Koritz, argued, "the powerless . . . cannot be reconciled to the powerful—

not without a fight." As Koritz finished his testimony, one of the commissioners thanked him for his words and noted that his (agonistic) perspective "wouldn't [have been] heard . . . were it not for this process."[114]

The GTRC created a public space for a more capacious, fractious, and less idealized version of the city's history within which more citizens could locate their experiences, even as they also were compelled by the process to reckon with other, unfamiliar experiences. For instance, the Woolworth's sit-in and similar, early civil rights–era activities had in many respects become consensual objects of attachment for Greensboro, whereas the events of November 3 were seen as aberrations to be downplayed or forgotten. By "facing shameful events honestly" and "lifting up this painful truth" about the events of November 1979, the commission hoped to more fully examine a "difficult chapter of Greensboro's history."[115] After the GTRC, the simplistic and stereotype-infused accounts of this event could not survive unchallenged. Empirical studies have correspondingly shown that, in the wake of the GTRC, elite-driven narratives of the Greensboro Massacre (for instance, the framing of the event as a "shootout") have lost some of their power.[116] The GTRC eroded the community cover story in part by revealing how the audience of a Periclean oration can *talk back* and develop a richer, more inclusive, and less amnesic story of civic life.

As a grassroots campaign involving ordinary citizens, the GTRC facilitated public engagement in ways that an official commission may not have been capable of doing—especially given levels of distrust toward public officials in the city. In this respect, the public nature of the GTRC proceedings—its visible presence in the community for a period of several years and its afterlife through follow-up public events—was just as important as the content of its final report. GTRC participants who were interviewed several years after the commission ended expressed both positive and negative assessments of the event. As one participant put it, the GTRC was "flawed but important."[117] Participants saw the open and inclusive process as "frustrating" since other participants "were saying things that I disagreed with," yet many also saw this frustration as a source of the GTRC's value because it went "beyond us."[118] Almost all of the participants viewed the commission as a moment or piece of a larger process of reconciliation or social recognition; it was a "really powerful first step" and a "first tiny step in a bigger process."[119] The democratic work of mourning, they might agree, is ongoing.

The GTRC was a multivocal civic process of working through that cannot be reduced to the terms of either agonism or consensualism. The process was framed by democratic norms and commitments that aspire to universal relevance within the (dangerous) game of consensus, but in this respect, I argue, it represents a Kleinian good object that, once internalized, licenses and creates space for public reflection on the shortcomings of those commitments. In other words, the partial idealization of the TRC is, paradoxically, what enables a salutary (and often agonistic) process of deidealization that clarifies historical and enduring social traumas. The good object, like the GTRC, is flawed but necessary. The GTRC offered a common narrative to which citizens can appeal as they address the problems of the city, but it also created a space where the contested nature of that process could be acknowledged.

Once again, Klein was not a political thinker, but we can use Klein to think politically. From this perspective the challenge is not to overcome agonistic voices of contestation but to filter them through a depressive awareness of whole object relations and the ambivalence within self, other, and world. The democratic work of mourning suggests the hope that past wrongs or traumas will be (more) openly and honestly discussed, without the presence of overwhelming bitterness or resentment, but it does not pretend that tragedies of social misrecognition can be finally surmounted or healed. To pretend so would be to fall into fantasies of omnipotence that keep us from the ongoing work of social and psychic integration. In this respect the democratic work of mourning is a commitment to addressing and working through particular traumas of misrecognition without pretending that social conflict as such can be transcended. As the *GTRC Final Report* puts it, the goal is to "take us some distance from half-truths, misunderstandings, myth, and hurtful interpretations," not to take us all the way to a beloved community.[120] The effect of these conjoined efforts in the case of Greensboro is that the traumatic event has now been situated in a political, social, and economic context such that distancing myths and defense mechanisms lose (some of) their power. The GTRC was able to erode the common narrative that had split off the Greensboro Massacre and the painful traumas of social misrecognition that formed the context in which the event took place.

Just as important, however, as the work of the Greensboro commission during its eighteen months of operation might be its democratic ripple effects within and beyond the city. Although the commission's formal recommendations have been largely neglected by city officials, the GTRC energized a variety of grassroots movements for social change in Greensboro, helped catalyze a regional alliance for racial reconciliation, and has inspired similar grassroots TRCs in places as different as Michigan and Maine. In Greensboro, multiple associations came to life through the community outreach events following the publication of the *GTRC Final Report*, including a minimum wage campaign, an affordable housing alliance, and an alternative currency project.[121] Although some of these efforts proved short-lived, the activists engaged in those associations have gone on to other efforts, including a local antiracism association.[122] None of these associations has proved to be as impactful or as long lasting as the Solms-Delta estate, but like that example they testify to the ever-present potential for public action as a rejoinder to social trauma.

Beyond the city of Greensboro, the GTRC inspired a regional Alliance for Truth and Racial Reconciliation, which provides an online gathering space for over twenty similar, local truth-gathering processes, sponsors conferences on racial reconciliation, and offers curriculum guides on race and civil rights.

The GTRC's biggest impact, however, might be far outside the former states of the Confederacy. Greensboro has become an example and a rallying cry for citizens motivated to examine and address local injustices or traumas of misrecognition. For instance, the Michigan Roundtable for Diversity and Inclusion, a nonprofit based in Detroit, organized a TRC surrounding the legacies of racial segregation and discrimination in Detroit and the surrounding metro area. In the state of Maine, the Wabanaki-State Child Welfare Truth and Reconciliation Commission was inaugurated in February 2013. The Maine commission is tasked with investigating and publicizing the historical persecution of native tribes in the area, including repeated episodes of forced relocation in which native children were taken from tribal areas to be raised in white homes. It is too early to tell what additional ripple effects such processes might inspire within these particular communities, but it is clear that the most powerful—and democratic—lesson of the GTRC is that citizens can organize around themes of truth and reconciliation in ways that can reshape the social circuitry of recognition and misrecognition. The effects of these actions are unpredictable—as is democratic action more generally speaking—but these events show how public processes of mourning can cultivate "depressive" modes of agency in which power is pluralized and extended beyond official institutions.[123]

The GTRC was a potential space that enabled communication and mediation that—while falling far short of social harmony—helped clarify the differences and fissures within and between the citizens of Greensboro. As the executive director of the GTRC, Jill Williams, argued, the process "opened up a space in which even the most privileged in town were engaged—willingly or not—in a dialogue about race and class disparities."[124] Just as within the South African example, it is these conversations and their unpredictable aftereffects that represent the greatest promise of a democratic work of mourning. The reverberations from the event are relatively faint, but clearly Greensboro has become a precedent and an opportunity for thinking about concrete practices of social recognition and repair—not only in the city but far afield.

Conclusion

The experience of Greensboro helps us to think about the democratic work of mourning as an ongoing practice within communities marked by historical and

enduring traumas of misrecognition. Learning from Greensboro, it seems crucial to cultivate political practices and spaces of mourning that invite a plurality
of voices into the process, not based on the premise that these voices can be subsumed within an all-encompassing consensus narrative of the past or on the agonistic idea that a clash of wills can yield a new hegemonic articulation through
a coalitional chain of equivalences. Public engagement on traumas of misrecognition is precarious, difficult, and unpredictable, but it can take place on the common ground created by good objects such as the GTRC. An appreciation of this
precariousness and ambivalence would emphasize that the democratic value of
the TRC process is not limited to its provision of a more complete account of the
past but extends to its ability to cultivate a capacious perspective that keeps the
essential complexity and contestability of these accounts in public view. Such an
emphasis, moreover, seems to capture best the "truth" about the TRC process—
namely, that it is not reconciliatory or redemptive in the ways often described. Instead of social closure or redemptive healing, then, perhaps we should see public
mourning processes more in the terms of the South African journalist Rian
Malan—as a process of "annihilating certainties" in order to create space and
agency through which individuals and communities can pick up the pieces and
begin again. TRCs are not magic salves for democratic problems. In fact, the experience of a TRC—and Greensboro is no exception—seems to be inherently
frustrating to almost all participants. Yet once again, perhaps this frustration or
disappointment is one of the most important features of these processes because
it can disrupt habits of projective identification, denial, and omnipotence and can
open up space for the development of new vocabularies and repertoires of
response.

It *can* do this. The conditional must be emphasized, given the simultaneous
emphasis on tragedy that must accompany an aspirational democratic morality.
The democratic work of mourning is precarious because we are always susceptible
to amnesic narratives of the past that intersect with psychological mechanisms of
self-deception. The reconciliation offered by TRCs, then, is not a terminable process of reaching unanimity or consensus. It should be viewed, rather, in the words
of GTRC Commissioner Cynthia Brown, as an interminable process of "putting
ourselves in places with people that we have disagreements with."[125] Doing so
often pulls apart or shatters our certainties and self-perceptions, yet by seeing conflict as chronic, we can discover better ways of living with it—ways that mitigate
the denial and splitting that feed a politics of demonization and paranoia.[126] The
democratic work of mourning is the search for coherence and recognition amid
ongoing disagreements and misrecognitions, carried out in part through these
disagreements. The consensualism of Pericles and the agonism of Antigone can
enliven one another under the reign of a Kleinian good object and within the

potential spaces created and re-created by citizens through a public work of mourning. This is a "splintering and shattering" activity that can be borne by a community aware of its fractures and fault lines, and the process of facing down these differences can in turn give birth to a better integrated community marked by spaces of mediation in which this fractious integration can be repeatedly formed, contested, and reformed over time.

Freud once wrote that, in order to avoid a painful process of self-examination, societies turn what is "disagreeable" into "what is untrue."[127] Yet if this were a timeless truth of social and psychic life, then we would not know the Greek experience of the Great Dionysia or, for that matter, would we have psychoanalysis itself. Moreover, if we convert Freud's acknowledgment of a deep-seated tendency into an axiom we will miss all that is promising in the experience of the Greensboro Truth and Reconciliation Commission and its afterlife in Greensboro and beyond. For the GTRC indicates the possibility that communities and citizens can face up to a difficult past amid the disagreements and conflicts in the present, without reifying those disagreements or falling into the traps of amnesia or manic reconciliation. The GTRC helps us to imagine social practices of understanding and working through misrecognition in ways that could enliven democratic practices and fulfill democratic norms.

The promise of the GTRC as a model for the democratic work of mourning is that such processes can create public space where the agonistic struggle for recognition and the civic search for consensual narratives might be combined in ways that mitigate—rather than provoke—paranoid-schizoid defenses. In the absence of their other, these discourses fashion a social world in their own image, in which disagreeable or difficult elements within their assumptions are split off and displaced onto a persecutory other. In isolation from one another, agonism and consensualism fulfill their own prophecies while leaving behind the messy work of democratic coexistence amid historical and enduring traumas of misrecognition. The democratic work of mourning, by contrast, holds together these disparate narratives in ways that can provoke depressive modes of agency by which citizens discover their power in concert with others—seeing those others as complex objects with whom a contentious coexistence is possible.[128] There are no guarantees of success, and the democratic work of mourning—like the integration of the Kleinian ego—will have to happen repeatedly. Yet the GTRC gives us both reasons for hope and room for action. It is precisely the kind of (good) object and (potential) space from which we might begin, again and again, to democratically mourn in the name of democracy.

BLACK LIVES MATTER AND THE DEMOCRATIC WORK OF MOURNING

The past is a life sentence, a blunt instrument aimed at tomorrow.

—Claudia Rankine, *Citizen*

Democracy is coming to the U.S.A. . . . It's coming to America first, the cradle of the best and of the worst.

—Leonard Cohen, *Democracy*

If Freddie Gray spent any time during his twenty-five years imagining his own funeral, it seems unlikely that he could have predicted the hours-long event that took place on April 27, 2015, at the New Shiloh Baptist Church in West Baltimore. Thousands of mourners were in attendance, including a U.S. cabinet secretary, a member of the U.S. House of Representatives, and multiple civil rights movement icons—not to mention a dozen or so television crews and even more newspaper and magazine journalists. The funeral took place just over a week after Gray's death as a result of injuries sustained while being arrested and detained by six officers of the Baltimore Police Department. He had been chased by several of those officers for "catching the eye" of one of them and running away. Somewhere between the moment when he was accosted, roughly loaded into a police van, and taken to the police station, he suffered a significant, "high-energy" injury to his neck and spine, and he died a week later.[1] Before that day, Freddie Gray was a relatively anonymous young man living in a neighborhood far outside the public consciousness of American society. Yet at his funeral on April 27 he was being described as a civil rights martyr by none other than Jesse Jackson.

Freddie Gray emerged from social anonymity only through social erasure. For Gray's family, friends, and neighbors, the loss was specific and concrete, and the grief was particular, but Gray's death was soon connected to the more diffuse public mourning taking place under the name of the emergent "Black Lives Matter" social movement. Freddie Gray's name and story quickly took on a larger political resonance next to those of Eric Garner, Michael Brown, Tamir Rice, Jamar Clark, and Trayvon Martin, which explains the media attention given to Gray's funeral. It also goes some distance to explaining why Gray's death provoked weeks of protests in Baltimore and elsewhere.

Voices at these protests expressed a range of frustrations. As one longtime resident put it, the marches, direct actions, and public gatherings emerged from "years and years of taking shit [and] now we're at a point where people just don't give a fuck."[2] Another protester claimed that "change" and "justice" could only take place through "revolution," although it was unclear in what name and by what means such a revolution might occur.[3] A local gang member insisted, "There is only so far that you can push people into a corner . . . we're frustrated and that's why we're out there on the streets."[4] Such voices in Baltimore echoed those heard in similar protests following the lack of grand jury indictments in the cases of Michael Brown and Eric Garner. As one resident of Staten Island put it during a December 2014 protest, "I thought there would be an indictment. I don't know what to do . . . I don't know what people can do, other than come to protests."[5] These views express not only specific grievances tied to the experiences of Freddie Gray or Eric Garner, they also express a generalized suspicion that the spaces and practices of political engagement are insufficient and untrusted, that there are few options for pursuing redress for grievances, and that the formal institutions of law and justice are normatively bankrupt or part of the problem—leading not only to uncertainty and frustration but cynicism and detachment.[6] One detects within these scenes of public grieving a genuine sense of impasse: a shared sentiment of injustice, disrespect, or misrecognition alongside a palpable confusion over how best to respond to such injustices.

The preceding chapters have argued that the intimate connection between politics and mourning reflects a broader, ongoing struggle for social recognition that takes place amid living legacies of violent misrecognition. Just as with the Greensboro Massacre of 1979 and its long aftermath, the recent Black Lives Matter protests reflect the complex politics of grief and grievance. In this afterword, I want to draw together the recent events in Baltimore, Staten Island, and Ferguson, and the larger Black Lives Matter social movement with the treatment given earlier of the Greensboro Massacre and the GTRC. For the poet Claudia Rankine, the Black Lives Matter protests represent not simply an effort to mourn the specific deaths of Freddie Gray, Trayvon Martin, or Michael Brown but an "attempt to keep mourning an open dynamic in our culture."[7] If this is the case, then such protests might be both illuminated and informed by the recent experiences in Greensboro and by the idea of a democratic work of mourning. As I have argued throughout in this work, the challenge of the democratic work of mourning is to locate and cultivate spaces and norms of public interaction that might erode some of the projections and pathologies attendant to ongoing relations of misrecognition. It is only from these spaces that feelings of impasse and despair might begin to gradually yield to a sense of democratic agency. The fact that such work is un-certain of success and excruciatingly difficult should not detract from its impor-tance, but only underline its urgency. However, the viability and desirability of a democratic practice of mourning hinges on a larger question—namely, whether the norms and ideals of democratic citizenship can still speak to the present mo-ment of social discontent and despair, a question to which I now turn.

Freddie Gray, Citizen?

In media accounts of his death and life, Freddie Gray was referred to in a variety of ways—identified by his race, his rap sheet, his place of residence (the Sandtown-Winchester neighborhood in West Baltimore), or his personality traits. Gray has also now been identified as a martyr and as a symbol (of social disrepair, or of mistrust between poor communities and the police force employed to protect them). Yet few commentators referred to Gray as "a democratic citizen," and this omission is revealing. By "citizen" here, I mean less the legal relationship of civic status and more the moral idea of citizenship as, in the terms of Jeffrey Stout, those "individuals who have a share of responsibility for the arrangements and policies undertaken by a republic."[8] Citizenship in this sense is predicated on both an in-ternalized feeling of agency and social recognition of this agency. Citizens are those who see themselves as entitled, in Stout's words, to "having a say" in their society, but they also must have this feeling of civic entitlement acknowledged by others around them. "To be a citizen," Stout argues, "is to be recognized by others as such."[9] If this recognition is withheld, then the internalized sense of civic en-titlement is under threat, and although the power of democratic citizens can only be actualized through association—the organized gathering of individual capacity—the feeling that such efforts are both possible and potentially impact-ful rests on a belief of ordinary citizens that they have the capacity to act and to effect change in their communities, through associational life itself or in concert with formal authorities and institutions. If citizenship as an internalized and so-cially recognized sense of generalized agency and capacity evaporates—if the moral idea of citizenship is no longer a widely held assumption or a viable standard—then democratic societies become more open to domination by per-petually organized and self-interested elites.

Citizenship is often overidentified with the idea of "rights," yet as Axel Honneth has argued, "rights" should themselves be understood as artifacts of social rec-ognition. To possess political rights is to be recognized as "being able to raise socially accepted claims"; they are a "way of making clear to oneself that one is respected by everyone else."[10] The struggle for rights is therefore a struggle over such "depersonalized symbols of social respect."[11] Respect, for Honneth, is not a question of empathy or sympathy; the question of citizenship is not necessarily linked to feelings of affection or social esteem. However, the absence of respect or the destruction of its symbols inevitably has psychological and interpersonal significance.[12] In other words, impersonal or abstract attributions of membership and civic capacity have deeply personal stakes. The implication is that the socio-political struggle for recognition as a citizen is an important aspect of an individual's psychological development within self-described democratic societies. If the denial of recognition in such contexts can lead to a "crippling feeling of social shame," then feelings of self-respect, agency, and capacity are necessarily tied to positive, mutualistic relations of recognition.[13] The ideals of democratic societies prescribe norms of generalized political capacity. Therefore, to not be recognized (by one's self or by others) as an actual or potential participant within collective life is to suffer a social injury, which can only be repaired through a shift in norms and patterns of civic efficacy and agency. In this respect, the language of citizenship, or of rights—while symbolically important—is by itself insufficient. To think of oneself or to be described as a citizen without the supporting circuitry of social recognition in place is to delude oneself or to be deluded. Appropriate institutions of mutual recognition, in Honneth's words, "are needed to promote the actual realization of individuals' reflexive freedom."[14]

In democratic societies, citizenship is what Sheldon Wolin refers to as a "birthright." Citizenship is a birthright because it is something that precedes our arrival and exists *in potentia* as an object of investment and attachment. To assert the birthright of citizenship is to assume what Wolin calls our "politicalness," or our "capacity for developing into beings who know and value what it means to participate in and be responsible for the care and improvement of our common and collective life."[15] A birthright is an inheritance that has to be claimed; it does not arrive as a gift but has to be made consciously our own. As Wolin puts it, "it is something to which we are entitled . . . but we have to . . . mix it with our mental and physical labor, undertake risks on its behalf, and even make sacrifices."[16] The "we" here, though, has to be read in the intersubjective and social terms of recognition as defined by Honneth and Stout. The political birthright of citizenship requires a collective labor in order to be claimed and carried forward; it is not something that can be individually assumed in isolation from participatory norms, settings, and culture. Citizenship, for Wolin, lives within the "ebb-and-flow of everyday activities, responsibilities and relationships."[17] Ordinary, daily interactions, expectations, and modes of comportment either reinforce a circuitry of civic recognition or they do not, and civic capacity cannot stand for long in the absence of these intersecting lines of support.

With this normative understanding of citizenship as a backdrop, perhaps it is unsurprising that the language of democratic citizenship has been absent from the accounts of Freddie Gray's life and death. There is no strong indication that Gray himself would have seen his life in terms of citizenship as defined by Stout, Honneth, or Wolin. Statistically speaking, the neighborhood in which he lived—Sandtown-Winchester—was, during Gray's lifetime, civically impoverished relative to even its surrounding neighborhoods. In 2008, Sandtown-Winchester had twice the unemployment, poverty, and homicide rates of Baltimore as a whole, four times the rate of lead paint violations, and significant educational gaps among both the youth and adult populations.[18] The structural economic, social, and political deficiencies in neighborhoods such as Gray's amount to what Darryl Pinckney calls the "holy trinity of disenfranchisement and dispossession."[19] In this respect, Gray's story reflects the experience of "millions of Americans who feel that they have no vested stake in this society."[20] In fact, as a convicted felon who at the time of his death had two pending drug charges against him, Gray would have been barred from the basic act of voting under Maryland's laws of felony disenfranchisement, which require offenders to complete their full sentences, including parole and probation, before they can reobtain the right to vote.[21] To be denied this most basic democratic act is already to fall outside the circuitry of civic recognition that Stout and Honneth describe. In such a situation, the language of citizenship might do little more than provide ideological cover for a situation in which *disenfranchisement* is the norm.

Politically debilitating patterns of interaction, settings, and norms in the present emerge from particular histories, and these histories in the case of Freddie Gray's neighborhood are intertwined with racial prejudice and discrimination written into America's legal tradition and expressed in a variety of more or less violent ways. Politicalness, in other words, is not the only birthright in American democracy. As Ta-Nehisi Coates has argued, American's political birthright is also marked by the "right to break the black body," or, as he puts it, "In America it is traditional to destroy the black body—it is heritage."[22] This heritage was expressed not only throughout the brutal centuries of forced labor and rape under slavery, but through a reign of terrorist violence in the former states of the Confederacy during which nearly four thousand African Americans were lynched between the years of 1880 and 1940.[23] In the latter half of the twentieth century, this heritage has found expression through more subtle means in racially coded housing, drug, police, and prison policies.[24] For Coates, then, incidents of police brutality or policies with differential racial impact should not be viewed primarily as violations of democratic norms. Instead, we should see these incidents as the expression of American democracy. Historically in America, norms of citizenship and whiteness have collapsed together in ways that have justified the violent exclusion of racialized others. Current criminal justice policies and the abuses of black bodies that have followed from these policies are not therefore deviations from but the "product of democratic will."[25]

Moreover, following from the normative concept of citizenship as expressed by Stout, Honneth, and Wolin, it is clear that the effects of a violent heritage of exclusion show up not only within stark experiences of disenfranchisement such as those experienced by convicted felons but also appear within everyday moments of disrespect or misrecognition. Such "microaggressions"—everyday slights or instances of disregard—reflect and carry forward historical patterns of exclusion while serving as more subtle reminders of the unconscious boundaries of political and social membership. Claudia Rankine's lyric *Citizen* collects a numbing variety of these moments: mundane interactions with friends, cash register attendants, real estate agents, strangers in line and service professionals. As personally painful as these moments might be (or even if they were *not* experienced as painful), they also contain civic or political content. If citizenship, as Wolin sees it, exists in the ebb-and-flow of everyday activities, then everyday experiences of disrespect and misrecognition carry an implicit message: *you are not a citizen.* Or, as Rankine puts it, "*this* is how you are a citizen . . . let it go. Move on."[26] Not to linger on these slights is an implicit clause within the contract of democratic citizenship, a clause that reinforces a circuitry of disrespect and disenfranchisement and that, in so doing, makes a mockery of stated democratic ideals.

If this view is accurate, then it should be asked what value the idea of citizenship could possibly have had for Freddie Gray, or what it might ever mean for the millions in similar social situations. As critical race scholars have shown, norms of "good" citizenship have often shielded assertions of racial, gender, and class privilege, which implies that individuals such as Gray have been structurally barred from such forms of recognition. This systemic exclusion also implies, however, that the very forms of civic recognition are an instantiation of privilege rather than a means of undoing or challenging it.[27] To be a "good citizen" is precisely to accede to norms of whiteness, regardless of the shade of one's skin color. If this is the case, then an attachment to norms or ideals of democratic citizenship might be little more than what Lauren Berlant calls "cruel optimism."[28] Berlant defines cruel optimism as a "desire [for] something that is actually an obstacle to your flourishing."[29] Akin to an addiction, cruel optimism is a structure of motivation and desire that locks the subject in pursuit of an object that cannot—and can *never*—fulfill the subject's actual desires. The subject, tragically, thinks that if they just try harder, or find different or novel ways to approach the object, that "this time" their disappointment will end and that they will achieve the long-awaited goal.[30] Cruel optimism reflects and does nothing to address a sense of social stuckness or impasse; instead, it simply returns us to a fantastical object of desire that is itself part of the problem. Given its history of intimate association with racial privilege and exclusion, perhaps democratic citizenship is a form of cruel optimism. Democratic optimism is cruel because it keeps individuals circling around the fantasy of generalized agency when the structural conditions of contemporary life radically preclude the realization of this dream.

One answer to this vexed situation, then, would be to reject the "birthright" of democratic citizenship as a fixed star of political aspiration and to detach political desires from the system of broken promises and bad dreams altogether (Rankine: "let it go"). By this light, the fact that millions of individuals in the American context have no vested stake in democratic society might be viewed as less a symptom of social pathology than as a necessary step toward significant rupture—the heralding of what Berlant calls an dramatic "event" that "shocks being into a radically open situation" of "ethical sociality."[31] Systems of privilege and structural injustice might only be overturned if we forsake the self-defeating fantasy of democratic citizenship, an impossible and cruel vision that perpetually postpones the possibility of radical change.

On this reading, generalized feelings of disenfranchisement are not primarily a symptom of civic distress but represent instead a powerful opportunity to alter dominant systems of political and social life. For Jodi Dean, the key to mobilizing such discontent is to understand and maintain the difference between democratic "drive" and the "desire" for actual equality (which Dean defines in terms of the communist idea of "from each according to their abilities, to each according to their needs").[32] Borrowing this distinction from Jacques Lacan, Dean argues that appeals to democracy take the structure of "drive," which "circle(s) around and around" the object of desire, and which receives small charges of enjoyment (*jouissance*) from doing so. We never reach our stated ends, but the small electric jolts of joy we get by our near misses distract and satisfy us just enough. Drive reflects "our stuckness in a circuit"—a ceding of our desire for the realization of our goal.[33] A will toward substantive equality gets splintered into a variety of microscopic democratic projects and dissipated through rhetorical bromides of citizenship. For Dean, the answer is not to fetishize or romanticize democracy, but to see through the fantasy of democracy as a goal or end in itself. We can do so by occupying "antagonism" as a "constitutive feature of human experience," in order to press our demands for a significant break or rupture from a system that fails on its own terms yet whose failure is perversely taken as the normal workings of that system.[34] Calls for democracy—more democracy, better democracy—are in actuality calls "for what is already there," when what is desperately needed is rupture, not continuity.[35] It follows, then, that the Freddie Grays of the world should not be distracted or taunted by the optimistic fantasy of democratic citizenship, but shaped instead into a collective mass of militant resistance. In other words, to quote Joe Hill, the activist leader of International Workers of the World, "Don't mourn—organize!"[36]

We arrive, then, at a critical juncture. Whether it is worthwhile to maintain mourning as an "open dynamic" within a culture aspiring toward democracy depends on whether the terms of democratic citizenship might still apply to our current condition or whether they represent forms of cruel optimism and the unjust postponement of radical change. The democratic promise of Black Lives Matter or similar undertakings of public mourning hinges on whether democracy itself actually has any promise—whether it heralds the realization of substantive equality, or whether its ideals are mainly cover for privileges that dissipate political desire and keep us stuck in a circuitry of misrecognition. The heritage of American democracy is undeniably ambivalent; it is replete with murder *and* repair, brutality *and* sacrifice, oppression *and* emancipation—and neither side of these terms can fully cancel out the other. Norms of citizenship have often been a cover for privilege and a means of reinforcing that privilege, yet they have also served as the occasion for overcoming exclusion and challenging unjust inequalities. In order to take some measure of this ambivalence, I turn in the following section to a closer reading of Rankine's *Citizen* and Coates's *Between the World and Me*. In the context of the contemporary politics of race, Rankine and Coates each reflect eloquently on the sense of ambivalence attendant on the terms of American identity and the ideals of democratic citizenship, and while neither author resolves (or even seeks to resolve) this ambivalence, they provide a structure of encouragement for efforts at social repair and a means of understanding the cruelty within democratic optimism (and within *all* objects of attachment) without forsaking that optimism for some mysterious ruptural event. Connecting the work of Rankine and Coates to that of Klein and Honneth and reading the Black Lives Matter protests through the perspective of theories of mutualistic civic interaction can in turn allow us to identify means by which the generalized feeling of social impasse might be patiently and persistently worn away.

"A Conscious Citizen of this Terrible and Beautiful World"

Ta-Nehisi Coates's *Between the World and Me* is written in the form of a letter to his son, but as a public rumination on histories of racial discrimination and disembodiment, its educative purpose is at the same time both intimate and social. The book identifies and works through the complexities of attachment to democratic ideals, while reflecting on the uneven experiences of recognition implied by those ideals. Coates is asking his audience to wrestle with the fact that norms and practices of American citizenship are deeply rooted in histories of exclusion whose lasting effects are still acutely felt. As he puts it, the question is "not whether Lincoln truly meant 'government of the people' but what our country has, throughout its history, taken the political term 'people' to actually mean."[37] As Coates writes to his son, "in 1863 [the people] did not mean your mother or your grandmother, it did not mean you and me."[38] These were not, of course, innocent omissions. The exclusion and violation of black bodies was not an unintended side effect of American democracy but "expressions" of democratic will.[39] The "Dream" of American democracy, therefore, historically and quite literally "rests on our backs, the bedding made from our bodies."[40] Moreover, current expressions of democratic will continue to have a differential racial impact even if they operate under a deracialized language of "fighting crime" or "safe communities." Those who speak this language are those whom Coates calls "Dreamers," who both experience and expect the security of social legibility and recognition but who live in denial of the radical insecurity of those excluded from this reality. Denial over this history and present is not the same crime as legal discrimination, but it is a necessary part of the same crime. The burden of the violent racial past that has not passed is intensified because it is disavowed. Civic forgetfulness or amnesia over America's racial history and present is "habit . . . another necessary component of the Dream."[41] Dreamers disavow this history through myths of reinvention and rebirth ("morning in America"), but doing so only obscures the fact that their security is purchased at the cost of continual exclusion, marginalization, and misrecognition. American citizenship, Coates argues, is rooted in fantasies of innocence and the projective identification of various black bodies that remain outside the people, such as Freddie Gray, Michael Brown, or Eric Garner—who are described as criminals, demons, or nuisances but never identified *as citizens*. The ideals of citizenship are used as cover, in fact, for these crimes of misrecognition; they are myths that form part of a larger "apparatus urging us to accept American innocence at face value and not to inquire too much."[42]

Despite all this, Coates does not find reason to relinquish the ideals of American democracy. While he insists that the "secret meaning of equality" has always been racial *inequality*—the right to "break the black body" in order to keep whole and secure the "Dream"—this secret meaning is not the only meaning of this ideal. Running through Coates's book is a conviction that the norms of equality, respect, and recognition contained within the ideals of democratic citizenship also represent a birthright to which everyone is entitled, a conviction articulated in the face of and despite the obvious living legacies of brutality, inequality, and misrecognition that limn the democratic tradition. American democracy's complex history of racial disrespect and disavowal does not, for Coates, defeat democratic aspirations. Instead, Coates assumes that these ideals have a motivating structure that exceeds their use as ideological cudgels. "Perhaps," he writes, on the basis of these "national hopes," the Dreamers "will truly become American and create a nobler basis for their myths."[43]

Coates, however, does not believe in any easy kind of civic reconciliation, nor does he have faith in the inevitable march of progress. The moral arc of the universe does not bend toward justice for Coates; it is "bent towards chaos."[44] As such he does not offer panaceas for despair, nor does he even downplay reasons for despair. Coates seems to have been compelled to write the book in part because of his son's reaction to the news that the killer of Michael Brown would not be indicted. Coates's son had stayed up late in order to hear the announcement of an indictment, and "when instead it was announced that there was none you said, 'I've got to go.'"[45] His son's response on hearing the decision of the Ferguson grand jury—"I've got to go"—is repeated later in the book (it is the only time that Coates's son is quoted directly), and it operates as a kind of standing challenge to which the entire book can be seen as a response, or as an elaboration of the *initial* response that Coates gave that night:

> You said 'I've got to go,' and you went into your room, and I heard you crying. I came in five minutes after and I didn't hug you, and I didn't comfort you, because I thought it would be wrong to comfort you. I did not tell you that it would be okay. . . . What I told you is what your grandparents tried to tell me: that this is your country, that this is your world, and that this is your body, and you must find some way to live within the all of it.[46]

In effect, Coates's response to his son is an affirmation of what Berlant might call impasse. "This is your country," has a double-edged meaning in the context of the Michael Brown case. On the one hand, it is a brutal reminder of the seemingly unaccountable violence to which black bodies are especially vulnerable (*this is your country*); on the other hand, it is a claim of membership, an assurance of belonging (this is *your* country). It is a bold assurance of citizenship that is not meant to be reassuring. Instead, Coates implies that an acknowledgment of the *lack* of reassurance is the best means of awakening from the Dream of security and innocence. As Coates puts it, "I did not tell you that it would be okay, because I have never believed that it would be okay."[47] Instead of feeding dreams of escape ("I've got to go"), Coates's double-edged assurance serves to underscore intolerable realities while it undermines a fantastical flight from these realities. It is only by acknowledging this discomforting situation that Coates's son might fulfill the author's parental aspiration: "I would not have you descend into your own dream. I would have you be a conscious citizen of this terrible and beautiful world."[48]

Citizenship, Coates implies, requires a consciousness of the ambivalence—the terror and beauty—of our democratic heritage. This consciousness is reminiscent of Wolin's arguments about the birthright of politicalness. For Wolin, this birthright is replete with "ambiguous historical moments," and in order to deal with these ambiguities "we need an interpretative mode of understanding that is able to reconnect past and present experience."[49] Democratic citizenship requires practices and settings through which citizens can "interpret the present experience of the collectivity, reconnect it to past symbols, and carry it forward."[50] Coates and Wolin seem to be calling for a kind of tragic, democratic consciousness, an emergence from the self-imposed immaturity of the "Dream" and from the fantasies of innocence or rebirth contained therein. As Coates puts it, "My education was a . . . process that would not award me any own especial Dream but would break all the dreams, all the comforting myths of Africa, of America, and everywhere, and would leave me only with humanity in all its terribleness. And there was so much terrible out there, even among us. You must understand this."[51]

Coates's formulation here echoes strongly with Melanie Klein's concept of the depressive position and the work of mourning. For Klein, the depressive position was the setting from which the ambivalence of self and other is acknowledged and conflicts within the world and self are faced with a greater degree of honesty and understanding. By internalizing whole, ambivalent objects ("there was so much terrible out there, even among us") and by coming to know and tolerate the ambivalence of the self ("Here was the lesson: I was not an innocent"),[52] we can better face up to the ambivalence of the terrible, beautiful world. Doing so creates the possibility of an appreciation for what Eve Sedgwick calls the "middle ranges of agency—the notion that you can be relatively empowered or disempowered without annihilating someone else or being annihilated."[53] On the other hand, the "Dreamers" are caught within a paranoid-schizoid fantasy of innocence and denial, pushed and pulled by intense anxieties of vulnerability that cannot be expressed and must be warded off through more or less violent means. Coates's prescribed response to the Dreamers (and we are *all*, Coates argues, potential Dreamers) is "to awaken them" by revealing "that they are an empire of humans and, like all empires of humans, are built on the destruction of the body. It is to stain their nobility, to make them vulnerable, fallible breakable humans."[54] This prescription resembles nothing so much as what Sedgwick saw as the "threshold" to the depressive position—"the simple, foundational, authentically very difficult understanding that good and bad tend to be inseparable at every level."[55] The search for what Coates calls "weaponized history" is the manic search for a way out of this depressive dilemma, but it only postpones the more difficult work of collaboratively building something more "noble" out of the rubble of our Dreams.

But perhaps Coates's depressive counsel is just another, more subtle, instance of cruel optimism. Coates walks some distance toward a complete rejection of the Dream—which "rests on our backs, the bedding made from our bodies"—yet at the last moment he pulls back toward resignation, advising his son to "find some way to live in the all of it" rather than grooming him for militant resistance. In the words of Berlant, Coates is like a "subject who acknowledges the broken circuit of reciprocity between herself and her world but who, refusing to see that cleavage as an end as such, takes it as an opportunity to repair both herself and the world."[56] The difficulty is that this (depressive) position seems to forsake a more radical, critical purchase on the object of attachment—it "attempts to sustain optimism for irreparable objects."[57] In the face of undeniable and seemingly unrelenting cruelty, it might be better to "suspend ordinary notions of repair and flourishing to ask whether the survival scenarios we attach to those affects weren't the problem in the first place."[58] However, here Berlant's analysis seems to assume the possibility of a simple causal attribution of harms, an easy determination that the survival scenarios available to us are the source of our problems and not an ambivalent (terrible *and* beautiful) birthright. More problematically, Berlant implies that there is somewhere else to go—another reality in which the problems of survival would be less acute and our attachments less cruel. Yet this seems to betray a fantasy of the perfect object, the hallucination of an all-giving "good breast." The idea of a simple attribution of guilt or innocence and corollary fantasies of escape are themselves cruel dreams that keep citizens from the authentically difficult labors of recognition and repair.

Claudia Rankine's *Citizen* drives home the difficulty of these labors. They are difficult because repair is not simply a matter of changes in public policy, such as ending felony disenfranchisement laws. While such actions might have a significant effect, Rankine shows how the circuitry of recognition and misrecognition reaches far beyond positive law and is reflected in everyday interactions that affirm one's place within (or outside) "the people." Rankine's poetic rendering of these microaggressions reveals how political relationships of recognition are intertwined with personal interactions, and vice versa. Experiences of disrespect travel across these theoretically distinct yet practically intertwined spaces. As skillfully expressed by Rankine, these experiences are layered and complex; they involve not only the slight itself but also the response (or the lack of a response) *and* the reception (or lack thereof) to that response. Experiences of disrespect take place within and reflect the basic coordinates of social recognition patterns, which means that the thematization of these experiences risks being misunderstood by the terms of (mis)recognition to which they are addressed. How does one communicate that the forms of communication currently in use are actually a form of *mis*communication, that they are a source of social injury? Rankine reflects on this difficulty on the third page of *Citizen*:

> Certain moments send adrenaline to your heart, dry out the tongue, and clog the lungs. . . . After it happened I was at a loss for words. . . . Haven't you said this to a close friend who early in your friendship, when distracted, would call you by the name of her black housekeeper? You assumed you two were the only black people in her life. Eventually she stopped doing this, though she never acknowledged her slippage. And you never called her on it (why not?) and yet, you don't forget.[59]

There are many layers of experience represented here. Within the passage, we detect the pain and resentment of the disrespected ("you don't forget"), the ways in which disrespect seeps into the everyday, and the difficulty of articulating any of this ("you never called her on it [why not?]"), even among friends. The uncertainty surrounding the author's reaction—"haven't you said this . . . ?" versus "you never called her on it"—reflects not only the humiliation of the slight but the painful difficulty of a response.

Even in those vignettes in *Citizen* where voice is found, or where witness to the slight is given, the subsequent interactions are often clipped and stunted, ending in silence or unanswered questions; for instance,

> Despite the fact that you have the same sabbatical schedule as everyone else, he says, you are always on sabbatical. You are friends so you respond, *easy.*
>
> What do you mean?
>
> Exactly, what do you mean?[60]

The responses, when they are given, are seen as a necessary form of confrontation: "The voice in your head silently tells you to take your foot off your throat because just getting along shouldn't be an ambition."[61] They are necessary because they seek to interrupt a circuitry of misrecognition, and they are necessarily a *confrontation* because they show how mundane modes of comportment and ways of speaking—forms of "getting along"—are themselves a source of social injury. Because of this, the energy required for a response—"to assert presence"—is often accompanied by "visceral disappointment: a disappointment in the sense that no amount of visibility will alter the ways in which one is perceived."[62] Responses to everyday instances of disrespect are necessary, difficult, and disappointing, and the "quotidian struggles against dehumanization" in turn give rise to understandable experiences of "anger."[63] Anger itself, however, is both a source of hope and a trap. The expression of anger, it is offered, "might . . . snap . . . [us] back into focus," getting us to pay attention to the concrete other with whom we are interacting, in part by calling attention to the racial projections that suffuse our quotidian lives and that have shaped our interactions heretofore.[64] Yet the cruelty of misrecognition can entrap anger in the very same circuitry of misunderstanding, where the reaction or response is siphoned into the category of the "angry black woman" who is seen to be acting out or "making a scene."[65] One of the frequent images and metaphors in *Citizen* is the game of tennis, with the responses to disrespect framed as angry (and hopefully effective) returns of serve. However, these backhands do not always necessarily sustain the volley (nor are they intended to); they are heated conclusions to interactions within an ongoing field of interactions that, unlike a tennis match, "doesn't have an ending."[66] The expression of anger is humanizing when it acts as a form of resistance against everyday acts of dehumanization and disrespect.

One hears within Rankine's sharp and angry responses (when they are offered) what Judith Butler has called the "carefully crafted 'fuck you.' "[67] Yet, once again, as *Citizen* makes clear, often the sharpest of these returns are misunderstood—ruled out of bounds—as the utterance gets waylaid among the circuitry of social misrecognition. The "lessons" on offer are not taken up by the world: "To live through the days sometimes you moan like deer. Sometimes you sigh. The world says stop that. Another sigh. Another stop that. Moaning elicits laughter, sighing upsets."[68]

In the face of these ordinary experiences of disrespect, the world only offers an impossible counsel: "Feel good. Feel better. Move forward. Let it go. Come on. Come on. Come on."[69] The counsel of letting go or forgetting, however, cannot be followed, in part because "the body has memory"[70] that is not susceptible to conscious erasure and in part because "the past is a life sentence, a blunt instrument aimed at tomorrow."[71] However, the edict to feel better and move on is also impossible because the counsel of forgetting is *itself* an injury—a fresh reminder of what is to be left behind.

It does not seem promising, then, that the price of being the "citizen" of Rankine's title is itself a similar commitment to impossible forgetting: "and this is how you are a citizen: Come on. Let it go. Move on."[72] Perhaps here Rankine is signaling that citizenship is a form of cruel optimism, a possibility that Rankine explicitly entertained in a 2014 interview:

> A year or two ago I read Lauren Berlant's *Cruel Optimism*. That's a book that gave me a kind of language to think about ideas like "the non-relation in the relation," which is a rephrasing of Berlant, for example.

When I read phrases like that in Berlant's work, it gives me a vocabulary
to understand incoherency. . . . In *Cruel Optimism*, Berlant talks about
things that we're invested in, despite the fact that they are not good for
us and place us in a non-sovereign relationship to our own lives. And I
thought, on a certain level, that thing that I am invested in that is hurt-
ing me would be this country [*laughs*].[73]

Rankine's laughter at the end of her reply could be interpreted as either a way
of carrying the burden of cruel optimism or as a way of indicating that cruelty is
not all that exists within this attachment. If it is the latter, we might go back to
the passage "and this is how you are a citizen" and see it as an attempt to challenge dominant norms of recognition while operating within them. For instance,
we might at first blush read the "come on" that follows as an incitation (perhaps
impatient) to short memory and easy civic reconciliation (come on . . . let it go).
Norms of citizenship encourage or require short memories in the name of civic
reconciliation, but if this is the case then clearly these norms are an obstacle to
our flourishing in a situation where our bodies carry the burden of memories and
the "past is a life sentence." But we might also read the "come on" as an aggressive sarcastic backhand ("*this* is what it means to be a citizen[?] *Come on*"). On
this reading, all the returns of serve that fight against the "furious erasures" within
dominant patterns of social recognition are not instances of cruel optimism but
an exhausting, often angry means of giving witness to the needs for recognition
and respect that are being denied.[74]

Rankine clearly expresses this desire for recognition located within the ideal
of citizenship. As she puts it, amid all the endless interactions, the countless vol-
leys, "you want the days to add up to something more than you came in out of
the sun and drank the potable water of your developed world."[75] The potable water
image is telling because it shows that the struggle for recognition exceeds the struggle for material well-being, that the creature comforts of advanced industrial
society—refrigerators, flat-screen televisions, or air conditioning—are ersatz substitutes for actual relations of recognition.[76] In fact, the passage following directly
from "this is how you are a citizen" testifies to the insufficiencies of material comforts
while lamenting the withholding of recognition: "Despite the air conditioning
you pull the button back and the window slides down into its door-sleeve. A
breeze touches your cheek. As something should."[77]

Once again, to attack compromised democratic ideals is an exercise of these ideals; it is the search for the "something more" than the current embodiment of those
norms and an opposition to their location in circuitry of social misrecognition that
furiously erases so many bodies. Perhaps then we can read the "come on" in a third

way—as an invitation toward something more than what is currently being offered. In *Citizen*, this "something more" is expressed by the idea of a "truce":

> Because words hang in the air like pollen, the throat closes. You hack away . . . a share of all remembering, a measure of all memory, is breath and to breathe you have to create a truce—a truce with the patience of a stethoscope.[78]

In the same 2014 interview quoted earlier, Rankine expanded on this idea:

> Truce . . . goes back to this idea of connection, community, and citizenship. You want to belong, you want to be here . . . you're constantly waiting to see that they recognize that you're a human being . . . and that together you will live—you will live together. The truce is that.[79]

Given the tennis metaphors in *Citizen*, it is tempting to read truce as the situation of *deuce*—not the end of a match, but a moment when the score has drawn even and each side's prowess has been recognized. Truce/deuce implies the creation of terms of interaction that are not predicated on the erasures of projective identification and stereotyping, but that are more open, honest, and collaborative. It does not imply the end of the match, but a continuation of social life in ways that affirm norms of connection, community, and citizenship amid ongoing and endless struggles for recognition.

Rankine's idea of truce reflects what Honneth might see as the anticipation of appropriate institutions and relationships caused by the friction of misrecognition or disrespect. Borrowing a distinction between "I" and "me" from the work of George Herbert Mead, Honneth argues that there exists an inner friction between a social self (the "me")—which is legible from within the dominant patterns of social recognition—and a "spontaneous reaction formation" (the "I") that cannot be grasped cognitively or contained within existing networks of recognition and modes of interaction.[80] Similarly, in *Citizen*, Rankine describes a battle between "the 'historical self' and the 'self-self.'" The historical self "arrive(s) with the full force of your American positioning," whereas the self-self interacts on the basis of "mutual interest" and open exploration.[81] For Honneth, "I" cannot realize—or even fully articulate—its desires by itself, yet by virtue of its existence it "anticipates a community in which one is entitled to have those desires satisfied."[82] *A breeze touches your cheek—as something should.* The "self-self" cannot fully articulate itself, but it reaches outward in anticipation of a community of reception in which it could be brought into being.

The power of Rankine's social criticism and the direction of social desire in her text rely on an attachment to recognition contained within the ideal of her lyric's title: *Citizen*. Ultimately, it does not seem as if Rankine could endorse Berlant's account of cruel optimism, nor would she seemingly welcome the kinds of militant discipline and politics on offer in Dean's *Communist Horizon*. Citizenship is more like a Kleinian good object, which holds idealizing presuppositions that in turn license a critical work of deidealization that challenges the ways in which social ideals are currently, and problematically, embodied (*"come on"*). For Rankine, *all* human attachments contain an aspect of cruelty: "We are invested in being together. In having friends. In joining our lives. And yet these are the people who also fail you."[83] If ambivalent humans are constitutionally capable of cruelty and replete with flaws, then the proper political task is not to imagine an absolute liberation from cruelty but to find ways of making the existing cruelty within patterns of social recognition conscious, communicable, and hence (potentially) reparable. As Rankine puts it, "Let's be flawed differently."[84]

If these readings of Rankine and Coates are plausible, then the challenge issuing from both of their books is the location of particular settings and viable practices of historical acknowledgment and social repair.[85] For Rankine, this is precisely the promise of the Black Lives Matter movement, which, for her "can be read as an attempt to keep mourning as an open dynamic in our culture."[86] Black Lives Matter, unlike "earlier black-power movements that tried to fight or segregate for self-preservations . . . aligns with the dead, continues the mourning and refuses the forgetting in front of all of us."[87] An open dynamic of mourning is a "mode of intervention and interruption," but it can also be seen as an American democratic tradition, in line with Mamie Till Mobley's refusal to keep private the grief over her slain son, Emmitt Till. By openly showing the brutal disfigurement of her son, Mobley sought "to make mourning enter our day-to-day world" by "refram[ing] mourning as a method of acknowledgment."[88] "Acknowledgment" here means not only to avow the disproportionate vulnerability of black bodies, but more importantly to recognize the circuitry of misrecognition that serves to disavow this vulnerability. It is to acknowledge the paranoid-schizoid defenses of splitting, denial, idealization, and demonization that circulate amid patterns of social recognition and poison social interactions. In other words, it is a Kleinian work of mourning, the collective pursuit of a social depressive position. As Rankine puts it, "the legacy of black bodies as property . . . continues to pollute the white imagination. To inhabit our citizenry fully, we have to not only understand this, but also to grasp it."[89] Grasping it, of course, means not simply achieving cognitive understanding of discomforting historical truths, but to wrestle with the dominant norms of recognition and the anxieties and defenses that limn the circuitry of social interaction. This, in shorthand, is the democratic work of mourning.

Reflexive Social Interaction and the Democratic Work of Mourning

Rankine's *Citizen* is a landmark in the exploration of America's contemporary racial topography, and Rankine herself is clearly a "poet" in the sense that James Baldwin used the term—as someone who reflects and refines experience in such a way that we can locate ourselves within it and wrest some fractious coherence out of incoherency. Yet interactions over the timing of sabbaticals and tennis metaphors might not speak directly to the experience of those—such as Freddie Gray—for whom Black Lives Matter is attempting to keep mourning an open dynamic in our culture. So thinking more concretely, what are the settings, norms, and practices that might respond to the feelings of discontent and impasse expressed in the protests for Freddie Gray or Eric Garner? If there is no choice but to pursue a flawed American democracy, how might we be "flawed differently"—where and how might citizens erode the democratically corrosive forms of disrespect and disavowal that limn relations of social recognition?

Social criticism and aesthetic illumination, however incisive, are not enough. As Axel Honneth argues in *Freedom's Right*, the only response to political "disenchantment"—owing to the "increasing decoupling of the political system from democratic will-formation"—would be to "bundle the public power of organizations, social movements and civil associations in order to put coordinated and massive pressure on the parliamentary legislature."[90] Civic and political "bundling," however, depends on sources of solidarity that were traditionally provided by a steadily dissipating "common background culture" and for which no viable alternative sources have been found.[91] The "load bearing structures" for a democratic culture of resistance and generalized agency, are the "practices, customs, and social roles" found within the everyday lifeworld.[92] And yet of course these are the same customs and modes of interaction that continue to produce the everyday experiences of disrespect, disenfranchisement, and disavowal noted by Coates and Rankine.

The inherent cruelty of democratic stuckness, then, requires building civic relationships that can simultaneously address concrete social problems while extending relations of mutual recognition across intransigent social divides, and to do so *from within* cultures and customs of misrecognition. Such forms of social togetherness are difficult and chancy, even among groups that are explicitly motivated to pursue them. In the sociologist Paul Lichterman's phrase, togetherness across social divides is "elusive," even if it is obtainable under the right conditions.[93] Groups that successfully reach outward to build crosscutting relationships display certain social customs and styles of interaction. In particular, group-building groups (civic "bundlers") develop norms and practices of what Lichterman calls "social reflexivity." Groups are socially reflexive when "they talk reflec-tively, self-critically, about their relations with the wider social context—the people, groups, or institutions they see on their horizon. A group can practice social reflexivity when its customs *welcome reflective talk about its concrete relationships in the wider social world*."[94] Communication about the communicative interactions that create social relationships matters greatly for the strength of those relation-ships. Social reflexivity in this sense is a more pluralistic, collective version of Rankine's disrespect-and-response tennis matches. It draws attention not only to what is or has been said, but also to why and how those utterances either draw people together or push them apart. Social reflexivity is a more public working through of the pained episodes of monologue (or fraught dialogue) gathered in *Citizen*, such as the following:

> The man at the cash register wants to know if you think your card will work. If this is routine, he didn't use it on the friend who went before you. . . . You want her to say something—both as witness and as a friend. She is not you; her silence says so. . . . Come over here with me, your eyes say. Why on earth would she? . . . What is wrong with you? This ques-tion gets stuck in your dreams.[95]

Being able to talk critically and self-reflectively about social interactions and the settings in which they take place would be the equivalent here of unpacking the silences and miscommunications intensifying this scene of disrespect. Rankine skillfully shows the clash of competing perceptual frameworks ("What is wrong with you?" and "Why on earth would she?") that have short-circuited the desired communicative act. The chance for solidarity across differences is missed, and the opportunity for mutual recognition is relegated to one's dreams. The civic and political challenge is to locate spaces and to cultivate norms that might allow citizens to reflect on such uncomfortable differences and to find voice to fill the present silences.

Civic bridge building takes more than a will to associate or a shared sense of commitment to addressing particular social problems, and it does not hinge on the sharing of common values or cultural frameworks. It depends instead on styles and customs of interaction and whether these allow for and encourage open com-munication about group boundaries, goals, and concrete relationships in the wider social world.[96] Lichterman studied different civic networks in Wisconsin—all of them affiliated with religious organizations—for a period of three and half years. All of the groups within these networks were motivated to "make a differ-ence" in their communities, and yet only one was able to effectively reach out-ward and build relationships beyond its original group of participants. What set this group—which Lichterman calls "Park Cluster"—apart from other, very similar groups was its ability to be flexible and critical about itself, its goals, the goals and orientations of others, and the social spaces in which it found itself and to which it ultimately traveled:

> Park Cluster was a flexible group . . . the Cluster wondered what Park residents themselves thought about the proposed neighborhood school that had seemed like such a good idea at the outset. They mulled over the biweekly free meals that had seemed at the start like an unquestionably nice thing for the neighborhood. They became more and more uneasy about talking about the good of the neighborhood without neighbors at the table. It became increasingly urgent to figure out how they could work with Charmaine, the neighborhood center director, instead of bypassing her. Fitfully, the Cluster *changed* as a group. They transformed their own style of togetherness as they cultivated new relationships beyond the group.[97]

As this example makes clear, customs of social reflexivity are not easy to practice. They lead to disappointment and cause self-doubt; they can be painful and embarrassing, as ideas and practices that seemed unquestionably beneficent take on a new light through engagements with those who had not been represented in their initial envisioning. Social reflexivity requires a comfort with uncertainty, ambiguity, and frustration. In fact, as Lichterman's study shows, it is *certainty* that threatens civic bridge building, whereas perplexity can facilitate it.[98]

The concepts and categories of object relations psychoanalysis seem a natural ally for this framework. Flexible, reflexive groups occupy a kind of collective depressive position—comfortable with ambivalence and uncertainty, tolerant of and even appreciative of difference, and less anxious about a lack of certain boundaries for the self and the group than they are about the damages that such boundaries can do. Bridge-building groups seem to exist within what Sedgwick calls the "middle ranges" of agency, in which power is seen as fluid, shared, and relational.[99] They have found ways to face down their own imperfections and to work through the complexities attendant to social interaction in a society with a terrible *and* beautiful democratic heritage.

On the other hand, the work of Melanie Klein and her successors sheds some light on why this kind of social togetherness is so elusive. Civic bridge building erodes psychologically easier sources of togetherness—stable group boundaries and clear lines of demarcation between inside/outside, good/evil. Reaching outward, as Lichterman notes, threatens "dominant definitions of good membership in the group. Reaching outward threatened the solidarity of the groups."[100] Solidarity rooted in the ideal object—Klein's "good breast"—cannot reach outward or build bridges because the group, under paranoid-schizoid pressures, cannot tolerate the pollution that occurs when the ideal is besmirched by the inclusion of "outsiders"—the resulting interactions are too uncomfortable, anxious, and painful. As Klein well knew, the shattering of projections associated with social reflexivity *hurts*, which is why the depressive position—the space from where this hurt can be experienced, rather than split off—requires that we work through the loss of these protective ideals and come to better terms with the perspectives and situations of others who had heretofore been one-sided, part objects in our psyche. The good object, by contrast, retains an aspect of idealization that bridges persecutory anxiety while preparing us for the unavoidable discomfort that limns communication across differences. Elusive togetherness requires what I have called "the work of mourning." Lichterman, in effect, has described the concrete politics of the depressive position, a means of practicing acknowledgment and social repair in the name of the good object of democratic citizenship.

Settings of Social Reflexivity: TRCs and the Work of Mourning

Insights about socially reflexive groups do not, by themselves, address problems of political impasse or disenchantment, nor do they address the intense feelings of disregard and distrust articulated by protesters in Baltimore, Staten Island, and Ferguson. What, then, about the countless citizens who are not already engaged in the labor of civic bridge building (however unsuccessfully), or what about citizens who are organized into more insular groups? Are there settings or spaces that might instigate habits of social reflexivity and democratic mourning in such places where these styles of interaction and reflection are far from customary? Lichterman's study shows how civic customs and expectations are important, but *settings* also matter. Communicative customs and interaction styles are powerfully shaped by the social spaces in which they take place, and American social life is suffused with social settings that deprivilege the kinds of exploratory, reflective, and outward-directed interactions that Lichterman has described.[101] This occurs—ironically and tragically—even among civic groups explicitly motivated to address the pathologies associated with social misrecognition.[102] Voluntary associations often actively police against difficult (or "controversial") subjects of conversation, rarely interrogate the boundaries of the group, and avoid disagreements that are seen as threatening to the obvious good of "doing good" within the community. The result is a stunted and self-limited form of civic participation: "Without reflecting on politics, organizers could encourage volunteers to bring a can of tuna to feed the hungry, but they could not encourage them to ponder the problems' sources."[103] It is hard to develop customs of social reflexivity when questions that might inspire reflection are seen as threatening to the social setting in which they are asked.

Here, then, we come full circle to the experience of the Greensboro Truth and Reconciliation Commission, introduced in chapter 1 and described more fully in chapter 5. I have argued that TRCs—even when they are, unlike the GTRC, official or state-sponsored processes—provide opportunities for what Lichterman describes as social reflexivity: communication about styles of social communication and interaction and the various wrongs carried out within or disavowed by patterns of social recognition. TRCs can inspire social reflexivity because they can challenge and even overturn anxiety-fueled projections surrounding social others. TRCs cannot destroy the need for such projections, but they can reshape modes of social perception and interaction, creating the basis for new political relationships—a "bundling" of socially reflexive associations, organizations, groups, and citizens that would be better positioned to address civic disenchantment and distrust than any alternative on the horizon.

TRCs can inspire social reflexivity because they challenge easy projections rooted in persecutory or paranoid fantasies. Both by allowing public space for a fuller and more open examination of public history and by commissioning an investigation of the past in ways that trace its subtle ramifications, TRCs can challenge stereotypes and projections that fuel social misunderstanding. For instance, as described in chapter 5, one of the effects of the GTRC was to challenge the widely circulated belief that the CWP were "outside agitators." Follow-up studies in Greensboro have shown that these effects have reached beyond individuals directly involved in the GTRC process. Elite-driven, institutional accounts of the Greensboro Massacre are increasingly contested in the city, and previously polarized narratives of the event have been weakened.[104] The GTRC, then, effectively shifted the narrative surrounding the events of 1979 and their aftermath in ways that clearly have improved the chances for social reflexivity. TRCs can have this effect because, by taking into account the broader context of social interaction that surrounds traumatic events, they facilitate communication about social communication and reflection on normal patterns of social interaction.

The effects of these efforts may be fleeting. The work of social acknowledgment and repair is difficult and chancy, in part because it requires an overhaul of the very circuitry of social recognition through which interactions are filtered— less akin to repairing the boat while on the high seas and more like jumping over our shadow. Yet just as we know that civic bridge building is possible, so too do we have evidence that the work of social acknowledgment taking place in TRCs can provide the basis for new social relationships in ways that dramatically erode patterns of misrecognition and maldistribution. Perhaps the most impressive example is that of the Solms-Delta wine estate, discussed in chapter 5. The owner of the estate, Mark Solms, whose family had been landowners in the area for six generations, was in a similar position to many of the civic organizations in our era of democratic disenchantment: he was dissatisfied with the current arrangements of power and powerlessness, yet his first attempts to address this situation met with abject failure and frustration. Solms wanted to build bridges, but his offers of dialogue and discussion were met with incredulity and antipathy. The workers on the estate would not engage with Solms or even look at him during these first, clearly uncomfortable, meetings. In response Solms effectively set up his own (very local) truth and reconciliation commission: along with the workers and a local archaeologist, Solms literally dug up the past of his estate, and the work of historical excavation proved to be only the first step in an still-unfolding process of social rearrangement at Solms-Delta.

Solms described the difficult and painful work of excavation and dialogue as "get[ing] your mind back."[105] On its face, this is a curious phrase, but it makes perfect sense from within the framework of object relations psychoanalysis that has guided this project. For the Kleinian analyst Hanna Segal, the depressive position is a state of mind in which the anxious, defensive projections of the paranoid-schizoid are withdrawn—"a state of mind where you know yourself and don't project, so that you can assess reality and know what can be achieved and what can't."[106] The withdrawal of outsized projections forces individuals "to face their own destructiveness, their inner conflicts and guilt, their internal realities."[107] The need to "face . . . the reality of history . . . exposes us to what is most unbearable."[108] Yet these painful and even humiliating examinations can, as they did for Solms and the estate workers, make social reflexivity possible—they can clarify the history of particular social positions and styles of interaction. The work of acknowledgment does not alter the past, but it can create new space for negotiations about power relationships going forward.

Conclusion: Black Lives Matter and the Work of Mourning

This brings us back to the case of Black Lives Matter and mourning as (ideally) an ongoing and open dynamic in American democracy. One of the weaknesses and inherent limitations of the TRC model as it is currently imagined and practiced is its *temporary* nature. However, if an open dynamic of mourning is indeed necessary in our time of democratic disenchantment, impasse, and suffering, then the most promising features of TRCs will have to be incorporated into ongoing associations, civic customs, and institutions. The developing Black Lives Matter social movement seemingly represents such an opportunity for the politics of mourning to become a broader form of democratic pedagogy. At the time of this writing, this opportunity is just that—an opportunity. It remains unclear in what directions Black Lives Matter will develop and what repertoires of agency it might manage to cultivate.

What is clear is that Black Lives Matter reveals the ongoing and intimate connection between mourning and politics. The movement began in a moment of grief, not just over the death of Trayvon Martin in 2012 but also over the acquittal of his killer, George Zimmerman, in 2013. Alicia Garza, a social activist with the Black Organization for Leadership and Dignity, described the Zimmerman acquittal as "a gut punch"—an intolerable signal that black lives did not seem to matter. In resistance to this idea, Garza and others created a virtual space in order that people could "share grief, share rage, [and] collaborate together."[109] Activists consciously drew connections between grief, mourning, and political action, following a familiar pattern that we have explored in this book.

As it developed over the summer and fall of 2015, however, Black Lives Matter increasingly came to be filtered through a framework of war and survival and corresponding tactics of militant resistance. In the wake of Michael Brown's death, Garza describes her realization that only direct action (such as shutting down a BART commuter train in San Francisco) could "stop the wheels" of the "war on black communities."[110] In light of the deaths of Brown, Freddie Gray, Trayvon Martin, Tamir Rice, and many, many others, this framework of war and militant resistance is understandable. Yet as this book has attempted to show, the democratic challenge is to avoid reducing the politics of mourning to either its angry, agonistic moments or to consensualist discourses or rituals. Grief and rage can be democratically generative, but they can also shut down social reflexivity and make coalitional politics and civic labors less likely. For these reasons, then, Black Lives Matter activists would have much to gain from a close examination and imitation of the pluralistic and dialogical work of efforts such as the GTRC. Such efforts can contextualize rage and grief within the social circuitry of recognition and misrecognition and make resistance more legible and successful. They also have the advantage of mitigating rigid moralism and acknowledging the complexity of our democratic political heritage in ways that instigate social reflexivity and labors of social repair.

The democratic work of mourning is an ongoing, difficult labor of building and rebuilding commonwealth. It presumes that democratic citizenship is a good object that, while inevitably idealized, enables the salutary work of deidealization. It seeks out the spaces and practices that enable reflexivity, recognition, and repair, and it does so amid living legacies of violence and bitter mistrust. It is an invitation: *this* is how we might be citizens. *Don't* let it go.

Notes

PREFACE

1. New York City Press Office, "Mayor de Blasio Holds Media Availability at Mt. Sinai United Christian Church on Staten Island," transcript, December 3, 2014.

2. Alicia Garza and L. A. Kauffman, "A Love Note to Our Folks: Alicia Garza on the Organizing of #BlackLivesMatter," *n+1 Magazine*, January 20, 2015.

3. Claudia Rankine, "The Condition of Black Life Is One of Mourning," *New York Times*, June 22, 2015.

4. Ibid.

5. Ibid.

6. Sigmund Freud, "Mourning and Melancholia," in *The Standard Edition of the Works of Sigmund Freud*, vol. 14, ed. and trans. James Strachey (London: Hogarth Press, 1976).

7. Claudia Rankine, "Blackness as the Second Person: Meara Sharma Interviews Claudia Rankine," *Guernica: A Magazine of Art and Politics*, November 17, 2014.

8. Mark Gibney, Rhoda E. Howard-Hassmann, Jean-Marc Colcaud, and Niklaus Steiner, eds., *The Age of Apology: Facing Up to the Past* (Philadelphia, PA: University of Pennsylvania Press, 2009). See also Imani Michelle Scott, ed., *Crimes against Humanity in the Land of the Free: Can a Truth and Reconciliation Process Heal Racial Conflict in America?* (Santa Barbara, CA: Praeger, 2014.)

9. Priscilla B. Hayner, *Unspeakable Truths: Transitional Justice and the Challenge of Truth Commissions* (New York: Routledge, 2011); Ronald Niezen, *Truth and Indignation: Canada's Truth and Reconciliation Commission on Residential Schools* (Toronto: University of Toronto Press, 2013); "Beyond the Mandate: Continuing the Conversation," Report of the Maine Wabanaki-State Child Welfare Truth and Reconciliation Commission, Hermon, ME, June 14, 2015.

10. James Baldwin, "As Much Truth as One Can Bear," *New York Times*, January 14, 1962.

11. Alexis de Tocqueville, *Democracy in America* (New York: Penguin Classics, 2003).

12. Bob Dylan, "It's All Over Now Baby Blue," *Bringing It All Back Home* (Warner Bros., 1965).

13. James Baldwin, "My Dungeon Shook," in *The Fire Next Time* (London: Vintage, 1992), 5.

14. James Baldwin, "Interview with Malcolm Presten," in *Conversations with James Baldwin*, ed. Fred L. Standley and Louis H. Pratt (Jackson: University of Mississippi Press, 1989), 26.

1. THE POLITICS OF MOURNING IN AMERICA

1. For this and other documents related to the CWP and the Greensboro Massacre, see the online repository of the Civil Rights Greensboro Project, http://library.uncg.edu/dp/crg.

2. The marchers had agreed, in tense negotiations with the police, to leave the shotguns unloaded. See Spoma Jovanovic, *Democracy, Dialogue and Community Action: Truth and Reconciliation in Greensboro* (Fayetteville: University of Arkansas Press, 2012).

3. Signe Waller, *Love and Revolution: A Political Memoir* (Lanham, MD: Rowman and Littlefield, 2002).

4. Quoted in Jovanovic, *Democracy, Dialogue, and Community Action*, 18, 18–19, 11–13.

5. Ibid., 7.

6. Francesca Polletta, *Freedom Is an Endless Meeting: Democracy in American Social Movements* (Chicago: University of Chicago Press, 2002).

7. William Chafe, *Civilities and Civil Rights* (Cambridge: Oxford University Press, 1993), 7.

8. As Chafe points out, civility often served an ideological function insofar as it offered a thin veneer of racial moderation that obscured the radical disparities and disagreements in Greensboro and elsewhere in the South. It is notable, for instance, that despite being one of the first cities to announce compliance with *Brown v. Board*, Greensboro still had over twenty schools in 1970 that were over 99 percent black or white. See the North Carolina State Advisory Commission on Civil Rights, "Trouble in Greensboro: A Report of the Open Meeting Concerning the Disturbances at Dudley High School and NCA&T State University," Raleigh, North Carolina, March 1970.

9. Edward Rothstein, "Four Men, A Counter and Soon, Revolution," *New York Times* January 31, 2010.

10. M. Kent Jennings, "Political Responses to Pain and Loss," *American Political Science Review* 93 (March 1999): 1–13.

11. "Fight Back, Fight AIDS: 15 Years of ACT UP," documentary, directed by James Wentzy, April 4, 2004 (ACT UP–DIVA TV, 2002), DVD; Scott Malone, "Michael Brown Protesters Stage "Die-in" in Missouri," Reuters news release, November 17, 2015, accessed December 31, 2014, http://www.huffingtonpost.com/2014/11/16/michael-brown-protesters-louis_n_6167714.html; Sara Helman and Tamar Rapoport, "Women in Black: Challenging Israel's Gender and Socio-political Orders," *British Journal of Sociology* 48 (December 1997): 681–700.

12. Jeffrey Stout, *Blessed Are the Organized* (Princeton, NJ: Princeton University Press, 2010), 219.

13. On the question of shared agency and the commemoration of sacrifice, see Danielle Allen, *Talking to Strangers* (Chicago: University of Chicago Press, 2004).

14. Judith Butler, *Precarious Life: The Powers of Mourning and Violence* (London: Verso, 2006), 34; see also Butler, *Frames of War: When Is Life Grievable?* (London: Verso, 2010).

15. Wendy Brown, "Political Idealization and Its Discontents," *Edgework: Critical Essays on Knowledge and Politics* (Princeton, NJ: Princeton University Press, 2006).

16. Libby Anker, *Orgies of Feeling: Melodrama and the Politics of Freedom* (Durham, NC: Duke University Press, 2014).

17. See David S. Gutterman and Andrew R. Murphy, "The 'Ground Zero mosque': Sacred Space and the Boundaries of American Identity," *Politics, Groups, and Identities* 2, no. 3 (2014): 368–85.

18. Butler, *Precarious Life*, xix.

19. Marguerite Guzman Bouvard, *Revolutionizing Motherhood: The Mothers of the Plaza de Mayo* (New York: SR Books, 1994). Ahmad Ashraf and Ali Banuazizi, "The State, Classes and Modes of Mobilization in the Iranian Revolution," *State, Culture, and Society* 1, no. 3 (1985): 3–40.

20. Bonnie Honig, *Emergency Politics: Paradox, Law, Democracy* (Princeton, NJ: Princeton University Press, 2009), 103. See also Honig, "Antigone's Laments, Creon's Grief: Mourning, Membership and the Politics of Exception," *Political Theory* 37 (February 2009).

21. See Stanley Cohen, *States of Denial: Knowing about Atrocities and Suffering.* (London: Polity Press, 2001). On commemoration and forgetting, see Sheldon Wolin, *The Presence of the Past: Essays on the State and the Constitution* (Baltimore: Johns Hopkins University Press, 1990). See also Jeffrey Olick, ed., *The Collective Memory Reader* (Oxford: Oxford University Press, 2011).

22. Lisa Magarrell and Joya Wesley, *Learning from Greensboro: Truth and Reconciliation in the United States* (Philadelphia: University of Pennsylvania Press, 2006), 212.

23. Mark Gibney, Rhoda E. Howard-Hassmann, Jean-Marc Colcaud, and Niklaus Steiner, eds., *The Age of Apology: Facing Up to the Past* (Philadelphia: University of Pennsylvania Press, 2007).

24. Louis Bickford, "Memoryworks/Memory Works," in *Transitional Justice, Culture, and Society: Beyond Outreach*, ed. Clara Ramirez-Barat, 491–528 (New York: Social Science Research Council, 2014). See also Stephen Winter, *Transitional Justice in Established Democracies: A Political Theory* (New York: Palgrave Macmillan, 2014).

25. Jean Axelrod Cahan, "Reconciliation or Reconstruction? Further Thoughts on Political Forgiveness," *Polity* 45 (April 2013): 174–97.

26. Axel Honneth, *The Right to Freedom* (New York: Columbia University Press, 2014), 66.

27. Ibid., 46.

28. Allen, *Talking to Strangers*, 5

29. Honneth, *Right to Freedom*, 63–67; see also Iris Marion Young, *Responsibility for Justice* (Oxford: Oxford University Press, 2011).

30. Young, *Responsibility for Justice*.

31. Raffi Khatchadourian, "A Century of Silence," *New Yorker*, January 5, 2015. See also Gesine Schwan, *Politics and Guilt: The Destructive Power of Silence* (Lincoln: University of Nebraska Press, 2001).

32. Vamik Volkan, *Blood Lines: From Ethnic Pride to Ethnic Terrorism* (Madeira Park, BC: Douglas and McIntyre, 1997).

33. Boltanski, *Love and Justice as Competences* (Cambridge: Polity, 2012), 42.

34. As Lawrie Balfour argues, law "does not reach as far" as social norms, meaning that patterns and habits of misrecognition cannot be legislated out of existence or approached primarily through juridical mechanisms. Balfour, *The Evidence of Things Not Said: James Baldwin and the Promise of American Democracy* (Ithaca: Cornell University Press, 2000), 79–80.

35. Along similar lines, Patchen Markell has argued that justice frameworks need to be supplemented by the idea "acknowledgment," in which the orientation is less toward the settlement of political controversies than toward a means of "aspect change" in which our awareness of plurality and nonsovereignty can be expanded. Markell, *Bound by Recognition* (Princeton, NJ: Princeton University Press, 2003). For a similar use of acknowledgment in the context of racial injustice, see Jack Turner, *Awakening to Race: Individualism and Social Consciousness in America* (Chicago: University of Chicago Press, 2012).

36. See Eddie Glaude, who discusses the "daunting challenge of work[ing] through the reality of our dead," in a country marked by legacies of chattel slavery, forced displacement of native peoples, and legal segregation. Glaude, *In a Shade of Blue* (Chicago: University of Chicago Press, 2008).

37. Judith Butler, *Antigone's Claim* (New York: Columbia University Press, 2002); Bonnie Honig, *Antigone Interrupted* (Cambridge: Cambridge University Press, 2013). Of course there have been many other interpretations and appropriations of Antigone within contemporary political theory. Jean Elshtain has offered a reading of *Antigone* in support of her theory of social feminism, although both Honig and Butler critique Elshtain for essentializing gender norms (Butler) or for a "mortalist humanism" that avoids the hard questions of politics (Honig). See Elshtain, "The Mothers of the Disappeared: An Encounter with Antigone's Daughters," in *Finding a New Feminism*, ed. Pamela Grande Jensen (Boulder, CO: Roman and Littlefield, 1996), 129–48. In a different vein, neo-Leninists such as Slavoj Zizek follow Jacques Lacan and valorize Antigone because she rejects the symbolic order and stays true to her (transgressive or revolutionary) desire. For Zizek, Antigone

provides an example of a purely positive act of assertion, and as such she is a model for radical ethico-political action in the teeth of communicative capitalism. Slavoj Zizek, "From Antigone to Joan of Arc," *Helios* 31, no. 1 (2004): 51–62. See also Yannis Stavraka-kis, *The Lacanian Left: Psychoanalysis, Theory, Politics* (Albany: State University of New York Press, 2007). In describing Antigone in terms of an agonistic, activist politics of resistance, I am not claiming that every interpretation of the play fits into this mold, but rather that agonism has styled its vision of politics in part beneath the shadow of Antigone's agon with Creon. On this point, see Honig, *Antigone Interrupted*, 13.

38. In Plato's *Menexenus*, Socrates sarcastically details the powerful narcotic effects of funeral oratory, saying that such speeches made him feel that he was living in the "Isles of the Blessed" rather than within an imperfect polis. *Plato: Complete Works*, ed. John M. Cooper and D. S. Hutchinson (Cambridge: Hackett, 1997).

39. Simon Stow, "Pericles at Ground Zero: Tragedy, Patriotism, and Public Mourning," *American Political Science Review* 101 (May 2007): 195–208.

40. Simon Stow, "From Upper Canal to Lower Manhattan: Memorialization and the Politics of Loss," *Perspectives on Politics* 10 (September 2012): 687–700.

41. Simon Stow, "Agonistic Homegoing: Frederick Douglass, Joseph Lowery, and the Democratic Value of African American Public Mourning," *American Political Science Review* 104 (November 2010): 681–97.

42. Nicole Loraux, *The Invention of Athens: The Funeral Oration in the Classical Greek City* (Cambridge, MA: MIT Press, 2006), 252.

43. Ibid., 252.

44. On the intersections between memory and justice, see W. James Booth, *Communities of Memory: On Witness, Identity, and Justice* (New York: Cornell University Press, 2006).

45. Discourses of reconciliation can serve as mechanisms of denial or as ideological displacements of political conflicts onto ethical terrain of "forgiveness." See George Shulman, "Acknowledgement and Disavowal as an Idiom for Theorizing Politics," *Theory and Event* 14, no. 1 (2011). By contrast, Hannah Arendt described forgiveness as a key political virtue and as a necessary complement to human action because it "releases us and others from the chain and pattern of consequences that all action engenders." Arendt, *The Human Condition* (Chicago: University of Chicago Press, 1998).

46. Erin B. Mee and Helene P. Foley, *Antigone on the Contemporary World Stage* (Oxford: Oxford University Press, 2011).

47. Robert Meister, *After Evil: A Politics of Human Rights* (New York: Columbia University Press, 2010). Compare Libby Anker's treatment of melodrama as a narrative genre through which citizens become affectively attached to an (impossible) ideal of sovereign freedom that only serves to intensify their experiences of unfreedom. Anker, *Orgies of Feeling*.

48. Meister's second chapter, "Ways of Winning," expresses the difficulty of this position sharply: "For me, the salient question would be how to reconcile the moral attitudes that make it possible (and legitimate) to engage in revolutionary struggle with the moral attitudes that make it possible (and legitimate) to stop." *After Evil*, 70. I return to this difficult question in chapter 5.

49. On this latter point, Meister quotes Reinhart Koselleck: "While revolution . . . was initially induced by its opponents as well as its proponents, once established in its legitimacy, it proceeded to continually reproduce its foe as a means through which it could remain permanent." Koselleck, "The Modern Concept of Revolution," in *Futures Past: On the Semantics of Historical Time*, trans. Keith Tribe (New York: Columbia University Press, 2004).

50. Wendy Brown, *States of Injury: Power and Freedom in Late Modernity* (Princeton, NJ: Princeton University Press, 1995), 73.

51. Wendy Brown, "The Desire to Be Punished: Freud's 'A Child Is Being Beaten,'" in *Politics Out of History* (Princeton, NJ: Princeton University Press, 2001), 54.

52. Frantz Fanon, *Black Skin, White Masks*, trans. Charles Lamn Markmann (New York: Grove Press, 1967), 229–31. For a counterweight to this argument, see W. James Booth, "'From This Far Place': On Justice and Absence," *American Political Science Review* 105 (November 2011): 750–64.

53. See Douglas Crimp, who argued that the militancy of AIDS activists was both a justified form of resistance and potentially a "means of dangerous denial." Crimp was concerned about a heroic posture of activist politics that obscured the complex sources of suffering with the gay community. Crimp, "Mourning and Militancy," *October* 51 (Winter 1989): 3–18. See also Tina Takemoto, "The Melancholia of AIDS: Interview with Douglas Crimp," *Art Journal* 62 (Winter 2003): 80–90. I return to Crimp's arguments in chapter 2.

54. For a counterpoint, see the work of Joel Olson, who argued that fanaticism's vigor to "draw lines" can be democratically generative. Olson, "Friends and Enemies, Slaves and Masters: Fanaticism, Wendell Phillips, and the Limits of Democratic Theory," *Journal of Politics* 71 (January 2009): 82–95.

55. See Meister, *After Evil*. Meister argues that the discourse of truth and reconciliation attempts to supplant the struggle for social justice with an ethical struggle for social harmony. I discuss the broader discourse of truth and reconciliation in chapter 5.

56. Wolin, *Presence of the Past*, 32–46.

57. Pamela Conover, "The Politics of Recognition: A Social Psychological Perspective," in *The Political Psychology of Democratic Citizenship*, ed. Eugene Borgida, Christopher M. Federico, and John L. Sullivan (Oxford: Oxford University Press, 2010), 176.

58. Axel Honneth, *The Struggle for Recognition: The Moral Grammar of Social Conflicts* (Cambridge, MA: MIT Press, 1995). For a useful critique of the politics of recognition, see Glen Sean Coulthard, *Red Skin, White Masks: Rejecting the Colonial Politics of Recognition* (Minneapolis: University of Minnesota Press, 2014).

59. Honneth, *Struggle for Recognition*, 103.

60. Axel Honneth, "Anxiety and Politics: The Strengths and Weaknesses of Franz Neuman's Diagnosis of a Social Pathology," *Pathologies of Reason* (New York: Columbia University Press, 2008).

61. For an argument that the well-being of psyche and socius are inseparable from each other (and that both are inseparable from a flourishing ecology), see Felix Guattari, *The Three Ecologies* (London: Bloomsbury Academic, 2008).

62. Nancy Luxon, *Crisis of Authority: Politics, Trust, and Truth-Telling in Freud and Foucault* (Cambridge, Cambridge University Press, 2013), 52.

63. Axel Honneth, "On Becoming Things: An Interview with Axel Honneth," *Platypus Review* 59 (September 2013).

64. Dominick LaCapra talks about working through as a "regulative ideal" that should govern processes of confronting social trauma, intended as a way of overcoming both social silence/denial and an endless fixation on the past. For LaCapra, mourning represents neither an "optimistic scenario of transcending the past" nor the idea of a "valorized" past operating as the "sole horizon of life." LaCapra, "Psychoanalysis, Memory and the Ethical Turn," in *History and Memory after Auschwitz* (Ithaca, NY: Cornell University Press, 1998). See also Seth Moglen, "On Mourning Social Injury," *Psychoanalysis, Culture, and Society* 10 (2005), 151–67.

65. On the idea of public work, see Harry Boyte, *Building America: The Democratic Promise of Public Work* (Philadelphia, PA: Temple University Press, 1996).

66. See Bonnie Honig's argument about a style of political agonism "between decision and deliberation." Honig, "Between Decision and Deliberation: Political Paradox in Democratic Theory," *American Political Science Review* 101 (February 2007): 1–17.

67. *Antigone* has been recently appropriated and performed in a wide variety of politically charged contexts, ranging from Argentina in the wake of its dirty war (1974–1983) to the Jenin Refugee Camp in Palestine to Northern Ireland, India, Taiwan, Turkey, and Poland. See Mee and Foley, *Antigone on the Contemporary World Stage*.

68. Chantal Mouffe, *Agonistics: Thinking Politics Agonistically* (London: Verso, 2013).

69. Honig, *Antigone Interrupted*, 13.

70. Gail Holst-Warhaft, *The Cue for Passion* (Cambridge, MA: Harvard University Press, 2000), 9, 197.

71. Ibid., 197.

72. Ibid., 16. Vamik Volkan sees this shared rage as part of a developmental need to "identify some people as allies and others as enemies," which itself grows from the individual's "efforts to protect his sense of self." Volkan, "The Need to Have Enemies and Allies: A Developmental Approach," *Political Psychology* 6, no. 2 (1985): 231–36.

73. On mourning's capacity to reconfigure political identity by widening the boundaries of a community, see Heather Pool, "The Politics of Mourning: The Triangle Fire and Political Belonging," *Polity* 44 (2012): 182–211. Pool describes the double-edged nature of this reconfiguration—the circle of community is often expanded only by the production of additional exclusions based on ethnicity, regional background, or other social markers.

74. Rose McDermott, "Emotional Manipulation of Political Identity," in *Manipulating Democracy*, ed. Wayne Le Chaminant and John Parrish (New York: Routledge, 2010), 130. See also Samantha Reis and Brian Martin, "Psychological Dynamics of Outrage against Injustice," *Peace Research: The Canadian Journal of Peace and Conflict Studies* 40, no. 1 (2008): 5–23.

75. Jeffrey Stevenson Murer, "Constructing the Enemy-Other: Anxiety, Trauma, and Mourning in the Narratives of Political Conflict," *Psychoanalysis, Culture, and Society* 14, no. 2 (2009): 109–30. Agonists such as William Connolly seek ways around this problem by advancing political virtues such as "agonistic respect." Chantal Mouffe also talks about the need to morph antagonism into a more respectful *agonism*, but she remains convinced that the friend/enemy distinction and the struggle for hegemony are unavoidable. Mouffe, *Agonistics*; William Connolly, *The Ethos of Pluralization* (Minneapolis: University of Minnesota Press, 1995).

76. See Julia Kristeva, *Powers of Horror: An Essay on Abjection*, trans. Leon S. Roudlez (New York: Columbia University Press, 1982).

77. On victim psychology and the slide toward eliminationist violence, see Mahmoud Mamdani, *When Victims Become Killers: Colonialism, Nativism, and the Genocide in Rwanda* (Princeton, NJ: Princeton University Press, 2001).

78. Julia Kristeva, *Hatred and Forgiveness* (New York: Columbia University Press, 2010), 183.

79. Committee to Avenge the CWP 5, "DCHS—Secret Supporters of the Klan," Blanche M. Boyd Papers, Duke University, http://library.uncg.edu/dp/crg/item.aspx?i =1192.

80. Compare with Michael Rogin's arguments about conservative (but not only conservative) "countersubversive demonology," which involves a conspiratorial, paranoid politics in which social subversives were disavowed or "lopped off" from the pure, virtuous center of American public life. Rogin, Ronald Reagan: *The Movie; And Other Episodes in Political Demonology* (Berkeley: University of California Press, 1988). What the case of the CWP demonstrates is that "subversives" can also practice a paranoid politics, even if sometimes— according to a quote often attributed to Woody Allen—"paranoia is knowing all the facts."

81. See Joel Olson, "Friends and Enemies, Slaves and Masters: Fanaticism, Wendell Phillips, and the Limits of Democratic Theory," *Journal of Politics* 71, no. 1 (January 2009): 82–95.

82. Meister, *After Evil*, 50.

83. Waller, *Love and Revolution*, 479, 476, 477.

84. Loraux, *Invention of Athens*, 252.

85. In *Mothers in Mourning*, Loraux argues that "the promotion of *lethe* (forgetting) [is] the basis of life in the city." *Mothers in Mourning* (Ithaca, NY: Cornell University Press, 1998), 92.

86. On how the Lincoln funeral turned the assassinated president from an object of almost unanimous consternation into an idealized object of admiration, see Barry Schwartz, "Mourning and the Making of a Sacred Symbol: Durkheim and the Lincoln Assassination," *Social Forces* 70 (December 1991): 343–64.

87. Renee C. Romano and Leigh Raiford, eds., *The Civil Rights Movement in American Memory* (Athens: University of Georgia Press, 2006).

88. Peter Dreier, "Rosa Parks: Angry, Not Tired," *Huffington Post*, February 2, 2013, accessed December 21, 2015, http://www.huffingtonpost.com/peter-dreier/rosa-parks-civil -rights_b_2608964.html.

89. Charles Payne, *I've Got the Light of Freedom: The Organizing Tradition and the Mississippi Freedom Struggle* (Berkeley: University of California Press, 2007).

90. Jacquelyn Dowd Hall, "The Long Civil Rights Movement and the Political Uses of the Past," *Journal of American History* 91 (March 2005): 1233–63.

91. Diane McWhorter, "Civil Rights Justice on the Cheap," *New York Times*, September 14, 2013.

92. For a sophisticated treatment of the themes of sacrifice and trust in the context of civil rights and American democracy, see Danielle Allen, *Talking to Strangers*.

93. On this lived struggle, see Polletta, *Freedom Is an Endless Meeting*.

94. Jenny Edkins, *Trauma and the Memory of Politics* (Cambridge: Cambridge University Press, 2003). See also Barbara Misztal, "The Sacralization of Memory," *European Journal of Social Theory* 7, no. 1 (2004).

95. On the question of grievable life, see Butler, *Precarious Life*, 20.

96. See John Bodnar's distinction between "national" and "vernacular" mourning. Bodnar, *Remaking America: Public Memory, Commemoration, and Patriotism in the Twentieth Century* (Princeton, NJ: Princeton University Press, 1993). Bodnar's distinction is discussed and utilized by Simon Stow in the context of public memorialization following September 11 and Hurricane Katrina. Stow, "From Upper Canal to Lower Manhattan."

97. Stow, "Agonistic Homegoing."

98. Ibid., 692

99. Paul Ricoeur, "Imagination, Testimony, and Trust: A Dialogue with Paul Ricoeur," in *Questioning Ethics: Contemporary Debates in Contemporary Philosophy*, ed. Mark Dooley and Richard Kearney (London: Routledge, 1999). See also Ricoeur, *Memory, History, Forgetting* (Chicago: University of Chicago Press, 2006).

100. Compare with the recuperation of "melancholia" as an insistent antidote to social amnesia. See D. L. Eng and David Kazanjian, eds., *Loss* (Berkeley: University of California Press, 2003); D. L. Eng, "The Value of Silence, *Theatre Journal* 54 (March 2002): 85–94; Marc Nichanian, "Between Genocide and Catastrophe," in Eng and Kazanjian, *Loss*, 99–124; Esther Sanchez-Pardo, *Cultures of the Death Drive* (Durham, NC: Duke University Press, 2003). For a critique of this melancholia turn, see Eric Santner, *Stranded Objects: Mourning, Memory, and Film in Postwar Germany* (Ithaca, NY: Cornell University Press, 1990); Harold Weilnbock, "The Trauma Must Remain Inaccessible to Memory," *Mittelweg* 36, no. 2 (2007); Wendy Brown, "Resisting Left Melancholy," *boundary* 26, no. 3 (1999); Dominick Lacapra, "Lanzmann's 'Shoah': Here There Is No Why," *Critical Inquiry* 23 (Winter 1997), 231–69; Dominick Lacapra, *Writing History, Writing Trauma* (Baltimore: Johns Hopkins University Press, 2001).

101. My turn to Klein is heavily indebted to the work of Fred Alford, who was one of the first political theorists to demonstrate that Klein's theory has political implications, despite the view that many of Klein's categories were not obviously or immediately social. Alford, *Melanie Klein and Critical Social Theory* (New Haven, CT: Yale University Press, 1989).

102. Alford, *Melanie Klein*, 11.

103. See Jürgen Habermas, who argued that naturalistic sciences of explanation had to be joined to the interpretive social sciences and to the "depth hermeneutics" of psychoanalysis in order to adequately understand social and political life. Habermas, *On the Logic of the Social Sciences*, trans. S. W. Nicholsen and J. A. Stark (Cambridge: Cambridge University Press, 1988).

104. Kovel, *White Racism: A Psychohistory* (New York: Columbia University Press, 1994), 7.

105. Kelly Oliver, *The Colonization of Psychic Space: A Psychoanalytic Social Theory of Oppression* (Minneapolis: University of Minnesota Press, 2004), xiii.

106. Meister, *After Evil*, 35.

107. For the psychoanalyst Hanna Segal (a student of Klein), there is a constant interaction between the dramas of the psyche and the polis. Political and social realities are suffused with projective identifications "imbued with deadly hostilities," and the conflicts with the psyche receive outlet and succor with the fantasies circulating social and political relations. Segal, *Yesterday, Today and Tomorrow*, ed. Nicola Abel-Hirsch (London: Routledge, 2007). In a similar vein, Noelle McAfee has argued that there can be no final, bright line between psychic and social spaces because, following the work of Kristeva, "the public sphere is also a semiotic space." McAfee, *Democracy and the Political Unconscious* (New York: Columbia University Press, 2008).

108. Melanie Klein, "On the Psychogenesis of Manic-Depressive States," in *Love, Guilt and Reparation: And Other Works 1929–1946* (New York: Free Press, 1975), 288; Melanie Klein, "Envy and Gratitude," in *Envy and Gratitude: And Other Works 1946–1963* (New York: Free Press, 1975), 188.

109. Thomas Ogden refers to Klein's theory of the positions in terms of inborn, organizing codes "by which perception is organized and meanings are attached to experience." Ogden, *Matrix of the Mind* (Boulder, CO: Rowman and Littlefield, 1986), 4.

110. Klein, "Notes on Some Schizoid Mechanisms," in *Envy and Gratitude*, 4.

111. Ibid., 4.

112. The formation of the first superego takes place through what Klein calls "projective identification." See Klein, "Some Theoretical Conclusions regarding the Emotional Life of the Infant," in *Envy and Gratitude*, 61–93.

113. Meira Likierman, *Melanie Klein: Her Work in Context* (London: Continuum, 2001).

114. Klein, *Envy and Gratitude*, 14

115. Likierman, *Melanie Klein*, 106.

116. Klein, "The Emotional Life of the Infant," in *Envy and Gratitude*, 74.

117. Ibid., 74.

118. Segal, *Yesterday, Today and Tomorrow*, 34.

119. Thomas Ogden refers to the "massive negation of the history of shared experience" within the paranoid-schizoid position, which amounts to "a continual rewriting of history in the service of maintaining discontinuities." Ogden, *Matrix of the Mind*, 63, 65.

120. Ogden calls the paranoid-schizoid position an "entrapment in the manifest" because "interpretation and perception are treated as identical processes." Ogden, *Matrix of the Mind*, 65.

121. Klein, "Mourning and its Relation to Manic-Depressive States," in *Love, Guilt, and Reparation*, 362.

122. Klein, "Notes on Some Schizoid Mechanisms," 6.

123. Klein, "The Theory of Anxiety and Guilt," in *Love, Guilt and Reparation*, 35.

124. Klein, "On the Sense of Loneliness," in *Envy and Gratitude*, 310.

125. Ibid., 301–2.

126. Klein, "Envy and Gratitude," 193.

127. See Simon Clarke, "Projective Identification: From Attack to Empathy?" *Kleinian Studies Ejournal*, http://www.psychoanalysis-and-therapy.com/human_nature/ksej /clarkeempathy.html.

128. Klein, "Envy and Gratitude," 232.

129. On this point, see the interview with Klein's student Hanna Segal, "Memories of Melanie Klein," pt. 1," http://www.melanie-klein-trust.org.uk/domains/melanie-klein -trust.org.uk/local/media/downloads/Memories_of_Melanie_Klein_Hanna_Segal.pdf.

130. Klein, "Mourning and Its Relation to Manic-Depressive States," 360.

131. Lior Barshack, *Passions and Convictions in Matters Political: Explorations in Moral Psychology* (New York: University Press of America, 2000).

132. Gal Gerson, "Object Relations Psychoanalysis as Political Theory," *Political Psychology* 25, no. 5 (2004): 769–94.

133. Eve Sedgwick, "Melanie Klein and the Difference Affect Makes," *South Atlantic Quarterly* 106 (Summer 2007): 631.

134. Ibid., 633.

135. "Ambivalence" comes from the Latin *ambi* (on both sides) and *valentia* (for capacity or strength). See Kenneth Weisbrode, *On Ambivalence* (Cambridge, MA: MIT Press, 2012).

136. Sedgwick, "Melanie Klein and the Difference Affect Makes," 631–32. Or, as Thomas Ogden puts it, "In the depressive position, phantasies of omnipotently annihilating one's rival no longer provide a satisfactory solution to a problem in a human relationship." Ogden, *Matrix of the Mind*, 91.

137. Sedgwick, "Melanie Klein and the Difference Affect Makes," 632.

138. D. W. Winnicott, "Some Thoughts on the Meaning of the Word 'Democracy,'" in *Home Is Where We Start From* (New York: W. W. Norton, 1986), 244.

139. Freud, "Mourning and Melancholia."

140. Winnicott, "The Value of Depression," in *Home Is Where We Start From*, 82.

141. Winnicott, "Meaning of the Word 'Democracy,'" 243.

142. Ogden, *Matrix of the Mind*, 7.

143. Ibid., 203.

144. Bonnie Honig, *Democracy and the Foreigner* (Princeton, NJ: Princeton University Press, 2001), 67–68, 70.

145. Ibid., 70.

146. See Marilyn Brewer, "Social Identity and Citizenship in a Pluralistic Society," *Political Psychology of Democratic Citizenship*, 163.

147. Ogden, *Matrix of the Mind*, 213. The literatures on deliberative minipublics and collaborative public work are promising sites for thinking about democratic potential spaces. See Simon Niemeyer, "The Emancipatory Effects of Deliberation: Empirical Lessons from Mini-Publics, *Politics and Society* 39 (March 2011): 103–40. Peter Levine, *We Are the Ones We Have Been Waiting For* (Oxford: Oxford University Press, 2013).

148. Ogden, *Matrix of the Mind*, 205. See also D. W. Winnicott, *Playing and Reality* (London: Routledge, 2005), 71–87.

149. Ogden, *Matrix of the Mind*, 207.

150. C. Fred Alford argues that politics is largely a paranoid-schizoid affair and that "psychoanalytic politics, if there is such a thing, is generally about who can best exploit the primitive terrors of the population." While I admire Alford's work greatly, I am convinced (or at least hopeful) that there are other possibilities available to democratic

citizens. See Alford, "The Possibility of Rational Outcomes from Democratic Discourse and Procedures: Comment," *Journal of Politics* 58, no. 3 (1996): 757–59.

151. Winnicott, *Home Is Where We Start From*, 253.

152. David Wong, *Natural Moralities: A Defense of Pluralistic Relativism* (Oxford: Oxford University Press, 2009).

153. See Kenneth Weisbrode, *On Ambivalence.*

154. Elliott Jacques, "On the Dynamics of Social Structure: A Contribution to the Psychoanalytical Study of Social Phenomena Deriving from the Views of Melanie Klein," *Human Relations* 6 (1953): 3–24.

155. Clarke, "Projective Identification." See also Michael Rustin, *The Good Society and the Inner World* (London: Verso, 1991).

156. The work of Judith Herman has become a touchstone for reflections on social trauma. See her *Trauma and Recovery: The Aftermath of Violence—from Domestic Abuse to Political Terror* (New York: Basic Books, 1997). Cathy Caruth has described traumas as "unclaimed experience" that require a witness in order to be claimed. See her *Unclaimed Experience: Trauma, Narrative, and History* (Baltimore: Johns Hopkins University Press, 1996). For a sharp critique of Caruth that is informed by object relations psychoanalysis, see Fred Alford, *Trauma and Forgiveness: Consequences and Communities* (Cambridge: Cambridge University Press, 2013). For a social constructivist perspective on trauma, see Jeffrey Alexander, *Trauma: A Social Theory* (New York: Polity Press, 2012). See also Ron Eyerman, Jeffrey C. Alexander, and Elizabeth Butler Breese, *Narrating Trauma: On the Impact of Collective Suffering* (Boulder, CO: Paradigm Publishers, 2013).

157. See Edkins, *Trauma and the Memory of Politics.* See also Patrick Hayes and Jim Campbell, *Bloody Sunday: Trauma, Pain, and Politics* (London: Palgrave Macmillan, 2005); Antonius Robben and Marcelo M. Suarez-Orozco, eds., *Cultures under Siege: Collective Violence and Trauma* (Cambridge: Cambridge University Press, 2009).

158. Herman, *Trauma and Recovery.*

159. On the politics of recognition, the most widely cited argument is that of Charles Taylor, *Multiculturalism: Examining the Politics of Recognition* (Princeton, NJ: Princeton University Press, 1994). My use of recognition owes a heavier debt to Axel Honneth than to Taylor, however. See Honneth, *The Struggle for Recognition.* For important critiques of the concept of recognition, see Patchen Markell, *Bound by Recognition* (Princeton, NJ: Princeton University Press, 2003); Kelly Oliver, *Witnessing: Beyond Recognition* (Minneapolis: University of Minnesota Press, 2001); Glen Sean Coulthard, *Red Skin, White Masks.*

160. Recognition is not an uncontroversial concept. For instance, Nancy Fraser has argued that discourses of recognition unjustly marginalize struggles for redistribution. The latter, perhaps, more accurately describes the CWP's organizing efforts. However, I follow Axel Honneth in conceptualizing a struggle for redistribution as part of a broader struggle for social recognition and standing. See the debate between Nancy Fraser and Axel Honneth in *Redistribution or Recognition? A Political-Philosophical Exchange* (London: Verso, 2004).

161. Ervin Staub, Laurie Anne Pearlman, Alexandria Gubin, and Athanase Hagengimana, "Healing, Reconciliation, Forgiving and the Prevention of Violence after Genocide or Mass Killing: An Intervention and Its Experimental Evaluation in Rwanda," *Journal of Social and Clinical Psychology* 24, no. 3 (2005): 297–334; Staub, "The Origins and Prevention of Genocide, Mass Killing, and Other Collective Violence," *Peace and Conflict: Journal of Peace Psychology* 5, no. 4 (1999): 303–36.

162. Vamik Volkan, "Tree Model: Psychopolitical Dialogues and the Promotion of Coexistence," in *The Handbook of Interethnic Coexistence*, ed. E. Weiner (New York: Continuum, 1998); Ervin Staub, "Breaking the Cycle of Genocidal Violence: Healing and Reconciliation," in *Perspectives on Loss*, ed. J. Harvey (Washington, DC: Taylor and Francis, 1998).

163. In this vein, Stow discusses the New Orleans Katrina Memorial as an instance of local, "vernacular" mourning that "enacts . . . a more productive form of remembering— one which looks forwards, not backwards by situating the body in its proper place as a precursor to social and political engagement." Stow, "From Upper Canal to Lower Manhattan," 692. On the value of joint projects and public action for eroding stereotypes and promoting values of social pluralism, see Staub, "Origins and Prevention of Genocide," 326.

164. Jovanovic, *Democracy, Dialogue and Community Action*, 152–54.

165. See David W. McIvor, "The Cunning of Recognition: Melanie Klein and Contemporary Political Theory," *Contemporary Political Theory* (October 2015), doi: 10.1057/cpt.2015.47.

166. Likierman, *Melanie Klein: Her Work in Context*.

2. TO JOIN IN HATE

1. For instance, the politics of mourning rove freely across well-worn distinction between "the public" and "the private." Moreover, while mourning rites are often associated with group boundaries, claims for grief can also erase previously rigid boundaries of identity. See Heather Pool, "The Politics of Mourning."

2. Charles Payne, *I've Got the Light of Freedom*; Marguerite Bouvard, *Revolutionizing Motherhood*; Deborah B. Gould, *Moving Politics: Emotion and ACT UP's Fight against Aids* (Chicago: University of Chicago Press, 2009).

3. Andres Fabian Henao Castro, "Antigone Claimed: 'I Am a Stranger!' Political Theory and the Figure of the Stranger," *Hypatia* 28 (Spring 2013): 308. On stigma, see Erving Goffman, *Stigma: The Management of Spoiled Identity* (New York: Simon and Schuster, 1986). On stigma and race, see Glenn Loury, *The Anatomy of Racial Inequality* (Cambridge, MA: Harvard University Press, 2002). On the struggle for recognition as a means of overcoming stigma, see Axel Honneth, *The Struggle for Recognition*, 164.

4. "A Theatre of Protest," *The Economist*, April 8, 2013.

5. Mee and Foley, *Antigone on the Contemporary World Stage*.

6. Mouffe, *Agonistics*; Chantal Mouffe, *On the Political* (London: Routledge, 2005); William Connolly, *Identity\Difference: Democratic Negotiations of Political Paradox* (Minneapolis: University of Minnesota Press, 2002); Bonnie Honig, *Political Theory and the Displacement of Politics* (Ithaca, NY: Cornell University Press, 1993).

7. Honig, *Antigone Interrupted*, 13.

8. Sedgwick, "Melanie Klein and the Difference Affect Makes," 632.

9. Honig, *Antigone Interrupted*, 8.

10. Elshtain, "The Mothers of the Disappeared"; Honig, "Antigone's Laments, Creon's Grief"; Jacques Lacan, *The Seminar of Jacques Lacan: The Ethics of Psychoanalysis* (New York: W. W. Norton, 1997); Peter Burian, "Gender and the City: Antigone from Hegel to Butler and Back," in *When Worlds Elide*, ed. Peter Euben and Karen Bassi (Lanham, MD: Rowman and Littlefield, 2010), 255–99.

11. See Nancy Kason Poulson, "In Defense of the Dead: *Antigona Furiosa*, by Griselda Gambaro," *Romance Quarterly* 59, no. 1 (2012): 48–54.

12. Crimp "Mourning and Militancy."

13. Ibid., 8.

14. Sophocles, *I: Antigone, Oedipus the King, and Oedipus at Colonus*, ed. and trans. David Grene and Richmond Lattimore (Chicago: University of Chicago Press, 1991). All references to this text are to the line number, not the page number.

15. Ibid., 10.

16. Carol J. C. Maxwell, "Coping with Bereavement through Activism: Real Grief Imagined Death, and Pseudo-Mourning among Pro-Life Direct Activists," *Ethos* 23 (December 1995): 437–52.

17. Ibid., 446.

18. Holst-Warhaft, *Cue for Passion*, 9, 197.

19. See Antonius Robben, "Death and Anthropology: An Introduction," in *Death, Mourning, and Ritual: A Cross-Cultural Reader* (Malden, MA: Blackwell Publishing, 2004).

20. Holst-Warhaft, *Cue for Passion*, 197.

21. Ibid., 16. Vamik Volkan sees this shared rage as part of a developmental need to "identify some people as allies and others as enemies," which itself grows from the individual's "efforts to protect his sense of self." Volkan, "The Need to Have Enemies and Allies."

22. Matilde Mellibovsky, *Circle of Love over Death* (Willimantic, CT: Curbstone Books, 1996).

23. Bouvard, *Revolutionizing Motherhood*, 60.

24. Loraux, *Mothers in Mourning*, 44.

25. Ibid., 11.

26. See Margaret Alexiou, *The Ritual Lament in Greek Tradition* (Cambridge: Cambridge University Press, 1974).

27. *Plutarch's Lives*, ed. Arthur Hugh Clough, trans. John Dryden, vol. 1 (New York: Modern Library Classics, 2001), 106–29.

28. For Nicole Loraux, the passion of grief claims eternity as its temporality, which amounts to a perpetual repetition of the loss. Electra embodies a permanent and excessive lamentation, which is expressed "in terms of 'forever.' " Loraux, *The Mourning Voice: An Essay on Greek Tragedy* (Ithaca, NY: Cornell University Press, 2002), 209.

29. See Samantha Reis and Brian Martin, "Psychological Dynamics of Outrage against Injustice," *Peace Research: The Canadian Journal of Peace and Conflict Studies* 40, no. 1 (2008): 5–23.

30. Loraux, *Mourning Voice*, 82.

31. Ibid., 23. See also Honig, "Antigone's Two Laws: Greek Tragedy and the Politics of Humanism," *New Literary History* 41 (Winter 2010): 1–33. In distinction to Honig, who reads Loraux as an embodiment of "mortalist humanism," I see Loraux as an agonist who in certain moments edges toward a Lacanian antihumanism. Loraux's emphasis on an "apolitical" membership for humans in the "race of mortals" (which Honig sees as an antipolitical claim redolent of mortalist humanism) has to be read alongside her emphasis on the bond of division, which shows that membership in the race of mortals is less a source of apolitical commonality than a constitutive outside to both the civic and noncivic "always." As I read it, Loraux's claim about the race of mortals is less a claim for substantive membership than a dissolvent of all community bonds, which are, according to her, internally conflicted and incomplete. In this way she comes closer to Lacan than to Elshtain or to the Butler of *Giving an Account of Oneself* and *Precarious Life*.

32. Loraux, *The Divided City: On Memory and Forgetting in Ancient Athens* (Cambridge, MA: MIT Press, 2006), 97.

33. Holst-Warhaft, *Cue for Passion*, 1.

34. Loraux, "Reflections of the Greek City on Unity and Division," in *City States in Classical Antiquity and Medieval Italy*, ed. Anthony Molho, Kurt Raaflaub, and Julia Emlen (Ann Arbor: University of Michigan Press, 1992), 48.

35. Mamdani, *When Victims Become Killers*.

36. Holst-Warhaft, *Cue for Passion*, 18.

37. bell hooks, *Killing Rage, Ending Racism* (New York: Holt, 1995), 17. See also Niza Yanay, *The Ideology of Hatred: The Psychic Power of Discourse* (Bronx, NY: Fordham University Press, 2012), 21.

38. hooks, *Killing Rage, Ending Racism*, 17.

39. James Baldwin, "Stranger in the Village," in *The Price of the Ticket: Collected Nonfiction 1948–1985* (New York: St. Martin's Press, 1985), 83.

40. Crimp, "Mourning and Militancy," 18.

41. Ibid., 18.

42. Klein, "A Contribution to the Psychogenesis of Manic-Depressive States," in *Love, Guilt, and Reparation*, 268.

43. Ibid., 268.

44. Sedgwick, "Melanie Klein and the Difference Affect Makes," 638.

45. Brown, *States of Injury*, 50.

46. Sedgwick, "Melanie Klein and the Difference Affect Makes," 635.

47. Klein, "Contribution to the Psychogenesis of Manic-Depressive States," 268.

48. Klein, "The Origins of Transference," in *Envy and Gratitude*, 52.

49. Crimp, "Mourning and Militancy," 18.

50. Sedgwick, "Melanie Klein and the Difference Affect Makes," 634.

51. The more common charge against Klein—that she reduces external experiences to the internal play of conscious and unconscious fantasy—is a red herring. While Klein does describe the power of conscious and unconscious fantasies to shape perception of reality, her theory is clearly concerned with the interaction between internal and external worlds, which mutually shape and influence each other.

52. Klein, "Mourning and Its Relation to Manic-Depressive States," 359.

53. As Eric Santner puts it, "mourning without solidarity is the beginning of madness." This also implies the obverse: the social recognition of loss is the precondition for sanity or health. Santner also sounds a Kleinian note when he argues that the "task of integrating damage, loss, disorientation, decentered-ness into a transformed structure of identity . . . is one of the central tasks of . . . the work of mourning." Santner, *Stranded Objects*, xiii.

54. Butler, *Antigone's Claim*, 2.

55. Judith Butler, *Gender Trouble: Feminism and the Subversion of Identity* (New York: Routledge, 2006), 45.

56. Ibid., 45.

57. Judith Butler, *The Psychic Life of Power: Theories in Subjection* (Stanford, CA: Stanford University Press, 1997), 147..

58. Butler, *Gender Trouble*, 81.

59. Butler, *Precarious Life*, 20.

60. Butler, *Antigone's Claim*, 28.

61. Butler, *Precarious Life*, 4.

62. Ibid., 4. See also Raymond Geuss, "The Politics of Managing Decline," *Theoria* 108, no. 52 (2005): 1–12.

63. Thomas Dumm, "Giving Away, Giving Over: A Conversation with Judith Butler," *Massachusetts Review* (June 2008), 98.

64. Ibid., 98. See also Anker, *Orgies of Feeling*.

65. Butler, *Antigone's Claim*, 29.

66. Ibid., 29.

67. Ibid., 24

68. Ibid., 5.

69. Ibid., 2.

70. Butler, *Frames of War*, 4.

71. In making her argument, Butler expressly rejects the reading of Antigone given by Jacques Lacan, who sees Antigone as a source of pure desire that resists its illegitimate channeling through the symbolic. However it is an open question whether or not Butler really distinguishes her approach fully from Lacan's. See Peter Burian, "Gender and the City." See also Heather Love, "Dwelling in Ambivalence," *Women's Review of Books*, 22, no. 2 (2004): 18–19.

72. Butler, *Psychic Life of Power*, 99.

73. Butler, *Antigone's Claim*, 79.

74. Ibid., 82.

75. Ibid., 80.

76. See Gillian Rose, *Mourning Becomes the Law: Philosophy and Representation* (Cambridge: Cambridge University Press, 1996).

77. Compare Moya Lloyd, "Radical Democratic Activism and the Politics of Resignification," *Constellations* 14 (March 2007), 129–46. Lloyd argues that Butler has perpetually understated the political and historical conditions necessary for successful acts of resignification or subversion. See also Lloyd, *Judith Butler: From Norms to Politics* (Cambridge: Polity, 2007).

78. Honig, *Antigone Interrupted*, 3

79. Honig, "Antigone's Laments, Creon's Grief," 17, 19.

80. Ibid., 7. See also Honig, "Between Decision and Deliberation," *American Political Science Review* 101 (February 2007): 1–15.

81. Honig, *Antigone Interrupted*, 40.

82. Honig, "Antigone's Laments, Creon's Grief," 31.

83. Honig, *Antigone Interrupted*, 46.

84. Ibid., 45.

85. Honig, "Antigone's Two Laws."

86. Jacques Lacan, *Seminar of Jacques Lacan*; Johann Wolfgang van Goethe, *Conversations of Goethe with Eckermann and Soret*, trans. John Oxenford (Whitefish, MT: Kessinger, 2005), 227.

87. Honig, "Antigone's Two Laws," 4.

88. Ibid., 10.

89. Ibid., 4.

90. Honig, *Antigone Interrupted*, 61.

91. Honig, "Antigone's Two Laws," 10.

92. Honig, *Antigone Interrupted*, 60.

93. Ibid., 61.

94. Ibid., 61.

95. Ibid., 62.

96. Takemoto, "Melancholia of AIDS: Interview with Douglas Crimp," 87.

97. Crimp, "Mourning and Militancy," 17.

98. Ibid., 17.

99. Honig now reads Freud slightly differently than Crimp, emphasizing the pleasure in life that "interrupts" mourning in a generative and productive (nonmelancholic) way. Yet this places a strong opposition between mourning and action that I think Crimp is refusing with his text.

100. Lacan, *Seminar of Jacques Lacan*.

101. Klein, Contribution to the Psychogenesis of Manic-Depressive States," 268.

102. Ibid., 268.

103. Ibid., 268.

104. Sedgwick, "Melanie Klein and the Difference Affect Makes," 637.

105. Melanie Klein, *Narrative of a Child Analysis* (New York: Free Press, 1975), 466.

106. Ogden, *Matrix of the Mind*, 91.

107. Honig, *Democracy and the Foreigner*, 67–68, 70.

108. Ibid., 70.

3. THE IMAGINARY CITY

1. On articulation (its dangers and its inevitability), see Charles Taylor, *Sources of the Self: The Making of Modern Identity* (Cambridge, MA: Harvard University Press, 1989), 97.

2. Jenny Edkins, *Trauma and the Memory of Politics*; John E. Bodnar, *Remaking America*.

3. Loraux, *Invention of Athens*.

4. See also Elizabeth Anderson, *The Imperative of Integration* (Princeton, NJ: Princeton University Press, 2010).

5. Charles Mills, *The Racial Contract* (Ithaca, NY: Cornell University Press, 1997), 19. See also Lawrie Balfour, *Evidence of Things Not Said*.

6. For similar critiques of Rawlsian theory, see Bonnie Honig, *Political Theory and the Displacement of Politics*; William Connolly, *Why I Am Not a Secularist* (Minneapolis: University of Minnesota Press, 1999); Sheldon Wolin, "The Liberal Democratic Divide: On Rawls's Political Liberalism," *Political Theory* 24, no. 1 (1996): 91–119.

7. Stow, "Agonistic Homegoing," 682.

8. Alford, *Melanie Klein*, 182–83.

9. Nicole Loraux, *The Divided City*, 101

10. Ricoeur, "Imagination, Testimony, and Trust."

11. On wholeness as a guiding democratic ideal, see Allen, *Talking to Strangers*. On the need for a superordinate identity in order to work through racial discrimination and inequality, see Anderson, *The Imperative of Integration*.

12. James Baldwin, Interview on *Faces* (television show). 1980. Available at https://www.youtube.com/watch?v=xb_NbdeE2zU.

13. Emile Durkheim, *Elementary Forms of Religious Life*, trans. Joseph Ward Swain (London: George Allen, 1964).

14. Antonius C. G. M. Robben, ed., *Death Mourning, and Burial: A Cross-Cultural Reader* (Oxford, UK: Blackwell, 2004).

15. Durkheim, *Elementary Forms*, 291–92.

16. Ibid., 297.

17. In this respect, I disagree slightly with Bonnie Honig in her interpretation of mourning as a reflection on "mere life." Mourning rituals are Janus-faced; they are concerned with "mere" and "more" life. Honig, *Antigone Interrupted*.

18. Durkheim, *Elementary Forms*, 298.

19. Ibid., 299.

20. Ibid., 299.

21. Simon Stow, "Pericles at Gettysburg and Ground Zero: Tragedy, Patriotism, and Public Mourning," *American Political Science Review* 101, no. 2 (2010): 195.

22. Sara Monoson, "Remembering Pericles: The Political and Theoretical Import of Plato's Menexenus," *Political Theory* 26 (August 1998): 505.

23. Thucydides, *History of the Peloponnesian War*, ed. M. I. Finley (New York: Penguin, 1972), bk. 2, sec. 35.

24. Ibid.

25. Durkheim, *Elementary Forms*, 297.

26. Thucydides, *History*, bk. 2, sec. 37.

27. Ibid., bk. 2, sec. 43.

28. Ibid.

29. Ibid., bk. 2, sec. 41.

30. Ibid.

31. Ibid., bk. 2, sec. 42.

32. "Menexenus," in *Plato: Complete Works*, ed. John M. Cooper and D. S. Hutchinson (Cambridge: Hackett, 1997). References are to line number.

33. Socrates actually claims that the speech was written by Aspasia, the metic wife of Pericles, in what is likely another dig at the Athenian leader. Ibid., 188.

34. Sigmund Freud, *The Ego and the Id* (London: W. W. Norton, 1990), 36.

35. See Joseph P. Forgas and Kipling D. Williams, eds., *The Social Self: Cognitive, Interpersonal and Intergroup Perspectives*, Sydney Symposium of Social Psychology Series (New York: Psychology Press / Taylor & Francis, 2003). See also Brewer, "Social Identity and Citizenship in a Pluralistic Society."

36. See Monoson, "Remembering Pericles," 505.

37. Loraux, *Invention of Athens*, 312.

38. Loraux, *Mourning Voice*, 19.

39. See Schwartz, "Mourning and the Making of a Sacred Symbol," 343–64.

40. Stow, "Pericles at Gettysburg," 682.

41. Michelle Alexander, *The New Jim Crow* (New York: New Press, 2010).

42. On the difference between moral stages and moral schemas, see the research done by James R. Rest, Darcia Narvaez, Muriel Bebeau, and Stephen Thoma, "A Neo-Kohlbergian Approach to Morality Research," *Journal of Moral Education* 29, no. 4 (2000): 381–95.

43. Klein, "Mourning and Its Relation to Manic-Depressive States," 350.

44. Klein, "On Mental Health," *Envy and Gratitude*, 270.

45. Mills, *The Racial Contract*, 14.

46. Ibid., 16.

47. Ibid., 18.

48. Ibid., 19.

49. Noel Ignatiev, *How the Irish Became White* (New York: Routledge, 1995). See also Joel Olson, *The Abolition of White Democracy* (Minneapolis: University of Minnesota Press, 2004).

50. John Rawls, *A Theory of Justice*, rev. ed. (Cambridge, MA: Belknap Press, 1999), 17.

51. Ibid., 149.

52. Mills, *Racial Contract*, 14.

53. Jody David Armour, *Negrophobia and Reasonable Racism: The Hidden Costs of Being Black in America* (New York: New York University Press, 1997); David B. Wilkins, "On Being Good and Black," *Harvard Law Review* 1924 (1999); Charles R. Lawrence III, "Two Views of the River: A Critique of the Liberal Defense of Affirmative Action," *Columbia Law Review* 101, no. 4 (2001): 928–75; Susan Storm and Lani Guinier, "The Future of Affirmative Action: Reclaiming the Innovative Ideal," *California Law Review* 84, no. 953 (1996).

54. Mills, *Racial Contract*, i.

55. Loraux, *Invention of Athens*, 251.

56. See Bill Galston, "Moral Personality and Liberal Theory: John Rawls's Dewey Lectures," *Political Theory* 10 (November 1982): 492–519; Raymond Geuss, "Liberalism and Its Discontents," *Political Theory* 30 (June 2002): 320–38; Raymond Geuss, *Philosophy and Real Politics* (Princeton, NJ: Princeton University Press, 2008).

57. Stow, "Agonistic Homegoing," 682, 692.

58. Derek Barker makes a similar argument when he notes that Rawls did not specify how individuals develop a sense of injustice. Barker, *Tragedy and Citizenship* (New York: State University of New York Press, 2009).

59. Thomas McCarthy, "Political Philosophy and Racial Injustice: From Normative to Critical Theory," in *Pragmatism, Critique, Judgment*, ed. Seyla Benhabib and Nancy Fraser (Cambridge, MA: MIT Press, 2004), 165. See also Laura Valentini, "On the Apparent Paradox of Ideal Theory," *Journal of Political Philosophy* 17, no. 3 (2009): 332–55; Mary Tjattas, "Psychoanalysis, Public Reason, and Reconstruction in the 'New' South Africa,"

American Imago 55, no.1 (1998): 51–75. On ideal theory more generally, see A. John Sim- mons, "Ideal and Non-Ideal Theory," *Philosophy and Public Affairs* 38 (2010): 5–36; Zofia Stemplowska, "What's Ideal about Ideal Theory?" *Social Theory and Practice* 34 (July 2008): 319–40.

60. In related fashion, Laura Valentini has argued that "keeping facts in sight" is essen- tial in order to produce a theory that is both "critical and action-guiding." Valentini, "Apparent Paradox of Ideal Theory." Compare also Jane Flax's argument that rationalistic approaches to justice split off the activity of thinking from the rest of subjectivity. Flax, "The Play of Justice: Justice as a Transitional Space," in *Disputed Subjects: Essays on Psychoanalysis, Politics, and Philosophy* (London: Routledge, 1993).

61. Rawls, *Theory*, 17.

62. Ibid., 399.

63. Ibid., 404.

64. Ibid., 433.

65. Ibid., 430, 433.

66. Ibid., 402–3.

67. Ibid., 408.

68. Ibid., 409.

69. Ibid., 412.

70. Ibid., 415, 414.

71. Ibid., 417.

72. See John Deigh, *The Sources of Moral Agency: Essays in Moral Psychology and Freud- ian Theory* (Cambridge: Cambridge University Press, 1996), 58.

73. Rawls, *Theory*, 473. See also Sigmund Freud, *Totem and Taboo*, trans. James Strachey (London: W. W. Norton, 1990); John Forrester, *Dispatches from the Freud Wars: Psycho- analysis and Its Passions* (Cambridge, MA: Harvard University Press, 1997).

74. Rawls, *Theory*, 467.

75. Ibid., 467.

76. Ibid., 466.

77. Ibid., 427, 433.

78. Freud's trajectory is not the only one that could be followed, of course. Habermas's dialogical updating of Kant's categorical imperative is one viable alternative. In fact, Haber- mas's dialogical theory of ethics is more compelling from a perspective of Kleinian psy- choanalysis, because it emphasizes the importance of a dialogical, intersubjective process of self- and social-formation, as opposed to Rawls's more monological original reasoning position. Also see Elizabeth Anderson's argument that racial integration is necessary because abstract principles of equality cannot, by themselves, overcome entrenched biases and inequalities. Anderson, *Imperative of Integration*, chap. 9.

79. Rawls, *Theory*, 120.

80. Ibid., 120.

81. Compare Rawls's published lectures on Joseph Butler, in which Rawls focuses his attention on Butler's principle of conscience. Conscience, on Rawls's reading, pro- vides judgments from which "there is no further appeal" and which form the basis of self-condemnation. The appeal to conscience—or the "supreme principle of reflec- tion—is "final; it settles the matter." Conscience is the supreme governing principle or faculty that allows the self to conquer its fractious passions and interests. This interpre- tation of conscience is strikingly similar to Rawls's description of the original position in *Theory* (and also, in *Liberalism*, to his concept of public reason, as I argue later chap- ter 3). John Rawls, *Lectures on the History of Moral Philosophy* (Cambridge: Harvard University Press, 2000).

82. Rawls, *Theory*, 514.

83. For more on purity as a form of border drawing, see Mary Douglas, *Purity and Danger: An Analysis of Concepts of Pollution and Taboo* (London: Routledge, 1966).

84. Alford, *Melanie Klein*, 182.

85. John Rawls, *Lectures on Political Philosophy* (Cambridge, MA: Belknap Press, 2008), 17.

86. Loraux, *The Divided City*, 101,

87. Bernard Williams, *Moral Luck* (Cambridge: Cambridge University Press, 1981).

88. John Rawls, *Political Liberalism*, rev. ed. (New York: Columbia University Press, 2005), xvii.

89. Ibid., xviii.

90. Ibid., xxvi.

91. Ibid., 10.

92. Ibid., 233.

93. Ibid., 87.

94. Ibid., 375.

95. Ibid., 87.

96. Freud, *Ego and the Id*.

97. Rawls, *Liberalism*, lx.

98. Rawls, *Lectures on Political Philosophy*, 8.

99. Ibid., 8.

100. Rawls, *Liberalism*, 243.

101. Ibid., 88.

102. Ibid., 133.

103. Freud, *Ego and the Id*, 57.

104. Rawls, *Liberalism*, 454.

105. Bonnie Honig argues that Rawls's approach reflects a vision of the responsible subject as one who is perpetually "anxious to distance himself from whatever pushes, pulls, attracts, or impels him from inside or outside." Hence, well-ordered subjects must be "comfortable in (and not also resistant to) their subscription to practices of self-containment and self-concealment." Honig, *Political Theory and the Displacement of Politics*, 155. Thomas McCarthy also suggests that Rawls constructs his theory around a Kantian vision of "self-abnegation." McCarthy, "Kantian Constructivism and Reconstructivism," *Ethics* 105 (October 1994): 44–63. See also Ed Wingenbach, "Unjust Context: The Priority of Stability in Rawls's Contextualized Theory of Justice," *American Journal of Political Science* 43 (January 1999): 225.

106. Rawls, *Liberalism*, 385–95.

107. Ibid., 247.

108. Ibid., 9.

109. In a similar fashion, Seyla Benhabib has criticized Rawls's approach for both its overrestricted social agenda and its theory of public discourse. See Benhabib, *Democracy and Difference: Contesting the Boundaries of the Political* (Princeton, NJ: Princeton University Press, 1996), 74–77.

110. Jonathan Lear, *Freud*, Routledge Philosophers Series (New York: Routledge, 2005), 186.

111. Sigmund Freud and Joseph Breuer, *Studies in Hysteria*, trans. James Strachey (London: Penguin Classics, 2004).

112. Shanto Iyengar, Solomon Messing, and Kyu S. Hahan, "Implicit Racial Attitudes: A Test of Their Convergent and Predictive Validity," paper presented at the annual meeting of the American Political Science Association (APSA) 2011, Seattle; Anthony G. Greenwald, "Implicit Bias: Scientific Foundations," *California Law Review* 94, no. 954 (July 2006).

113. T. D. Wilson, S. Lindsey, and T. Y. Schooler, "A Model of Dual Attitudes," *Psychological Review* 107 (2000): 101–26; David M. Amodio and Saaid A. Mendoza, "Implicit Intergroup Bias: Cognitive, Affective, and Motivational Underpinnings," in *Handbook of Implicit Social Cognition*, ed. B. Gawronski and B. K. Payne (New York: Guilford Press, 2010); Richard R. Lau and Caroline Heldman, "Self-Interest, Symbolic Attitudes, and Support for Public Policy: A Multilevel Analysis," *Political Psychology* 30, no. 4 (2009): 513–37.

114. Jim Sidanius, Felicia Pratto, Colette Van Laar, and Shana Levin, "Social Dominance Theory: Its Agenda and Method," *Political Psychology* 25 (December 2004): 845–80; Serge Guimond, *Social Comparison and Social Psychology: Understanding Cognition, Intergroup Relations, and Culture* (Cambridge: Cambridge University Press, 2005).

115. Christina Suthammanont, David A. M. Peterson, Christ T. Owens, and Jan E. Leighley, "Taking Threat Seriously: Prejudice, Principle, and Attitudes toward Racial Policies," *Political Behavior* 32, no. 2 (2010): 231–53.

116. Simon Clarke, "Projective Identification"; Anne Anlin Cheng, *Melancholy of Race: Psychoanalysis, Assimilation, and Hidden Grief* (Oxford: Oxford University Press, 2001).

117. On social institutions as a defense against paranoid-schizoid anxiety, see Elliott Jacques, "On the Dynamics of Social Structure: A Contribution to the Psychoanalytical Study of Social Phenomena Deriving from the Views of Melanie Klein," *Human Relations* 6 (1953): 3–24.

118. James Baldwin, "Interview with Studs Terkel," in *Conversations with James Baldwin*, 8.

119. Ibid., 8.

120. Baldwin, "Interview with Kenneth Clark," in *Conversations with James Baldwin*, 44.

121. Baldwin, "Interview with Kalamu ya Salaam," in *Conversations with James Baldwin*, 183.

122. Baldwin, "Interview with Henry Louis Gates," in *Conversations with James Baldwin*, 269.

123. Baldwin, "Interview with Kalamu ya Salaam," 179.

124. Baldwin, "Interview with David Estes," in *Conversations with James Baldwin*, 280.

125. Baldwin, "Interview with John Hall," in *Conversations with James Baldwin*, 100.

126. Baldwin, "Interview with Wolfgang Binder," in *Conversations with James Baldwin*, 208.

127. Baldwin, "Interview with John Hall," 108.

128. Ange-Marie Hancock, *The Politics of Disgust* (New York: New York University Press, 2004).

129. Baldwin, "Interview with Kenneth Clark," 45.

130. James Baldwin, "The World I Never Made," remarks at DC Press Club, http://www.c-span.org/video/?150875-1/world-never-made.

131. Baldwin, "Interview with Studs Terkel," 6.

132. Baldwin, "Many Thousands Gone," 78. See also George Shulman, *American Prophecy: Race and Redemption in American Political Culture* (Minneapolis: University of Minnesota Press, 2008).

133. Stow, "Agonistic Homegoing," 682.

134. Ibid., 682.

135. Ibid., 683.

136. Richard Seaford, "Historicizing Tragic Ambivalence: The Vote of Athena," in *History, Tragedy, Theory: Dialogues on Greek Drama*, ed. B. Goff (Austin: University of Texas Press, 1995), 202.

137. Stow, "Agonistic Homegoing," 681.

138. Ibid., 688.

139. Frederick Douglass, "Oration in Memory of Abraham Lincoln," in *From Many, One: Readings in American Political and Social Thought*, ed. Richard C. Sinopoli (Washington, DC: Georgetown University Press, 2007), 271.

140. Stow, "Agonistic Homegoing," 667.

141. Ibid., 687.

142. Ibid., 687.

143. Likierman, *Melanie Klein*, 109.

144. Ibid., 114–15.

145. Ibid., 78.

146. Ibid., 121.

147. See the support for Rawlsian liberalism by Susan Okin and Drucilla Cornell on (somewhat) similar terms. As Okin puts it, reasoning from the original position "in which the parties do not know their sex can yield important insights." Okin, "Political Liberalism, Justice, and Gender," *Ethics* 105 (1994): 38; Okin, *Justice, Gender, and the Family* (New York; Basic Books, 1991), 174–86. Cornell argues that Rawlsian liberalism permits individuals to passionately invest in an overlapping political consensus while allowing us to keep some of our selves outside the terms of this agreement. In other words, Rawls's theory seems to leave more room for the unconscious and for our negotiations with this inexhaustible layer of being. "Response to Thomas McCarthy: The Political Alliance Between Ethical Feminism and Rawls's Kantian Constructivism," *Constellations* 2, no. 2 (1995): 189–206. For an imaginative repurposing of Rawls's original position within a nonideal theory context, see Glenn Loury, "Why Are So Many Americans in Prison?" *Boston Review* (July/August 2007).

148. Rawls, *Lectures on Political Philosophy*, 420.

149. Ibid., 423.

150. Ibid., 430.

151. Hannah Arendt wrote about conscience as a similar dialogical "two-in-one," although Arendt would have resisted the claim that this was a psychoanalytic insight. See Arendt, *Life of the Mind* (New York: Mariner Books, 1981).

152. Klein, "The Emotional Life of the Infant," in *Envy and Gratitude*, 73.

153. Isaac Balbus, *Mourning and Modernity* (New York: Other Press, 2005), 66.

154. Segal, *Yesterday, Today, and Tomorrow*, 49.

155. Sheldon Wolin, *Politics and Vision* (Princeton, NJ: Princeton University Press, 2004). Wolin's reading of the tradition of liberalism is, of course, not the consensus view. However, one does not have to agree with the extremes of Wolin's argument in order to acknowledge that liberalism has historically sought means of controlling or containing the dangerous passions supposedly let loose in any form of participatory politics. Recall Madison's famous dismissal of Athenian democracy: "Had every Athenian citizen been a Socrates, every Athenian assembly would still have been a mob." In addition to this Madisonian strain in the liberal tradition, liberalism is also predominantly a view that seeks to limit the scope of what politics, as a domain, can include or address. Rights-based liberal theories describe a zone of inviolability that ought to be secure from political interference (originally by an encroaching government, but also by one's fellow citizens). And the laissez faire-*cum*-capitalist strand of liberal ideology also favors a contraction of the political sphere, on the grounds that markets are superior to political decisions in efficiently allocating resources. Thus, to the fear of raucousness, we can add the fear of predation and the fear of waste as paradigmatic liberal anxieties.

156. For a similar argument about the necessity of actual social integration to promote racial equality and nondiscrimination, see Anderson, *The Imperative of Integration*.

157. Loraux, *Invention of Athens*, 220.

158. Segal, *Yesterday, Today and Tomorrow*.

159. Ogden, *Matrix of the Mind*, 193.

160. Alexander, *New Jim Crow*, 118.

161. Ibid., 141.

162. Ibid.,124.

163. For instance, evidence from public deliberation shows that when citizens deliberate about prison policies they shift markedly against the idea that incarceration reduces crime and they become more protective of defendants' rights. See James S. Fishkin, *The Voice of the People: Public Opinion and Democracy* (New Haven, CT: Yale University Press, 1995), 215–16.

164. Baldwin, "Many Thousands Gone," 78.

165. Baldwin, "The Black Scholar Interviews James Baldwin (1973)," in *Conversations with James Baldwin*, 155.

166. Wilfred Bion, *Experiences in Groups* (London: Routledge, 1991).

4. "THERE IS TROUBLE HERE. THERE IS MORE TO COME"

1. On conditions of loss becoming conditions for action, see George Shulman, "Interpreting Occupy," *Possible Futures*, December 20, 2011. On the challenge of accepting vulnerability and overcoming penchants for misrecognition, see Markell, *Bound by Recognition*.

2. Thomas McCarthy, "Coming to Terms with Our past, Part 2: On the Morality and Politics of Reparation for Slavery," *Political Theory* 32, no. 6 (2004): 9.

3. Rosemary Nagy, "Reconciliation in Post-Commission South Africa: Thick and Thin Accounts of Solidarity," *Canadian Journal of Political Science* 35, no. 2 (2002): 330.

4. On "wholeness" rather than fantastical "oneness" as a driving ideal of democratic politics, see Allen, *Talking To Strangers*. On the importance of the social recognition of difference and heterogeneity along with a superordinate idea of the public, see Iris Marion Young, *Justice and the Politics of Difference* (Princeton, NJ: Princeton University Press, 1990).

5. Gordon W. Allport, *The Nature of Prejudice* (Cambridge, MA: Addison-Wesley, 1954); Thomas Pettigrew and Linda Tropp, "A Meta-Analytic Test of Intergroup Contact Theory," *Journal of Personality and Social Psychology* 90 (May 2006): 751–83. On dialogue and interactive problem solving, see H. C. Kelman and R. J. Fisher, "Conflict Analysis and Resolution," in *Political Psychology*, ed. D. Sears, L. Huddy, and R. Jervis (Oxford: Oxford University Press, 2003). Marc Howard Ross and Joy Rathman, eds., *Theory and Practice in Ethnic Conflict Management: Theorizing Success and Failure* (New York: St. Martin's Press, 1999).

6. On the *Oresteia* as a drama of reconciliation, see Markell, *Bound by Recognition*, 96. On relational power and civic agency, see Stout, *Blessed Are the Organized*.

7. For the idea that tragedy and psychoanalysis can speak to each other on the topos of mourning, see Olga Taxidou, *Tragedy, Modernity and Mourning* (Edinburgh: Edinburgh University Press, 2004). I should make it clear at the outset that I am not interested in tracing the representations of mourning in the extant tragedies or in seeing the origin of the tragic festival in the sublimation of banned affect following Solon's edicts outlawing certain practices of lament in the polis. There is, however, a rich literature on these two themes. For the former, see Margaret Alexiou, *The Ritual Lament in Greek Tradition*; Robert Garland, *The Greek Way of Death* (Ithaca, NY: Cornell University Press, 2001); for the latter, see Robert Garland, "The Well-Ordered Corpse: An Investigation into the Motives behind Greek Funerary Legislation," *Bulletin of the Institute of Classical Studies*, 36, no. 1 (1990): 1–15; Nicole Loraux, *Mothers in Mourning*.

8. Christian Meier, *The Political Art of Greek Tragedy* (New York: Polity Press, 1993).

9. Josiah Ober, *Athenian Legacies* (Princeton, NJ: Princeton University Press, 2007), 129.

10. For the development of Athenian democracy (which provided the context for tragedy's own development), see Cynthia Farrar, *The Origins of Democratic Thinking.* (Cambridge: Cambridge University Press, 1988); M. I. Finley, *Democracy Ancient and Modern* (New Brunswick, NJ: Rutgers University Press, 1988); A. H. M. Jones, *Athenian Democracy* (Baltimore: Johns Hopkins University Press, 1986); Kurt Raaflaub, Josiah Ober, and Robert Wallace, eds., *Origins of Democracy in Ancient Greece* (Berkeley: University of California Press, 2007).

11. Simon Goldhill, *Love, Sex, and Tragedy: How the Ancient World Shapes Our Lives* (Manchester, UK: John Murray, 2004), 227.

12. As Helene Foley sees it, the tragic genre "permits excessive behavior that was seemingly discouraged in the practice of the [Athenian] society." Foley, "The Politics of Tragic Lamentation," in *Tragedy, Comedy and the Polis*, ed. Alan H. Sommerstein (Bari, IT: Levante Editori, 1993). Froma Zeitlin sees the predominance of female representations in the tragedies in a similar light. By "playing the other," Athenian males were able to question, explore, and (ultimately) reinforce and patrol the boundaries of civic/masculine identity. Zeitlin, "Playing the Other: Theater, Theatricality, and the Feminine in Greek Drama," in *Nothing to Do with Dionysus? Athenian Drama in Its Social Context*, ed. John J. Winkler and Froma I. Zeitlin (Princeton, NJ: Princeton University Press, 1990).

13. For a (sympathetic) review of the literature in this vein, see Sara Monoson, *Plato's Democratic Entanglements* (Princeton, NJ: Princeton University Press, 2000), 88. For a critical view of this developing consensus, see Jasper Griffin, "The Social Function of Tragedy," *Classical Quarterly* 48, no. 1 (1998): 39–61; P. J. Rhodes, "Nothing to Do with Democracy: Athenian Drama and the Polis," *Journal of Hellenic Studies* 123 (2003): 104–19.

14. Monoson, *Plato's Democratic Entanglements*, 89.

15. Josh Beer, *Sophocles and the Tragedy of Athenian Democracy: Greek Tragedy and Political Theory* (Westport, CT: Greenwood, 2004), xii.

16. J. Peter Euben, introduction to *Greek Tragedy and Political Theory* (Berkeley: University of California Press, 1986), 22–23.

17. Helene Foley, "Tragedy and Democratic Ideology," in Goff, *History, Tragedy, Theory.*

18. That is, until acting became more professionalized at the close of the fifth century. See Pat Easterling and Edith Hall, eds.,, *Greek and Roman Actors: Aspects of an Ancient Profession* (Cambridge: Cambridge University Press, 2002).

19. Justina Gregory, *Euripides and the Instruction of the Athenians* (Ann Arbor: University of Michigan Press, 1991).

20. Monoson, *Democratic Entanglements*, 88. Yet see David Kawalko Roselli's *Theater of the People: Spectators and Society in Ancient Athens* (Austin: University of Texas Press, 2011), which cautions against a reading of the Athenian audience that elides the multiple perspectives and contested group boundaries within the audience. As Roselli puts it, "The citizen body was not homogenous, and many noncitizens resided in Athens and were active in the theater," 9.

21. Josiah Ober, *Mass and Elite in Democratic Athens* (Princeton, NJ: Princeton University Press, 1989).

22. Euben, introduction, 23. Euben cites William Arrowsmith, who wrote that tragedy was "a democratic *paideia* [or education] complete in itself." Arrowsmith, "A Greek Theater of Ideas," *Arion* 2 (Autumn 1963): 33.

23. Christian Meier, *The Political Art of Greek Tragedy* (New York: Polity Press, 1993), 18.

24. Goldhill, *Love, Sex, and Tragedy*, 179. See also P. E. Easterling, ed., *The Cambridge Companion to Greek Tragedy* (Cambridge: Cambridge University Press, 1997).

25. Goldhill, *Love, Sex, and Tragedy*, 214.

26. Ibid., 273.

27. Euben, introduction, 23.

28. Monoson, *Plato's Democratic Entanglements*, 88–90.

29. Mark Griffith, "Families and Inter-City Relations," in *Why Athens: A Reappraisal of Tragic Politics*, ed. D. M. Carter (Oxford: Oxford University Press, 2011), 17.

30. Ibid., 177. For differences within the audience of spectators, see also Roselli, *Theater of the People*.

31. Josiah Ober and Barry Strauss, "Drama, Political Rhetoric and the Discourse of Athenian Democracy," in Winkler and Zeitlin, *Nothing to Do with Dionysus*. See also Ober, *Democracy and Knowledge* (Princeton, NJ: Princeton University Press, 2008).

32. Ober, *Athenian Legacies*, 129.

33. Peter Euben, John R. Wallach, and Josiah Ober, eds., introduction to *Athenian Political Thought and the Reconstitution of American Democracy* (Ithaca, NY: Cornell University Press, 1994), 17.

34. Bruce Heiden, "Emotion, Acting, and the Athenian Ethos," in Sommerstein, *Tragedy, Comedy and the Polis*.

35. Ober, *Democracy and Knowledge*, 31. See also Ober, *Mass and Elite in Democratic Athens*.

36. Ober refers to this capacity as "a sort of political expertise . . . in the operations of self-government." *Democracy and Knowledge*, 121.

37. Ober, *Athenian Legacies*, 129.

38. Michael Rustin, *Good Society and the Inner World*; Georgina Born, "Anthropology, Kleinian Psychoanalysis, and the Subject in Culture," *American Anthropologist* 100, no. 2 (1998): 373–86.

39. Murray Edelman, *Constructing the Political Spectacle* (Chicago: University of Chicago Press, 1988).

40. Wilfred Bion, "Attacks on Linking," in *Melanie Klein Today: Developments in Theory and Practice*, vol. 1, *Mainly Theory*, ed. Elizabeth Bott Spillius (London: Routledge, 1988).

41. C. Fred Alford, "Hanna Segal—A Memorial Appreciation," *Psychoanalysis, Culture and Society* 17 (2012): 322.

42. Klein, "Mourning and Its Relation to Manic-Depressive States," 362. See also Likierman, *Melanie Klein*, 109.

43. Rustin, *Good Society and the Inner World*, 66. On melodrama as a political syndrome, see Libby Anker, *Orgies of Feeling*.

44. Foley, "Tragedy and Democratic Ideology," 144.

45. Goldhill, "Great Dionysia and Civic Ideology," 74.

46. "Misrecognition" is, of course, one possible translation of Lacan's concept of *méconnaissance*. But Lacan's misrecognition is quite different from the psychological experience to which I refer here. Whereas Lacan's *méconnaissance* is the formation of the ego through a displacement or misrecognition of the symbolic determinants of subjectivity (including discourse), the misrecognition that gets exposed in tragedy (and Kleinian analysis) is how our fantasies and fears have been projected onto the other and kept us from knowing him or her better. For Lacan, the subject comes into being through *méconnaissance*; for Klein, the subject comes into (depressive) being through recognition of its misrecognitions—through avowal of its disavowals.

47. Klein, *Narrative of a Child Analysis*, 120.

48. Aristotle, *Poetics*, trans. Anthony Kenney (Oxford: Oxford University Press, 2013), chap. 6.

49. Martha Nussbaum, "Tragedy and Self-Sufficiency: Plato and Aristotle on Fear and Pity," *Essays on Aristotle's Poetics*, ed. Amelie Oksenberg Rorty (Princeton, NJ: Princeton University Press, 1992), 267.

50. Ibid., 121. Nussbaum's example is Achilles's (momentary) reconciliation with Priam in Homer's *Iliad*. Elsewhere Nussbaum argues that it is appreciation of imperfection in the tragic hero that allows us to face and accept our own imperfections. Identification, on this understanding, is not taking the hero as an exemplary model for action but as the means of better acknowledging our own faults and lacks. Martha Nussbaum, *Fragility of Goodness* (Cambridge: Cambridge University Press, 1986), 387.

51. Klein, *Narrative of a Child Analysis*, 120.

52. Freud likened the analytic procedure to Sophocles's skillful telling of Oedipus's discovery of his origins. Sigmund Freud, *The Interpretation of Dreams*, trans. and ed. James Strachey (New York: Basic Books, 2010), 279.

53. Aristotle, *Poetics*, bk. 11.

54. Klein, *Narrative of a Child Analysis*, 28.

55. Ibid., 99.

56. Klein, "Love, Guilt, and Reparation," in *Love, Guilt and Reparation*, 350.

57. The chorus, on seeing the blinded Oedipus, says, "Indeed I pity you, but I cannot look at you . . . I shudder at the sight of you." Sophocles, *Oedipus the King*, trans. David Greene (Chicago: University of Chicago Press, 1991), lines1302–5.

58. All lines are from *The Complete Greek Tragedies: Aeschylus*, ed. and trans. David Grene and Richmond Lattimore (Chicago: University of Chicago Press, 1991).

59. The phrase is Lacan's. See Slavoj Zizek, "The Act and its Vicissitudes," http://www .lacan.com/symptom6_articles/zizek.html. Zizek notes the connection between the *passage a l'acte* and suicide, that is, that the aggressive action toward the others is actually intended against the self.

60. "Denial . . . is a potent defense against the persecutory anxiety and guilt which result from destructive impulses never being completely controlled . . . denial . . . may stifle feelings of love and guilt, undermine sympathy and consideration both with the internal and external objects, and disturb the capacity for judgment and the sense of reality." Melanie Klein, "Some Reflections on the Oresteia," *Envy and Gratitude and Other Works 1946–1963*, 293. This description fits well with Aeschylus's portrayal of both Agamemnon and Clytemnestra.

61. Whether or not the imputation of guilt to Orestes is an anachronism depends on how much we share the thesis that Greek culture was a "shame" culture that only later developed a category of emotion consonant with "guilt." Bernard Williams, *Shame and Necessity* (Berkeley: University of California Press, 1993).

62. Klein, *Narrative of a Child Analysis*, 28.

63. It is true that Orestes still clings to Apollo ("he declared I could do this and not be charged with wrong") and imagines that the god will provide sanctuary and absolution through which Orestes might "escape this blood that is my own" (1032). Yet this comes after Orestes has acknowledged the impurity of his action. Even the language used, "the blood that is my own," implies that Orestes' hoped-for absolution will not be redemptive.

64. Seaford, "Historicizing Tragic Ambivalence," 208.

65. Ibid., 208.

66. Christopher Rocco, *Tragedy and Enlightenment: Athenian Political Thought and the Dilemmas of Modernity* (Berkeley: University of California Press, 1997).

67. Ibid., 25. Whether or not Rocco has constructed a "rationalist" straw man is another story. His identification of this narrative with Habermas is a problematic leveling of the latter's understanding of enlightenment.

68. Ibid., 25.

69. Ibid., 26.

70. Rocco is carrying forward William Connolly's emphasis on disruption and disturbance. For a critique of Connolly that develops the given argument, see McIvor, "The Politics of Speed: Connolly, Wolin, and the Prospects for Democratic Citizenship in an Accelerated Polity," *Polity* 43, no. 1 (2011): 58–83.

71. As Helene Foley puts it, tragedy "holds up to view contradictions in *polis* ideology." Foley, "Tragedy and Democratic Ideology," 144.

72. There are, of course, countless other interpretations of the *Oresteia* that could be discussed. Seaford's and Rocco's map the central tension between ritual closure and anomic disturbance (forgetting/fixation), but onto this schema other powerful readings could be mapped. For instance, there is similar tension between Christian Meier's view that the *Oresteia* is paradigmatic for education into democratic citizenship and Nicole Loraux's view that the trilogy is more representative of the (patriarchal) containment of excess through the incorporation of female mourning affect into a civic ritual that "forgets" the conflicts at the root of the polis. Meier, *Political Art of Greek Tragedy*; Loraux, *Voice of Mourning* and *Mothers in Mourning*. Yet neither Meier nor Loraux acknowledge the ambiguity of collective suffering (Meier sees it as costless; Loraux sees it as pure ideology). Peter Euben is an exemplary figure in a middle position. For Euben, the image of justice that emerges from the *Oresteia* has four crucial components: reconciliation of diversities, reciprocity, recognition, and judgment. These elements exist in tense balance with one another. As Euben puts it, "by making the tensions and sheer formlessness of human life lucid and thus intelligible without slighting the contingency of politics, the permeability of human constructs, the irony of action, or the duality of passion, Aeschylus seconds the prodigious integration of life his trilogy commends." Euben, *The Tragedy of Political Theory* (Princeton, NJ: Princeton University Press, 1990), 91.

73. Goldhill, "Civic Ideology and the Problem of Difference," 49.

74. Klein, "Some Reflections on the Oresteia," 298.

75. Murer, "Constructing the Enemy-Other"; Staub, "Reconciliation after Genocide, Mass Killing, or Intractable Conflict: Understanding the Roots of Violence, Psychological Recovery, and Steps toward a General Theory," *Political Psychology* 27, no. 6 (2006): 867–94.

76. Meira Likierman sees the tragic and the moral as "simultaneous narratives" that "work on two levels within the Kleinian texts." In effect, the moral is not a response to or redemption of the tragic because the moral needs the tragic in order to retain "its sense"— "for morality must assume the possibility of irrevocable loss all the time." Likierman, *Melanie Klein*, 121.

77. D. W. Winnicott, "Concept of a Healthy Individual," in *Home Is Where We Start From*, 21–34.

78. The quote is from Peter Euben, *Tragedy of Political Theory*, 90. C. Fred Alford ties the Athenians' willingness to share one another's pain to Pericles' paean to the Athenian public spiritedness toward self-government in Thucydides's *History of the Peloponnesian War*: "Since a state can support individuals in their suffering, but no one person by himself can bear the load that rests on the state, is it not right for us all to rally to her defense?" (Thucydides, *History*, bk. 2, sec. 60); C. Fred Alford, *Psychoanalytic Theory of Greek Tragedy* (New Haven, CT: Yale University Press, 1992), 150.

79. Ogden, *Matrix of the Mind*, 213.

80. Winnicott, *Playing and Reality*, 71–87.

81. Oddone Longo, "The Theater of the Polis," in Winkler and Zeitlin, *Nothing to Do with Dionysus*.

82. Ibid., 19.

83. Goldhill, *Love, Sex, Tragedy*, 231.

84. Jonathan Lear, "An Interpretation of Transference," in *Open Minded: Working Out the Logic of the Soul* (Cambridge, MA: Harvard University Press, 1998), 70.

85. Ibid., 72.

86. Winnicott, "Concept of a Healthy Individual," 36.

87. For Fred Alford, Klein's emphasis on depressive integration and whole-object relations implies—above all else—the political and subjective acceptance of pollution: "Whole object relations refer to the self's ability to avoid splitting its objects into all good and all bad part-objects. Such relations require the toleration of ambivalent feelings toward others." Alford, *Psychoanalytic Theory of Greek Tragedy*, 18.

88. Ibid., 7.

89. Mark Griffith has argued that Greek tragedy is best approached through a series of paradoxes or "contradictory principles" of interpretation. For instance, Griffith argues that the tragedies were both part of a "polis-organized Dionysian ritual" and "theatrical entertainment," received as both a kind of "instruction (moral, civic, aesthetic, existential) about how to live" in the world and "a kind of fantasy . . . and temporary escape from (and distortion of) mundane reality." The second of Griffith's contradictory principles, however—that the plays provided both "(a) individual psychological/mental stimulus for each viewer and (b) a collective psycho-social behavioral impact on the mass audiences in the theater"—while framed as a paradox, could also be seen as an accurate description of the intertwinement between the psychological and political dramas of reconciliation. Griffin, introduction to *Why Athens? A Reappraisal of Tragic Politics*, ed. D. M. Carter (Oxford: Oxford University Press, 2011), 2.

90. Herodotus, *Histories*, trans. David Grene (Chicago: University of Chicago Press, 1988), chap. 6, sec. 21.

91. Ibid.

92. P. J. Wilson, "Tragic Rhetoric: The Use of Tragedy and the Tragic in the Fourth Century," in *Tragedy and the Tragic*, ed. M. S. Silk (Oxford: Oxford University Press, 1998), 311.

93. As Thornton Lockwood has usefully reminded me, Aeschylus's *Persians* also dealt with an episode of Athens' recent memory insofar as it depicted the consequences of the Greek victory over the invading Persian army in 479 BCE. However, *Persians* seems to focus less on the polis's misfortunes than on a celebration (if also reflective and perhaps self-critical) of Athenian success and daring. With this emphasis, it is a very different play than Phrynichos's *Capture of Miletos*.

94. Freud, "Mourning and Melancholia," 244.

95. Lear, "Interpretation of Transference," 57.

96. Ibid. Lear thinks that Socrates's great mistake was to ignore transference; he "acted as though the meaning of his activity would be transparent to others, and he thus provoked a transference storm." This argument does seem to comport with the evidence that Socrates was influential mainly among the Athenian youth because those who are coming of age often have a more fluid psychic structure and, as a result, fewer resistances tied to transference.

97. Klein, "Emotional Life of the Infant," 91.

98. Ibid., 91.

99. Lear, *Freud*, 36.

100. See Lear, "Catharsis," in *Open Minded*.

101. See Lear, "An Interpretation of Transference," where he compares the early Freud with Socrates: "Socrates, like Freud, began with an essentially cathartic method . . . overcoming conflict could, for him, only be a matter of eliciting and expelling false belief," 58.

102. For a review of this literature, see Nussbaum, "Tragedy and Self-Sufficiency."

103. Leon Golden, "Catharsis," *Transactions of the American Philological Association* 93 (1962); Leon Golden, "The Purgation Theory of Catharsis," *Journal of Aesthetics and Art Criticism* 31, (Summer 1973): 473–79; Leon Golden, "Epic, Tragedy, and Catharsis," *Classical Philology* 71 (January 1976): 77–85.

104. Nussbaum, "Tragedy and Self-Sufficiency."

105. Steven Salkever, "Tragedy and the Education of the *Demos*: Aristotle's Response to Plato," in Euben, *Greek Tragedy and Political Theory*.

106. See Lear, "Catharsis," 202. Lear does not entirely reject this account, but sees cognitive pleasure as a "step which occurs en route to the production of the proper pleasure of tragedy," which Lear associates with the recognition of "certain emotional possibilities which in ordinary life we ignore," 216.

107. Amelie Rorty, "The Psychology of Aristotelian Tragedy," in *Essays on Aristotle's Poetics*.

108. Salkever, "Tragedy and the Education of the *Demos*."

109. Ibid., 300.

110. Goldhill, *Love, Sex, and Tragedy*, 222. Emphasis added.

111. Euben, *Tragedy of Political Theory*, 90.

112. James Gibson, "The Contributions of Truth to Reconciliation: Lessons from South Africa," *Journal of Conflict Resolution* 50, no. 3 (2006): 409–32. See also James Gibson, "Truth, Reconciliation, and the Creation of a Human Rights Culture in South Africa," *Law and Society Review* 38, no. 1 (2004): 5–40.

113. Eric Doxtader and Fanie du Toit, introduction to *In the Balance: South Africans Debate Reconciliation* (Auckland Park, SA: Jacana Press, 2010), xii, 1.

114. Yael Farber, *Molora* (London: Oberon Books, 2008), 48.

115. Ibid., 12.

116. Ibid., 83.

117. Ibid., 83.

118. Ibid., 86.

119. Ibid., 87.

120. Glenn A. Odom, "South African Truth and Tragedy: Yael Farber's *Molora* and Reconciliation Aesthetics," *Comparative Literature* 63, no. 1 (2011): 47–63.

121. Compare with Hannah Arendt's famous description of the public "world" as an "in-between" space that "relates and separates men at the same time." Arendt, *Human Condition*, 52.

5. A SPLINTERING AND SHATTERING ACTIVITY

1. Martha Minow, *Between Vengeance and Forgiveness* (Boston: Beacon Press, 1999), 1. On the justice cascade, see Kathryn Sikkink, *The Justice Cascade: How Human Rights Prosecutions Are Changing World Politics* (New York: W. W. Norton, 2011). On the age of apology, see Mark Gibney, ed., *The Age of Apology: Facing Up to the Past* (Philadelphia: University of Pennsylvania Press, 2009).

2. The TRC method, inspired by the South African experience, has in many ways displaced the previously hegemonic Nuremberg method, which focused on the prosecution of perpetrators by the new ruling party or by occupying forces. See Priscilla Hayner, *Unspeakable Truths: Transitional Justice and the Challenge of Truth Commissions* (London: Routledge, 2010).

3. Quoted in Andre du Toit, "Experiences with Truth and Justice in South Africa: Stockenstrom, Gandhi, and the TRC," *Journal of Southern African Affairs* 31, no. 2 (2005): 419–48.

4. See Claire Moon, *Narrating Political Reconciliation: South Africa's Truth and Reconciliation Commission* (Lanham, MD: Lexington Books, 2009).

5. For a treatment of the various meanings of reconciliation as used by the TRC's advocates, critics, and participants, see Nagy, "Reconciliation in Post-Commission South Africa." See also Marek Kaminski, "Judging Transitional Justice: A New Criterion for Evaluating Truth Revelation Procedures," *Journal of Conflict Resolution* 50, no. 3 (2006): 383–408.

6. Desmond Tutu, *No Future without Forgiveness* (New York: Doubleday, 1999), 165.

7. Meister, *After Evil*, v. Lauren Berlant similarly argues the human rights discourses "over-identify" social justice with the eradication of pain rather than structural social changes, reflecting (and feeding) a liberalism of fear. Berlant, "The Subject of True Feeling: Pain, Privacy, and Politics," in *Cultural Pluralism, Identity Politics, and the Law*, ed. Austin Sarat and Thomas R. Kearns (Ann Arbor: University of Michigan Press, 1999), 49–84. See also Lauren Berlant, *Cruel Optimism* (Durham, NC: Duke University Press, 2011).

8. Meister, *After Evil*, 53.

9. As Meister puts it, "Those of us who are troubled by this assumption [that an evil such as apartheid can be dead while beneficiaries continue to prosper] will find it natural to respond by reverting to the revolutionary logic of justice-as-struggle . . . 'The evil still lives,' we will say, 'the struggle continues.'" *After Evil*, 54.

10. Aletta Norval, *Aversive Democracy: Inheritance and Originality in the Democratic Tradition* (Cambridge: Cambridge University Press, 2007).

11. Heidi Grunebaum, *Memorializing the Past: Everyday Life in South Africa after the Truth and Reconciliation Commission* (New Brunswick, NJ: Transaction, 2011).

12. Tutu, *No Future without Forgiveness*, 40.

13. *Greensboro Truth and Reconciliation Commission Final Report* (May 25, 2006). Available online at www.greensborotrc.org.

14. Klein, "Mourning and Its Relation to Manic-Depressive States," 355.

15. Ibid., 362.

16. Ibid., 348.

17. International Center for Transitional Justice, "Truth and Memory," May 2014, accessed May 5, 2015, https://www.ictj.org/our-work/transitional-justice-issues/truth-and-memory.

18. Ricoeur, "Imagination, Testimony, and Trust."

19. Martha Minow, *Breaking the Cycles of Hatred* (Princeton, NJ: Princeton University Press, 2002).

20. Thomas McCarthy, "Vergangenheitsbewältigung in the USA: On the Politics of the Memory of Slavery," *Political Theory* 30, no. 5 (2002): 623–48.

21. Jürgen Habermas, "On the Public Use of History," *New German Critique* 44 (1988), 44.

22. Ibid., 44.

23. Ibid., 45.

24. Quoted in Magarrell and Wesley, *Learning from Greensboro*, 163.

25. Elizabeth Kiss, "Moral Ambition within and beyond Political Constraints," in *Truth v. Justice: The Morality of Truth Commissions*, ed. Robert I. Rotberg and Dennis Thompson (Princeton, NJ: Princeton University Press, 2000), 79.

26. Iris Marion Young, *Responsibility for Justice*, 97.

27. Nagy, "Reconciliation in Post-Commission South Africa." See also Rosemary Nagy, "After the TRC: Citizenship, Memory, and Reconciliation," *Canadian Journal of African Studies* 38, no. 3 (2004): 636–53.

28. Quoted in Oliver Ramsbotham, Tom Woodhouse, and Hugh Miall, *Contemporary Conflict Resolution* (Cambridge: Polity Press, 2011), 230.

29. Richard A. Wilson, *The Politics of Truth and Reconciliation in South Africa: Legitimizing the Post-Apartheid State* (Cambridge: Cambridge University Press, 2001), 54.

30. Nancy Potter, ed. *Trauma, Truth, and Reconciliation: Healing Damaged Relationships* (Oxford: Oxford University Press, 2006), 4.

31. Jay A. Vora and Erika Vora, "The Effectiveness of South Africa's Truth and Reconciliation Commission: Perceptions of Xhosa, Afrikaner, and English South Africans," *Journal of Black Studies* 34 (January 2004): 301–22.

32. Mahmoud Mamdani, "Reconciliation without Justice," *Southern African Review of Books* 10 (November–December 1997), 4.

33. Elizabeth Stanley, "Evaluating the Truth and Reconciliation Commission," *Journal of Modern African Studies* 39, no. 3 (2001): 543.

34. Johan Galtung, "After Violence, Reconstruction, Reconciliation and Resolution: Coping with Visible and Invisible Effects of War and Violence," in *Reconciliation, Justice and Coexistence*, ed. Mohammad Abu-Nimer (New York: Lexington Books, 2001).

35. On the struggle for recognition as a "moral grammar" for social conflicts, see Honneth, *The Struggle for Recognition.* On the idea that the struggle for recognition has to countenance human capacities for and interest in misrecognition, see David W. McIvor, "The Cunning of Recognition: Melanie Klein and Contemporary Political Theory," *Contemporary Political Theory* (online publication October 27, 2015), doi: 10.1057/cpt.2015.47.

36. Meister, *After Evil*, 5.

37. Sonali Chakravarti, *Sing the Rage: Listening to Anger after Mass Violence* (Chicago: University of Chicago Press, 2014).

38. Ibid., 19.

39. Norval, *Aversive Democracy*, 197.

40. Ibid., 198.

41. Ibid., 205.

42. Ibid., 207.

43. Ibid., 205.

44. Wendy Brown, *Undoing the Demos: Neoliberalism's Stealth Revolution* (New York: Zone Books, 2015).

45. Grunebaum, *Memorializing the Past*, 9.

46. Jacques Ranciere, *Dissensus: On Politics and Aesthetics* (London: Bloomsbury Academic, 2010), 42.

47. Alexander Keller Hirsch, introduction to *Theorizing Post-Conflict Reconciliation: Agonism, Restitution, and Repair*, ed. Alexander Keller Hirsch (London: Routledge, 2012), 3. On the search for common ground and the value of mutual respect, see Amy Gutmann and Dennis Thompson, "Moral Foundations of Truth Commissions," in *Truth v. Justice: The Morality of Truth Commissions*, ed. Robert I. Rotberg and Dennis Thompson (Princeton. NJ: Princeton University Press, 2000).

48. Stanley, "Evaluating the Truth and Reconciliation Commission," 527.

49. Grunebaum, *Memorializing the Past*, 40.

50. Ibid., 40–41.

51. Ibid., 8.

52. Ibid., 8.

53. Leigh Payne, *Unsettling Accounts: Neither Truth nor Reconciliation in Confessions of State Violence* (Durham, NC: Duke University Press, 2006).

54. Ibid., 12.

55. Doxtader and Du Toit, introduction, xii.

56. Ibid., xii.

57. Paul Muldoon and Andrew Schaap, "Confounded by Recognition," in Hirsch, *Theorizing Post-Conflict Reconciliation*, 182. See also Adrian Little, "Between Disagreement and Consent: Unraveling the Democratic Paradox," *Australian Journal of Political Science* 42, no. 1 (2007): 143–59.

58. Jonathan Allen, "Balancing Justice and Social Unity: Political Theory and the Idea of a Truth and Reconciliation Commission," *University of Toronto Law Journal* 49 (Summer 1999): 320.

59. See David Mendeloff, "Truth-Seeking, Truth-Telling, and Postconflict Peacebuilding: Curb the Enthusiasm?" *International Studies Review* 6, no. 3 (2004): 355–80.

60. LaCapra, "Lanzmann's 'Shoah.'"

61. Minow, "Breaking the Cycles of Hatred."

62. Charles Villa-Vicencio and Wilhelm Verwoerd, eds., *Looking Back, Reaching Forward* (London: Zed Books, 2000).

63. Michael Ignatieff, quoted in Audrey R. Chapman and Patrick Ball, "The Truth of Truth Commissions: Comparative Lessons from Haiti, South Africa, and Guatemala," *Human Rights Quarterly* 23, no. 1 (2001): 1–43.

64. Brandon Hamber and Richard Wilson, "Symbolic Closure through Memory, Reparation and Revenge in Post-Conflict Societies," *Research Papers*, Paper no. 5, University of Connecticut, accessed December 25, 2015, http://digitalcommons.uconn.edu/hri _papers/5.

65. Meister, *After Evil*, x.

66. Ibid., 8.

67. Ibid., 60. See also Mark Sanders, *Ambiguities of Witnessing: Law and Literature in the Time of a Truth Commission* (Stanford, CA: Stanford University Press, 2007).

68. Meister, *After Evil*, 62.

69. Wendy Brown, "Resisting Left Melancholy," 19–27.

70. Meister, *After Evil*, 70.

71. Ibid., 344n76.

72. See James L. Gibson, *Overcoming Apartheid: Can Truth Reconcile a Divided Nation?* (New York: Russell Sage Foundation, 2004).

73. David K. Androff, "Reconciliation in a Community-Based Restorative Justice Intervention," *Journal of Sociology and Social Welfare* 39 (December 2012); Gibson, "Contributions of Truth to Reconciliation," 415.

74. Pablo de Grieff, "On Making the Invisible Visible: The Role of Cultural Interventions in Transitional Justice Processes," in *Transitional Justice, Culture, and Society: Beyond Outreach*, ed. Clara Ramirez-Barat (New York: Social Science Research Council, 2014).

75. Hayner, *Unspeakable Truths*, 14.

76. Paul Gready, *The Era of Transitional Justice: The Aftermath of the Truth and Reconciliation Commission in South Africa and Beyond* (London: Routledge, 2011), 12.

77. Quoted in Hayner, *Unspeakable Truths*, 186.

78. Geoffrey Yor, "South African Winery Owner Uncorks Long-hidden History of Slavery," *Globe and Mail*, August 19, 2011.

79. Ibid.

80. Matt Goulding, "The Long Harvest," December 2012, accessed May 5, 2015, http://roadsandkingdoms.com/author/mdgoulding.

81. Ibid., 10.

82. Ibid., 8.

83. Ibid., 7.

84. Yor, "South African Winery Owner," 2.

85. Ibid., 2.

86. Louis Bickford, "Memoryworks/Memory Works," in Ramirez-Barat, *Transitional Justice, Culture, and Society*, 497.

87. Gibson, "Contributions of Truth to Reconciliation," 412; James Gibson, "Truth, Reconciliation, and the Creation of a Human Rights Culture in South Africa," *Law and Society Review* 38, no. 1 (2004): 5–40.

88. John Paul Lederach, *Building Peace* (Washington, DC: U.S. Institute of Peace, 1997); Gibson, *Overcoming Apartheid*.

89. Gibson, "Contributions of Truth to Reconciliation," 429.

90. Ibid., 412.

91. Eric Doxtader, "The Potential of Reconciliation's Beginning: A Reply," *Rhetoric and Public Affairs* 7 (Fall 2004): 387.

92. Magarrell and Wesley, *Learning from Greensboro*, 1.

93. Louis Bickford, "Unofficial Truth Projects," *Human Rights Quarterly* 29 (2007): 994–1035.

94. David Cunningham, Colleen Nugent, and Caitlin Slodden, "The Durability of Collective Memory: Reconciling the Greensboro Massacre," *Social Forces* 88 (June 2010): 1–26.

95. *Greensboro Truth and Reconciliation Commission Final Report*. This point was drive home by a Freudian slip committed by the former mayor of Greensboro, Jim Melvin, who was in office during the period of the Greensboro Massacre and its aftermath. When Melvin was interviewed for a documentary film about the GTRC, he described the process as a "waste of time" and went on to say, "We don't have much time for these people . . . I don't care what the civil right, er, truth and reconciliation commission people say. They didn't sit through the trial, they didn't hear all the evidence." The transposition in Melvin's mind between civil rights advocates and the Greensboro TRC is powerful testimony to the subterranean struggles over race in the South and elsewhere. Adam Zucker, "Greensboro: Closer to the Truth," documentary film, 2007, http://www.greensborothe movie.com.

96. Recently the phrase "City of Civil Rights" was an entry in a contest to select a new slogan for Greensboro. Eric Ginsburg, "Lacking Cohesive Marketing, Greensboro Seeks Plan," *Triad City Beat*, March 18, 2015.

97. Chafe, *Civilities and Civil Rights*.

98. Quoted in Zucker, "Greensboro: Closer to the Truth."

99. Jill Williams, "Legitimacy and Effectiveness of a Grassroots Truth and Reconciliation Commission," *Law and Contemporary Problems* 72 (Spring 2009): 148.

100. Ibid., 148.

101. Magarrell and Wesley, *Learning from Greensboro*, 183–84.

102. Ibid., 205.

103. *Greensboro Truth and Reconciliation Commission Final Report*, 45.

104. Magarrell and Wesley, *Learning from Greensboro*, 30.

105. Ibid., 30.

106. On framing, see Michael Ignatieff, "Articles of Faith," *Index on Censorship* 25 (September 1996): 110–22.

107. *Greensboro Truth and Reconciliation Commission Final Report*, 82.

108. See Jacquelyn Dowd Hall, "The Long Civil Rights Movement and the Political Uses of the Past," *Journal of American History* 91 (March 2005): 1233–63.

109. Gibson, "Contributions of Truth to Reconciliation," 415; Daniel Bar-Tal, "A Socio-Psychological Conception of Collective Identity," *Personality and Social Psychology Review* 13 (2009): 356.

110. Klein, "Notes on Some Schizoid Mechanisms," in *Envy and Gratitude*, 6.

111. See Clarke, "Projective Identification."

112. Ed Whitfield, quoted in Magarrell and Wesley, *Learning from Greensboro*, 28.

113. Gibson, "Contributions of Truth to Reconciliation," 417.

114. Deanna Wylie Mayer, "From Fear to Truth," *Sojourners*, February 2006.

115. *Greensboro Truth and Reconciliation Commission Final Report*, 15.

116. Cunningham, Nugent, and Slodden, "The Durability of Collective Memory." 1.

117. David K. Androff, "Reconciliation in a Community-Based Restorative Justice Intervention," *Journal of Sociology and Social Welfare* 39 (December 2012): 84.

118. Ibid., 87.

119. Ibid., 85.

120. *Greensboro Truth and Reconciliation Commission Final Report*, 13.

121. Jovanovic, *Democracy, Dialogue and Community Action*, 153.

122. Dismantling Racism: A Resource Book for Social Change Groups, http://www .westernstatescenter.org/tools-and-resources/Tools/Dismantling%20Racism. Accessed November 15, 2015.

123. On the unpredictability of action, see Arendt, *The Human Condition*.

124. Jill Williams, "Truth and Reconciliation Comes to the South: Lessons from Greensboro," *Public Eyes Magazine* 21 (Spring 2007). http://www.publiceye.org/magazine/v21n2 /reconciliation.html.

125. Cynthia Brown, quoted in Zucker, "Greensboro: Closer to the Truth."

126. Gibson, "Contributions of Truth to Reconciliation," 415; Daniel Bar-Tal, *Intractable Conflicts: Socio-Psychological Foundations and Dynamics* (Cambridge: Cambridge University Press, 2013).

127. Sigmund Freud, *Introductory Lectures on Psychoanalysis*, trans. James Strachey (London: W. W. Norton, 1989).

128. On "contentious coexistence" in the context of truth commissions, see Payne, *Unsettling Accounts*.

AFTERWORD

1. Will Greenberg, "Leaked Autopsy Report Finds Freddie Gray Suffered 'High-Energy' Injury," *Washington Post*, June 24, 2015.

2. Joel Anderson, "Baltimore Erupts after Funeral for Man Who Died in Police Custody," *Buzzfeed News*, April 27, 2015.

3. Sheryl Gay Stolberg, "After Thousands Rally in Baltimore, Police Make Some Arrests as Curfew Takes Hold," *New York Times*, May 2, 2015.

4. Ron Nixon, "Amid Violence, Factions and Messages Converge in a Weary and Unsettled Baltimore," *New York Times*, April 27, 2015.

5. J. David Goodman and Al Baker, "Wave of Protests after Grand Jury Doesn't Indict Officer in Eric Garner Chokehold Case," *New York Times*, December 3, 2014.

6. According to #BlackLivesMatter activist Alicia Garza, the social media campaign was initiated partly in response to expressions of cynicism after the acquittal of George Zimmerman in the Trayvon Martin case. As Garcia put it, "I [wasn't] satisfied with the 'I told you so' and I [wasn't] satisfied with the nihilistic 'it'll never happen' kind of thing." Garza and Kauffman, "Love Note to Our Folks."

7. Claudia Rankine, "The Condition of Black Life Is One of Mourning," *New York Times*, June 22, 2015.

8. Stout, *Blessed Are the Organized*, 10.

9. Ibid., 11.

10. Honneth, *Struggle for Recognition*, 120.

11. Ibid., 121.

12. Ibid., 110.

13. Ibid., 121.

14. Honneth, *Freedom's Right*, 65.

15. Wolin, *Presence of the Past*, 139.

16. Ibid., 139–40.

17. Wolin, *Politics and Vision*, 604.

18. Alisa Ames, Mark Evans, Laura Fox, Adam Milam, Ryan Petteway, and Regina Rutledge, *2011 Neighborhood Health Profile: Sandtown-Winchester/Harlem Park*, Baltimore City Health Department, December 2011.

19. Darryl Pinckney, "In Ferguson," *New York Review of Books*, January 8, 2015.

20. Yohura Williams, "You're Nobody 'Till Somebody Kills You: Baltimore, Freddie Gray and the Problem of History," *Huffington Post*, April 29, 2015.

21. Monica Potts, "The Freddie Gray's of West Baltimore Who Can't Vote," *Daily Beast*, May 5, 2015.

22. Ta-Nehisi Coates, *Between the World and Me* (New York: Spiegel and Grau, 2015), 103–4.

23. *Lynching in America: Confronting the Legacy of Racial Terror*, Equal Justice Initiative, Montgomery, Alabama, 2015. http://www.eji.org/lynchinginamerica.

24. Ta-Nehisi Coates, "The Case for Reparations," *Atlantic*, June 2014; Alexander, *New Jim Crow*.

25. Coates, *Between the World and Me*, 79.

26. Rankine, *Citizen: An American Lyric* (Minneapolis, MN: Graywolf Press, 2014), 151. Emphasis added.

27. Evelyn Nakano Glenn, *Unequal Freedom: How Race and Gender Shaped American Citizenship and Labor* (Cambridge, MA: Harvard University Press, 2004); George M. Fredrickson, "The Historical Construction of Race and Citizenship in the United States," in *Diverse Nations: Explorations in the History of Racial and Ethnic Pluralism* (Boulder, CO: Paradigm, 2008).

28. Berlant, *Cruel Optimism*.

29. Ibid., 2.

30. Ibid., 2.

31. Ibid., 5.

32. Jodi Dean, *The Communist Horizon* (London: Verso, 2012).

33. Ibid., 66.

34. Ibid., 120.

35. Ibid., 65.

36. Franklin Rosemont, *Joe Hill: The IWW and the Making of a Revolutionary Working-class Counterculture* (Chicago, IL: Charles H. Kerr Publishing Company, 2003), 17.

37. Coates, *Between the World and Me*, 6.

38. Ibid., 6.

39. Ibid., 79.

40. Ibid., 11.

41. Ibid., 11.

42. Ibid., 8.

43. Ibid., 7.

44. Ibid., 28.

45. Ibid., 11.

46. Ibid., 11–12.

47. Ibid., 12.

48. Ibid., 108.

49. Wolin, *Presence of the Past*, 141.

50. Ibid., 141.

51. Coates, *Between the World and Me*, 52.

52. Ibid., 30.

53. Sedgwick, "Melanie Klein and the Difference Affect Makes," 631–32. Or, as Thomas Ogden puts it, "in the depressive position, phantasies of omnipotently annihilating one's rival no longer provide a satisfactory solution to a problem in a human relationship." Ogden, *Matrix of the Mind*, 91.

54. Coates, *Between the World and Me*, 143.

55. Sedgwick, "Difference Affect Makes," 637.

56. Berlant, *Cruel Optimism*, 259.

57. Ibid., 259.

58. Ibid., 49.

59. Rankine, *Citizen*, 7.

60. Ibid., 47.

61. Ibid., 55.

62. Ibid., 24.

63. Ibid., 24.

64. Ibid., 30.

65. Ibid., 35.

66. Ibid., 159.

67. Butler, *Frames of War*, 182.

68. Rankine, *Citizen*, 59.

69. Ibid., 66.

70. Ibid., 28.

71. Ibid., 72.

72. Ibid., 151.

73. Claudia Rankine, "Blackness as the Second Person." https://www.guernicamag.com /interviews/blackness-as-the-second-person/.

74. Rankine, *Citizen*, 142.

75. Ibid., 156.

76. This view that the struggle for recognition exceeds the struggle for material well-being offers a challenge to many voices on the right who claim that poverty in the United States is an illusion because even the poor have televisions, refrigerators, etc. See Robert Rector and Rachel Sheffield, "Air Conditioning, Cable TV, and an Xbox: What Is Poverty in the United States Today," *Heritage Foundation*, July 18, 2011.

77. Rankine, *Citizen*, 151.

78. Ibid., 156.

79. Rankine, "Blackness as the Second Person."

80. Honneth, *Struggle for Recognition*, 83.

81. Rankine, *Citizen*, 14.

82. Honneth, *Struggle for Recognition*, 83.

83. Rankine, "Blackness as the Second Person."

84. Ibid.

85. See Jack Turner, *Awakening to Race* (Chicago: University of Chicago Press, 2012). Turner uses the work of Stanley Cavell to argue that white Americans' failure to recognize racial inequality is a problem of acknowledgment; that is, it is not a question of knowledge but of what is done with that knowledge. For Turner, the failure to acknowledge racial inequality constitutes a failure of democratic individualist virtue.

86. Rankine, "Condition of Black Life."

87. Ibid.

88. Ibid.

89. Ibid.

90. Honneth, *Freedom's Right*, 326.

91. Ibid., 327.

92. Ibid., 66.

93. Paul Lichterman, *Elusive Togetherness: Church Groups Trying to Bridge America's Divisions* (Princeton, NJ: Princeton University Press, 2005).

94. Ibid., 15.

95. Rankine, *Citizen*, 54.

96. Lichterman's study extends the literature on social capital while challenging some of this literature's assumptions about how social capital forms and how it can be effective. Other, similar studies show that the density of associational life is less important than bridges or connections between associational nodes. See, for instance, Sean Safford, *Why the Garden Club Couldn't Save Youngstown* (Cambridge, MA: Harvard University Press, 2009). See also Peter Levine, *We Are the Ones We Have Been Waiting For*.

97. Lichterman, *Elusive Togetherness*, 256.

98. Ibid., 256–57.

99. Sedgwick, "Difference Affect Makes," 637.

100. Lichterman, *Elusive Togetherness*, 15.

101. Nina Eliasoph, *Avoiding Politics: How Americans Produce Apathy in Everyday Life* (Cambridge: Cambridge University Press, 1998).

102. Nina Eliasoph, *Making Volunteers: Civic Life after Welfare's End* (Princeton, NJ: Princeton University Press, 2011).

103. Ibid., 87.

104. Cunningham, Nugent, and Slodden, "The Durability of Collective Memory."

105. Mark Solms, "Land Ownership in South Africa: Turning Neuropsychoanalysis into Wine," *TEDxObserver*, April 1, 2011, http://www.theguardian.com/tedx/mark-solms-south -africa-neuropsychoanalysis-wine.

106. Segal, *Yesterday, Today and Tomorrow*, 251.

107. Ibid., 41.

108. Hanna Segal, "From Hiroshima to the Gulf War and After: Socio-political Expressions of Ambivalence," in *Psychoanalysis, Literature and War* (London: Routledge, 1995), 167.

109. Garza and Kauffman, "Love Note to Our Folks."

110. Ibid.

Index

CPSIA information can be obtained at www.ICGtesting.com
Printed in the USA
BVOW08*0647061016

464028BV00002B/4/P